The Four Foundations of Mindfulness

The Four Foundations of Mindfulness

Venerable U Sīlānanda

Edited by Ruth-Inge Heinze, Ph.D.

Wisdom Publications · Boston · London · Sydney

Dr. Ruth-Inge Heinze, who transcribed and prepared Venerable U Sīlānanda's talks for publication, sponsored the printing of this book in memory of her parents, Otto and Louise Heinze.

First published in 1990

Wisdom Publications
361 Newbury Street, Boston, MA 02115, USA
402 Hoe Street, London E17 9AA, England
PO Box 1326, Chatswood, NSW 2067, Australia

Library of Congress Cataloging-in-Publication Data

Ven. U Sīlānanda
  The four foundations of mindfulness.
  1. Meditation (Buddhism)
  I. Title
  BQ5612   1990   294.3'443   90-70043

ISBN 0 86171 092 4

Printed and bound by Eurasia Press of Singapore.

Acknowledgements

The publication of this book on the *Mahā Satipaṭṭhāna Sutta*, would not have been possible without the help of many people.

First, I wish to thank Dr. Ruth-Inge Heinze who has worked tirelessly to support the *Dhamma*. She transcribed, prepared and edited my talks for this publication, and I am grateful for this and all her efforts over the years.

I want also to thank my students whose dedication and support has been very important since I first came to live in the United States. It is a great joy to study the *Dhamma* with them.

I am glad that Wisdom Publications has published this book so that it can reach many people I have never met.

All proceeds from this book will be donated to the Dhammachakka Meditation Center whose goals are to offer meditation retreats and spread the *Dhamma* in the West.

The late Venerable Mahāsi Sayadaw of Burma was a living example of the Buddha's teachings. I had the privilege of being his student for over twenty years. I am extremely grateful to the Venerable Mahāsi Sayadaw for his guidance, through which I am able to transmit the Buddha's teachings purely. Any failure to do so is my own.

Contents

Foreword

It gives me great joy to provide some preliminary comments to Ven. U Sīlānanda's *The Four Foundation of Mindfulness,* a clear and thorough treatment of the Buddha's *Mahā Satipaṭṭhāna Sutta.* This *sutta* is vital to the practice of *vipassanā* meditation and also means a great deal to me personally. I have studied and benefitted from a wide variety of religious scriptures — often quite rich and evocative from a religious as well as literary point of view. The *Satipaṭṭhāna Sutta* (at least in English translation) in contrast is dry and plain, a kind of extended spiritual telegram. It is also, for me, the single most valuable text encountered in this life. Over the years, I have studied many of its translations, questioned many of its teachers, and many times tested its validity in my own meditation practice. It has all been extraordinarily beneficial, especially so after hearing Ven. U Sīlānanda's lectures on this, by now, familiar text.

These lectures (the basis for the present volume) and many personal discussions with the author provided me with greatly appreciated clarity in terms of the meaning of the *sutta* and its significance for *actual meditation practice.* Ven. U Sīlānanda, being a scholar yogi, is able to harmonize doctrine and practice, so that there are no gaps between the two realms. In addition, the rich commentarial literature is used to deepen profoundly our understanding of the *sutta.* This is no small accomplishment as it discourages us from making a rigid and even oppositional distinction between the *sutta* and commentaries about it. The approach is rather one of seeing the benefit of carefully and cautiously drawing upon these ancient reflections in order to help us grasp the original sense of the *sutta.*

The author also brings to this work a very rich contemporary influence — that of his teacher, Ven. Mahāsi Sayadaw of Burma. This body of teachings and practice has an especially strong impact on current *vipassanā* practice in the West. The many yogis who practice in the style of Ven. Mahāsi Sayadaw will, of course, find this rendering of the *Satipaṭṭhāna Sutta* of great value. It will also be of considerable interest to prac-titioners of other schools because of the wealth of doctrinal and practical *Dhamma* treasures it contains. The general reader will find it useful because of the unrelenting manner in which this *sutta* reminds us of the wide variety of oppor-tunities that come along each day for us to choose attention rather than blindness.

Ven. U Sīlānanda's text is clear, thorough, and systematic. Intellectual understanding and reflection upon the centrality of mindfulness in this text can help prepare the heart for the great meditative journey that moves from sorrow to liberation.

May all beings put the Buddha's Teaching into practice!

Dr. Larry Rosenberg
Cambridge Insight Meditation Center
Cambridge, Massachusetts
April, 1990

Part One
Commentary

Introduction

The Great Discourse on the Foundations of Mindfulness is important for those who practice *vipassanā* meditation, because all
instructions are directly or indirectly based on the teachings
contained in the *sutta*. If you are serious about *vipassanā*
meditation, you should know this *sutta* well.

We will use a revised translation of the original *Mahā
Satipaṭṭhāna Sutta*. I call it "revised," because I used several
translations and selected whatever was agreeable to me and
combined my findings with my own translation. In this way,
I came up with a somewhat new translation.

This exposition is based on the ancient commentary, the
sub-commentary, and the Burmese commentary written by
the Venerable Mahāsi Sayadaw. At the invitation of the Insight Meditation Society in Barre, Massachusetts, he visited
this country in 1979. The Venerable was a famous and successful meditation teacher, perhaps the best known Burmese
meditation teacher in the West. Before he passed away in
August, 1982, he gave many talks on *vipassanā* meditation and
other discourses of the Buddha. Records of his talks and some
of his books have been translated into English and published
in this country.

The full name of this *sutta* in Pāli is *Mahā Satipaṭṭhāna Sutta*,
which means *The Great Discourse on the Foundations of Mindfulness* or *The Setting Up of Mindfulness*. In this *sutta*, the Buddha
gave instructions on how to practice *satipaṭṭhāna vipassanā*
meditation. There are four foundations of mindfulness explained in this *sutta* and also in this exposition.

Whenever Buddhists undertake something, they first pay
homage to the Buddha, the *Dhamma*, and the *Sangha*. Therefore, whenever people write about a Buddhist topic, they first
put the words, *Namō Tassa Bhagavato Arahato Sammā-sambud-*

13

dhasā, at the beginning of the book. We also will begin with "Homage to the Blessed One, the Worthy One, the Fully Enlightened One."

Thus have I heard.[1]

Every *sutta* in the *Collection of Discourses* is introduced with the words, "Thus have I heard." The word "I" refers to the Venerable Ānanda who was the first cousin of the Buddha. Ānanda was His permanent personal attendant for twenty-five years. It is said that he was of the same age as the Buddha because he was born on the same day as the Buddha. The Buddha taught for forty-five years, but for the first twenty years had no permanent attendant. Sometimes, one *bhikkhu* served as His attendant and, at other times, another *bhikkhu*. From the twenty-first year onward, however, the Venerable Ānanda became his permanent personal attendant.

It is interesting to learn how the Venerable Ānanda was given this position. In the twenty-first year of His teaching, the Buddha announced that He needed a personal attendant. When He made this announcement, many of His chief disciples sought to become His attendant, but the Buddha refused to accept them. Then, in the assembly, some *bhikkhus* asked Ānanda to offer his services to the Buddha, but Ānanda said, "If Buddha really wants me to be His attendant, He will ask me Himself. I will not offer myself unless I am asked by the Buddha." So, eventually, the Buddha asked Ānanda to become His attendant.

Ānanda replied that he would accept the position only on certain conditions. There were actually eight conditions. The first four we call "rejections," and the other four "acquisitions." The four rejections were: First, the Buddha must not give him any robes for being His attendant. Second, he should not be given good food received by the Buddha, for being His attendant. Third, he should not be asked to stay in the Buddha's fragrant cell or have a separate cell for himself. Fourth, if anyone should invite the Buddha to visit his house and partake of food, Ānanda should not be included in the invitation. These are the "four conditions of rejection." Venerable Ānanda did not want in anyway to materially benefit from his relationship to the Buddha.

The "four conditions of acquisition" are: First, he must have the right to accept any invitation for the Buddha and, once

Ānanda had accepted the invitation, the Buddha must go to the place He had been invited to. Second, he should be permitted to bring to the Buddha, at any time, a devotee coming from a far-off place. Third, he should be permitted to place before the Buddha any problem as soon as it arose. If Ānanda had any doubt about anything, he should have the right to approach the Buddha and ask Him to remove his doubts. That means, Buddha must always be available to him to answer any questions. Fourth, the Buddha should repeat to him any discourse delivered in Ānanda's absence. This last point is very important with respect to the words, "Thus have I heard."

Because the Buddha agreed to these conditions and the Venerable Ānanda became the personal attendant to the Buddha on these conditions, the Buddha always repeated to Ānanda any discourse delivered in the latter's absence. Therefore, the Venerable Ānanda knew all the discourses and teachings delivered by the Buddha.

In the book called *Expositor,* the commentary to the first book of the *Abhidhamma,* you find these words of praise for the Venerable Ānanda:

> The Elder was indeed of wide experience, a student of the Three *Pitakas* [the Three Divisions of the Buddha's Teachings]. He could learn, recite and preach, as he stood [that means, in one standing, he could learn, recite or preach] one thousand and five hundred stanzas or sixty thousand feet, as easily as though he were gathering creepers and flowers. That was the Elder's single course of exposition. None but the Buddha was able to teach or attain the distinction of teaching, so that this Elder knew the actual text word by word.[2]

Ānanda possessed a quick and keen intellect. The Buddha was the only person who could teach him, so, the Venerable Ānanda came to know everything the Buddha taught.

These words, "Thus have I heard" and the following were uttered by the Venerable Ānanda at the First Buddhist Council, held about three months after the death of the Buddha. After the Buddha had died, the Chief Disciple, Mahā Kassapa, decided to hold a council and chose five hundred *arahats* to participate. At that council, all teachings of the Buddha were collected and carefully scrutinized. Only when the assembly was satisfied that these were the authentic teachings of the Buddha were these teachings admitted to the collection and recited in unison. Reciting in unison indicated that the teachings had been accepted unanimously by the council to be the authentic words of the Buddha. Because, at that time, it was not the practice to write down the Buddha's teachings, they were recorded by way of recitation.

Not only were the teachings recorded, but they were also classified into different collections. The most popular division was the division into *Pitakas*. These are the *Vinaya Pitaka*, the Division of Rules for Monks and Nuns; the *Sutta Pitaka*, the Division of Discourses; and the *Abhidhamma Pitaka*, the Division of the Higher Teachings. The *Mahā Satipaṭṭhāna Sutta* belongs to the Division of Discourses.

The collection of the teachings thus recorded was handed down from generation to generation by word of mouth until about five hundred years after the death of the Buddha when they were written down on palm leaves in Sri Lanka.

As mentioned above, at the First Buddhist Council, the Venerable Mahā Kassapa raised questions about the authenticity of the Buddha's teachings and there were two venerables who answered the questions of Mahā Kassapa. For the *Vinaya*, Division of Rules for Monks and Nuns, the Venerable Upali gave the answers and it was the Venerable Ānanda who responded for the *suttas*, the 84,000 sermons the Buddha taught.

When the Venerable Mahā Kassapa posed questions about the *Mahā Satipaṭṭhāna Sutta*, the Venerable Ānanda gave answers beginning with "Thus have I heard." By saying, "Thus have I heard," the Venerable Ānanda effaced himself and bore witness to the Master. He finalized the Buddha's words and established the *Dhamma* as the guide. When disclaiming that the words were his own invention and disclosing that he had previously heard these words uttered by the Buddha, he annihilated lack of faith in this *Dhamma* in gods and human beings. He instilled excellence of faith by saying: "This was acquired by me in the very presence of the Blessed One, so there need be neither hesitation nor doubt about meaning or ideas or phrases or syllables."

Thus have I heard: At one time, the Blessed One was living in Kurus, where there was a market town of the Kurus, named Kammasadamma.

"At one time": Although the exact time of delivering this *sutta* was known to the Venerable Ānanda, for the sake of brevity he only said, "at one time." For him it is a saving of labor, perhaps, but for us who belong to another era, it is definitely not a blessing, because we do not know exactly when this *sutta* was taught, at what time and in what year. If the Venerable Ānanda had mentioned all these details, we would be able to put this *sutta* and all the other teachings in chronological order, but now we cannot. We can only guess which *suttas* might have been taught before the others.

"In Kurus": "Kurus" is the name of a district or a small country in India. The Pāli term requires that the word be in the plural. Originally, it was the name of the people who first inhabited this district. When the name later was applied to the district, the plural lingered on. So, although the district was only one, in Pāli it requires the plural, hence, *kurusu*, "in Kurus."

"Where there was a market town of the Kurus, named Kammasadamma": The market town was called "Kammasa-damma" because a cannibal king by the name of Kammasa-pada ("Speckled Foot") was subdued there. Some preferred the spelling "Kammāsa-dhamma" and explained that it was called *"kammāsa-dhamma"* because the traditional virtuous practice of the Kurus had been stained (*kammāsa*).

There the Blessed One addressed the bhikkhus thus: "bhikkhus," and the bhikkhus replied, "Venerable Sir." And the Blessed One spoke as follows:

The Buddha always addressed the monks as *bhikkhus*. *Bhikkhus* were the excellent persons who accepted His teachings. But this does not mean that, in saying *bhikkhus*, other people who were not monks were not addressed. Moreover, anybody who accepts and follows the Buddha's teachings can be called a *bhikkhu* (in Pāli). So, when the Buddha said, *"bhikkhus,"* it must be understood that monks as well as nuns and lay people are addressed.

> *This is the only way, bhikkhus, for the purification of beings, for the overcoming of sorrow and lamentation, for the disappearance of pain and grief, for reaching the Noble Path, for the realization of Nibbāna, namely, the Four Foundations of Mindfulness.*

"This is the only way": To understand the explanation you should know the Pāli words for the "only way." It is in Pāli, *ekāyāna*. *Eka* means "one," and *ayāna* means "way," so *ekāyāna* means "one way." The word *ekāyāna* is explained in five ways.

The first explanation is that it is the "single way" that does not branch off. There are no branches in this way, so that you can follow this way with assurance from beginning to deliverance.

The second explanation is that this way has to be trodden "alone." In practicing meditation, you are making this journey alone, without companions. You may be in a group, you may be in a retreat, but actually you are going your own way. You are alone. Nobody is with you. Nobody can give his or her concentration or wisdom to you and you cannot give any of your concentration or wisdom to anybody else. So, although you may be in a group, you are really practicing alone. Therefore, this is the "only way," the "way to be trodden alone."

The third explanation is that this is the "way of the One." The "way of the One" means the "way of the Excellent One," the way discovered by the Buddha.

The fourth explanation is that it is the "only way" because it is the way that leads only to one destination," i.e., to *nibbāna*. So, when you go along this way, you will surely reach the destination. *Nibbāna* will be the only destination you reach, when you go along this way.

The fifth explanation is that this is the "only way to reach *nibbāna*." There is no other way. The *satipaṭṭhāna* or mindfulness way is the only way to *nibbāna*, the end of suffering, the destruction of mental defilements.

"For the purification of beings": That means for the purification of the minds of all beings. The minds of all beings are tainted with or contaminated by different defilements. Most of the time your minds are not pure. There are attachments or craving, greed, hatred or anger, ignorance, pride, envy, jealousy, and so forth. Attachments defile your minds.

The *satipaṭṭhāna* method helps to purify your minds. This is the only way for the purification of the minds of all beings. When you practice *vipassanā* meditation, you do not have greed or hatred or delusion or pride or other defilements. All these things are absent from your mind during meditation. When you have reached the destination, then your mind will be absolutely free from mental defilements. By going along this path, you will reach the highest stage of attainment and your mind will be absolutely pure.

"For the overcoming of sorrow and lamentation": Sorrow and lamentation can be overcome by this meditation. When you practice *vipassanā* meditation, you are instructed to be aware of everything that is happening to you, to notice everything that comes to you at the present moment. When you are aware of everything, when you observe everything during meditation, the defilements will disappear. When you reach the final stage of arahathood, you will have overcome sorrow and lamentation altogether. After you have reached such a stage, sorrow and lamentation will never come to you again. There are many persons whose sorrow and lamentation have been overcome by the practice of *satipaṭṭhāna vipassanā* meditation.

"For the disappearance of pain and grief": Pain means physical pain and grief means mental pain. Physical pain and mental pain can be overcome by *vipassanā* meditation. When you have sat for some time, you feel pain in the body; but when you persevere in watching the pain or taking note of pain, and your concentration becomes powerful, then the pain will go away and you will have overcome pain. You can also overcome grief through the practice of *vipassanā* meditation. When you have reached the highest stage, you will have overcome pain and grief once and for all.

"For reaching the Noble Path": The Noble Path here means a type of consciousness which appears at the moment of realization. When meditators realize the truth, which is *nibbāna*, there arises in them a type of consciousness which is called "path consciousness." It is called "path consciousness" because when you have reached this stage of consciousness, you can be certain to reach *nibbāna* on this path. It surely will lead there.

There are four stages of realization and so there are four types of path consciousness. Each path consciousness eradicates some mental defilements completely so that after reaching the fourth path consciousness, all of them are altogether eradicated. The defilements eradicated by path consciousness will not return to you. For reaching the Noble Path, for attaining this type of consciousness which can eradicate the mental defilements altogether, *satipaṭṭhāna* is the only way.

"For the realization of *nibbāna*": We can say that reaching the Noble Path means reaching the "state of path consciousness" and realizing *nibbāna* means reaching the "state of fruition consciousness." Immediately after the path consciousness comes the fruition consciousness. Some knowledge of the *Abhidhamma* will help you to understand this more clearly. Suffice it to say that both the path consciousness and the fruition consciousness take *nibbāna* as their object, they both perceive *nibbāna* directly. Either of these two moments can be called moments of realizing *nibbāna*.

In brief, the Buddha said, this is the only way to purify your mind, to overcome sorrow and lamentation, to overcome pain and grief, to reach the Noble Path and to realize *nibbāna*. And what is this only way? This only way is none other than the way of the Four Foundations of Mindfulness.

> *What are the four? Herein [in this teaching], bhikkhus, a bhikkhu dwells contemplating the body in the body, ardently, clearly comprehending and mindful, removing covetousness and grief in the world.*

This is, briefly, the statement of mindfulness meditation. Meditators are contemplating the body in the body. This is how they practice mindfulness meditation. You contemplate or keep yourself mindful of the body in the body. Here the word "body" is repeated to make sure that you contemplate the body in the body and not in the feelings, not in the consciousness, and not in the *dhammas*.

"Ardently, clearly comprehending and mindful": This is important, because it shows how you should meditate. When you meditate, when you contemplate the body in the body, i.e, when you make yourself aware of everything that is in the body, you must do it ardently, clearly comprehending and mindful. "Ardently" means, you must be energetic, put forth effort to be mindful or to watch whatever is in the body. "Ardently" refers, therefore, to the energy or effort you invest.

Without effort you cannot keep your mind on the object, you cannot meditate. So a certain amount of energy or effort is needed to practice meditation. It is not an easy thing to keep your mind on the object. Therefore, energy or effort is a requirement for the practice of meditation.

You must be "clearly comprehending and mindful." When you practice meditation, you must always be mindful. You must be mindful of your breath, the movements of your abdomen, the different deportments and the small activities of the body. Mindfulness is something like a stone hitting a wall. In order to throw a stone, you must put out energy. You throw the stone with energy and it hits the wall. Like the stone hitting the wall, mindfulness hits the object. Whatever the objects are — the breath, or the movements of the abdomen, or the activities of the body — your mind, as it were, goes to these objects. That hitting of the object is mindfulness.

When you have mindfulness, combined with energy or effort, your mind stays with the object for some time. The stone, after hitting the wall, when it is a wet mud wall, stays with the wall. It gets stuck in the wall. In the same way, the mind goes to the object and, when it is helped by energy and mindfulness, stays with the object. That staying of the mind with the object is what we call concentration. So, when you have mindfulness, you will achieve concentration. Only when you have developed concentration, will you have wisdom and the understanding of the nature of things. You will have clear comprehension of things. So when it is said that you should be mindful and clearly comprehending, this means, you also must have concentration. It is indispensable to clear comprehension, which is wisdom.

Moreover, mindfulness and concentration belong to the group of concentration. There are eight factors of the Path, namely, Right Understanding, Right Thought, Right Speech, Right Action, Right Livelihood, Right Effort, Right Mindfulness, and Right Concentration. These eight factors are divided into three groups, namely, the morality group, the concentration group, and the wisdom group. Effort, mindfulness, and concentration belong to the concentration group. When one is practiced, the others have also to be practiced. Therefore, mindfulness here also means concentration.

When you have concentration, when your mind stays with the object for some time, you come to see the nature of mind and body. You see that they are impermanent, unsatisfactory, insubstantial. You will come to see the rising and passing of things, when you have sufficient concentration. Different thoughts come to you. You take note of them and they go away. You come to see this clearly only when you have the necessary concentration.

Four things are needed so that your meditation is good. First, you have to ardently make effort. Second, you have to practice mindfulness. Third, you have to develop concentration. And fourth, you have to understand and comprehend. These four constituents are indispensable for good meditation. By saying, "ardently, clearly comprehending and mindful," the Buddha showed you how to meditate, how to observe things, how to watch your breath, the movements of your abdomen and other activities of your body as well as your feelings, consciousness and the *dhammas*. Therefore, it is important when you meditate to have energy to back up mindfulness, so that you can generate sufficient concentration to penetrate the nature of things.

"Removing covetousness and grief in the world": When the Buddha said, "in the world," it means here the body, the aggregates of clinging. "Covetousness" means craving or greed or attachment, and "grief" means ill will or hatred or anger or depression. By these words, the Buddha showed the constituents which have to be removed. He showed the results of meditation, the results of being ardent, clearly comprehending, and mindful, the results of having concentration.

When you make effort, are mindful, have concentration and a penetrating knowledge or wisdom, then you can remove covetousness and grief. You can remove greed and hatred which are the two gross hindrances. There are altogether five hindrances, but these are the grosser ones. When you can remove the two grosser ones, you will be able to remove the other ones as well. When you clearly comprehend your breath or the movements of your abdomen or your feelings or other activities in your body, you will have neither craving nor attachments, neither ill will nor hatred at that time. At every moment, you remove these factors from your mind.

There are two kinds of removal. Let us call them "momentary removal" and "temporary removal." During "momentary removal," the hindrances are removed momentarily. At one moment, they will not be present, but the next moment, they may show up again. They are removed only at the moment when they make room for wholesome mental states. "Temporary removal" means removal for some time, longer than momentary removal. Mahāsi Sayadaw explained the temporary removal as follows:

> When a meditator is constantly observant of every mental and physical phenomenon and comprehends each [of the phenomena] clearly as impermanent, unsatisfactory, insubstantial and not beautiful, effort, mindfulness, and concentration will develop in him. Because of this development, the mind becomes so refined that even on the non-observed objects, attachment and ill will don't arise.

> Even when he is resting, gross attachment and ill will do not arise in him to such an extent that he comes to think that gross attachment and ill will cannot arise in him at all. Thus, the subdued state of defilements even on the non-observed objects, by the fact of observing the present objects, is what is called "temporary removal," by the group of concentration members present at each observing act.

> This is temporary removal of greed and hatred. A meditator experiences these two kinds of removal — momentary removal on the objects observed and temporary removal on the non-observed objects, every time he is observing. To get these two benefits of removal, a meditator must practice contemplation of his body, observing every physical phenomenon which is evident at the present moment. This is what the Buddha meant.

The meditation instructions of Mahāsi Sayadaw are described in more detail in Part Three.

Now, when you keep your mind on your breath, for example, and mentally note "in-out," "in-out," even before you get steady concentration, you will have moments of concentration. Then you will have distractions and then concentration again and then distractions, and so on. At that time, your removal of covetousness and grief is said to be "momen-tary." At one moment, you remove the defilements and, the next moment, they may be present in your mind again.

After some time, when you build up your practice and can keep your mind on the object for a longer time, you will be able to remove the defilements temporarily, i.e., for a longer period of time. You will come to see that, even on the objects not observed, the defilements remain subdued. When you have reached this stage, you are said to have gotten rid of your defilements by "temporary removal." Since this removal is temporary, the defilements will come back to you, when you give up meditation altogether.

There is one more removal, and that is "total removal." It is achieved at the moment of path consciousness, at the moment of realizing *nibbāna*. So, when you reach path consciousness, you remove, abandon, annihilate or eradicate the hindrances and other defilements altogether. Once removed, they will not come back to you at all. This "total removal" is not referred to here, since only the mundane and not the supramundane path is shown. (The word "removal" is used here in the technical sense of "not letting the defilements arise.")

> *He dwells contemplating the feeling in the feelings, ar-dently, clearly comprehending and mindful, removing covetousness and grief in the world.*

When the Buddha said, "in the world," it means here "in the feelings." Meditators are mindful of their feelings. They ob-serve and take note of their feelings. There are three kinds of feelings, namely, pleasant feelings, painful feelings, and indif-ferent feelings. Meditators are aware of any of their feelings which are present at the moment. You contemplate on your feelings as you contemplate on your body.

> *He dwells contemplating the consciousness in the con-sciousness, ardently, clearly comprehending and mindful, removing covetousness and grief in the world.*

When the Buddha said, "in the world," it means here "in the consciousness." The object of meditation here is to observe the different types of consciousness. There is consciousness accompanied by greed, by hatred, by delusion, and so on.

When you want something and you are aware of this want, as "wanting, wanting, wanting" you are contemplating on the consciousness which is accompanied by greed. Similarly, when you are angry, and so forth.

> *He dwells contemplating the dhammas in the dhammas, ardently, clearly comprehending and mindful, removing covetousness and grief in the world.*

When the Buddha said, "in the world," it means here "in the *dhammas*." The word *dhammas* denotes many things. It is the most difficult word in Pāli to translate into any other language. Some translate it as "mental objects." Although this is not altogether wrong, it does not cover what is covered by *dhammas*. So, it is better to leave this word untranslated.

You will know what *dhammas* (see glossary) are when you reach the section on the Contemplation of the *dhammas*. In brief, they are the five mental hindrances, the five aggregates of clinging, the six internal and six external sense-bases, the seven factors of enlightenment, and the Four Noble Truths. When you have desire in your mind and you are aware of that as "desire, desire, desire," you are contemplating on the *dhammas*. They are mental hindrances. The same is true for anger, etc.

This is a brief statement of the Four Foundations of Mindfulness, which are the Contemplation of the Body, the Contemplation of the Feelings, the Contemplation of the Consciousness, and the Contemplation of the *dhammas*.

You will find many repetitions in the *sutta*. They cannot be avoided. You should understand that this *sutta* and all other teachings belong to the age where there were no books, so teachings had to be memorized. When you memorize a passage, you have to repeat it again and again. By these repetitions, you gain deeper understanding of it. Also, when you are listening to a talk, you cannot go back, as you can when you are reading. Repetitions help you to understand more fully so that you can grasp the meaning more thoroughly. Although repetitions may be tedious, they cannot be left out.

1 Contemplation of the Body in the Body

The First Foundation of Mindfulness is the Contemplation of the Body in the Body. The Buddha described it in fourteen different ways. In other words, he taught fourteen different topics for the Contemplation of the Body in the Body. The first of these topics is breathing. The Buddha said,

> *And how, bhikkhus, does a bhikkhu dwell, contemplating the body in the body? Here now, bhikkhus, a bhikkhu having gone to the forest, to the foot of a tree, to a secluded place, sits down cross-legged, keeps his upper body erect, and directs his mindfulness to the object of his meditation. Ever mindful, he breathes in, ever mindful, he breathes out.*

With the words, "having gone to the forest, to the foot of a tree, to a secluded place," the Buddha indicated suitable places for meditation. The first is the "forest," meaning any kind of forest which offers the bliss of seclusion. Since the place must be secluded, it should be a forest where nobody lives, away from the sounds and noises of people living in villages, towns, or cities. In some texts, a forest is defined as a place about five-hundred-bow lengths away from human habitation. One bow length is equivalent to six feet, so it means about three thousand feet away from any human habitation. When a place is that faraway from people, seclusion can be found there. These days, it is difficult to find a really secluded place. Even in a forest you may still hear the noise of air planes.

The second place mentioned in the sutta is "the foot of a tree." The foot of any tree is a suitable place for meditation, but it should be in as quiet a place as a forest. The third place is just "a secluded place." It may be in a city or a village, but has to be secluded. With regard to these places, seclusion is the most important condition. Therefore, any place which offers seclusion is a suitable place for meditation.

In other *suttas*, traditional lists of secluded places are given: a forest, the root of a tree, a rock, a hill cleft, a mountain cave, a charnel ground (cemetery), a jungle thicket, open space, and a heap of straw.[3] With reference to these lists, the last seven places, beginning with "a rock," are also to be taken as "secluded places."

These places are mentioned because they are most suitable for beginners who need a place which is both quiet and free from distractions. A retreat center or meditation monastery may provide a secluded environment for practice. For those who have experience and whose concentration has matured to some extent, any place is the right place for meditation.

"[He] sits down cross-legged, keeps his upper body erect and directs his mindfulness to the object of his meditation": With these words, the Buddha showed how you should prepare yourself for meditation, and what posture you should select. He mentions the traditional posture of sitting "cross-legged." People in the East are accustomed to sitting on the floor, so sitting cross-legged comes naturally to them. They have no difficulty sitting in this position. It is a very good posture for meditation and it is a peaceful one, neither conducive to idleness nor to agitation.

There are three different forms of sitting cross-legged. The first one is the "full-lotus position" which is most difficult to maintain. When you have no practice, you cannot sit in this posture for a long time. When your legs are intertwined, you will feel pain after you have sat in this position for a few minutes. The second posture is the "half-lotus position." You put one leg on top of the other, but they are not intertwined. You can sit longer in this position; however, you will still feel some kind of pressure and your feet will get numb after some minutes. The third is the "easy position." In this position, you sit with one leg in front of and not on the other. This position is described in some books as the "Burmese position." In Burma, most people sit this way. This posture may be the best for beginners. Since it is the most comfortable one, beginners will be able to sit in this posture for a longer period of time, without much discomfort.

Some people find it very painful to sit cross-legged, so painful that it interferes with their practice of meditation. Such people may sit on a cushion, a chair, or a bench, since some degree of comfort is necessary for practicing meditation. Though there should not be too much comfort, some is necessary to continue with the practice of meditation.

"He keeps his upper body erect," means meditators keep their body straight when they sit cross-legged. When you sit straight, your spine is also straight. When your spine is straight, the eighteen vertebrae in the spine are resting one on top of the other. When you sit straight, your muscles, sinews, skin, and flesh are not twisted, so painful feelings do not so readily arise as when your muscles, etc., are twisted. Your mind can become unified in meditation and, instead of collapsing when the pain increases, can attend to the growth of mindfulness.[4]

Sitting cross-legged and keeping your upper body erect is, therefore, a very suitable position which is conducive to concentration.

MINDFULNESS OF BREATHING

"He directs his mindfulness to the object of meditation," means that practitioners focus their mind on the object of meditation. Here, the object of meditation will be the breath. So, you set your mind, i.e., you focus, on the incoming and outgoing breath.

"Ever mindful, he breathes in, ever mindful, he breathes out": This explains the practice of meditation. When you practice meditation, you keep your mind on the breath. You breathe in and out mindfully. Actually, you put your mind at the entrance of your nostrils and observe the breath as "in-out, in-out," and so on. Your mind must stay at the tip of your nose, it must not follow the breath into and out of your body. You must try to see the in-breath and the out-breath as two separate things. The in-breath is not existing at the time of breathing out and the out-breath is not existing at the time of breathing in.

When you practice breathing meditation, you can observe your breath in many different ways.[5] Four of these ways are shown in this *sutta.*

Breathing in a long breath, he knows, "I am breathing in long"; breathing out a long breath, he knows, "I am breathing out long."

During the course of observing their breath, meditators sometimes happen to breathe long breaths. Then meditators should know, "we are breathing in long." That means they do not fail to notice it when they pay sufficient attention to the breath. It does not mean that you should deliberately breathe long in order to know that you are breathing long. To "know" here means to know thoroughly and not superficially.

Breathing in a short breath, he knows, "I am breathing in a short breath"; breathing out a short breath, he knows, "I am breathing out a short breath."

Sometimes, meditators happen to breathe short breaths. At such a time, they know thoroughly that they are breathing short breaths; they do not fail to notice that they are doing so. Here also, it must be understood that you should not deliberately make your breaths short. You should just know that you are breathing short breaths.

"Making clear the entire in-breath body, I shall breathe in," thus he makes efforts [literally, he trains himself]; "making clear the entire out-breath body, I shall breathe out," thus he makes efforts.

When you observe your breaths, you must try to see all the breaths clearly. "Making clear" means making the breaths known, making them plain, trying to see them vividly. In the original Pāli text, the word for "the entire in-breath body" is *sabbakāya* which literally means the entire body. But *kāya* or body here does not mean the entire physical body. It means the breath body. The Pāli word *kāya* can mean the physical body as well as a group. It is similar to when you talk about a body of members. Here it means not the entire physical body but just the breath, and "entire" here means, the beginning, the middle and the end. So, meditators must try to see thoroughly the beginning, the middle, and the end of each breath. You must also not forget that this section is on mindfulness of breathing so that the object of this meditation must be the breathing and not the entire physical body.

The following explanation is given in *The Path of Purification:*

> He trains thus, "I shall breathe in making known, making plain the beginning, middle, and end of the entire in-breath body. I shall breathe out making known, making plain, the beginning, middle, and end of the entire out-breath body," thus he trains himself. Making the breaths known, making them plain, in this way, he both breathes in and breathes out with consciousness, associated with knowledge.[6]

You must have noticed the future tense in this passage. It is to show that in the previous observations of the breath, you did not need so much knowledge, so much effort to distinguish the long from the short breaths, but from here on, you must make effort to gain knowledge, to see the breaths clearly and thoroughly. That is why the future tense is used here and in the following passages.

It does not mean that meditators should breathe more vigorously so that the breathing may become clear to them. Their concentration and knowledge or understanding are said to be deep and thorough only when they can perceive the beginning, the middle, and the end of each breath clearly. When they see the breaths clearly because they breathe more vigorously, that means they see the breaths clearly not because of their concentration and knowledge but because of the grossness of the object. Therefore, meditators should not breathe more vigorously just to see their breaths more clearly. When they do so, they will tire themselves out in a short time. Therefore, breathing should be normal.

When you practice this kind of meditation, you should try to put forth effort and gain knowledge in order to see all in-breaths and out-breaths clearly, while you breathe normally. How many things do you need in order to see the breaths clearly? How many factors are involved in each act of clear observation? You need effort, mindfulness, concentration, and understanding.

> *"Calming the gross in-breath [literally, body-conditioned things], I shall breathe in," thus he makes efforts; "calming the gross out-breath, I shall breathe out," thus he makes efforts.*

In this passage, the breath is called "body-conditioned thing." The Pāli word for "body-conditioned thing" is *kāya sankhāra*. *Kāya* means "body" and *sankhāra* means "conditioned." Therefore, it means a "thing conditioned by the body." It is said that breath is caused by consciousness or the mind. But when there is no body, there cannot be any breath. So, although it is caused by the mind, the breath depends on the body for its arising, i.e., for its appearance. Therefore, it is called *kāya sankhāra*, a "thing conditioned by the body."

Sankhāra is a difficult word in the Pāli language. It can mean many things, depending on the context. Sometimes it means "volition," which we call *kamma*. In the teachings of the Dependent Origination, *sankhāra* means just this. Sometimes, it means the "fifty mental factors," headed by volition, as in *sankhāra khandha*, the aggregate of *sankhāra*. Sometimes, *sankhāra* means "everything in the world, everything that is conditioned," for example, when you say, "all *sankhāra* are impermanent." Sometimes, it means "encouraging" or "prompting," as in the *Abhidhamma* term, *asankhārika*. Here, it has the meaning of "conditioning." So, *kāya-sankhāra* here means the "breath which is conditioned by the body."

This word *kāya sankhāra* has also been translated in different ways. In the *Buddhist Dictionary*, it is translated as "bodily functions," while Soma Thera, in *The Way of Mindfulness*, translated it as "activities of the body." Nyānamoli, in *The Path of Purification*, translated it as "bodily formations," and Nyānaponika, in *The Heart of Buddhist Meditation*, translated it as "bodily functions." Nyānasatta Thera sees it as "the activities of the body." What is meant here by the term is just "the breath." Here it should be taken as the gross breath, because it has to be calmed down.

The expression, "calming the gross in-breath," should not be taken to mean that meditators should deliberately calm down, inhibit, and still their breath. What is meant is that when the breath becomes very subtle, meditators must try hard, pay attention, and apply more effort to discern it. The breath is not like the other objects of meditation which become clearer and clearer with the increase in concentration and understanding. When meditators progress further and further, the objects, e.g., the *kasina* (earth disks) or other meditation objects become clearer and clearer in their mind. It is not the same with the breath which becomes subtler and more and more difficult to perceive, according to your progress.

When you are not meditating, your mind and body are not restful. Your breaths, which depend on the condition of your mind and body, will then arise in gross form. But when you continue to meditate, your mind and body become rested and tranquil and the breaths become subtle. The more you progress toward the achievement of concentration, the subtler your breaths become, so much so that you have to investigate whether they exist or not. They may become so subtle that, at one point, you will doubt whether they are there at all. Since you do not find anything to perceive, you may think the breath is simply lost. At such a time, you should say to yourself, "I am not dead, I have not drowned. I am still alive. But I cannot perceive the breaths because they are too subtle and my concentration and understanding are not keen and developed enough. Therefore, I must develop them more, pay more attention to the meditation object, and try to perceive these subtle breaths." When you continue with your efforts and gain more understanding, you will be able to perceive the breaths however subtle they may be.

When, in the course of meditation, the breaths become imperceptible, do not give up your meditation. You must encourage and exert yourself to perceive the subtle breaths until they become clear to you again. This is what is meant by "calming the gross in-breath." You must increase your effort.

In the *sutta*, the Buddha has shown four ways of breathing meditation. When you practice this meditation, you should perceive fully the long breaths, the short breaths, the duration of the breaths, and the subtle, almost imperceptible, breaths.

Thus, you have now four ways of breathing mindfully. First, when breathing in with a long breath, you must note that you are breathing in with a long breath. Second, you must note when you are breathing out with a long breath. Third, you note when you are breathing in with a short breath. Fourth, note when you are breathing out with a short breath. These are the four rules of breathing mindfully.

The Buddha gave a simile so that the *bhikkhus* could understand this teaching more clearly. When he said,

> as a skillful operator of a lathe and his apprentice are making a long turn,

"making a long turn" means, when making something big like a drum, operators have to make a long turn on the lathe. "When making a short turn" means, when making something small, such as ivory needles, operators have to make short turns on the lathe. Making these turns, practitioners should be aware of what turn is being made.

> *Thus, he dwells contemplating the body in the body internally, or... externally, or...[both] internally and externally.*

What is meant by "contemplating internally?" It means that meditators contemplate or keep themselves mindful of their own in-breaths and out-breaths. When they keep their mind on their own breathing, they are said to be "contemplating the body in the body internally." When you have gained some practice in keeping your mind on your own breaths, occasionally you may think of other people's breaths as well. "Just as my breaths have a beginning and an end, appear and disappear, so do the breaths of other people." In this way, you contemplate on the breaths of other people. In doing this, you are said to be "contemplating the body in the body externally." It does not mean that you look at other people and contemplate their breathing. However, when you happen to contemplate other people's breaths, you should be mindful of them, too. Sometimes, you contemplate your own breathing and then the breathing of other people and then your own breathing again. You go back and forth between your breathing and that of others. When you do that you are said to be "contemplating the body in the body internally and externally." It doesn't mean that you should look at your and other people's breathing.

> *He dwells contemplating the origination factors of the breath body, or he dwells contemplating the dissolution factors of the breath body, or he dwells contemplating both, the origination and dissolution factors of the breath body.*

Here, "origination factors" mean the factors which bring about the breath. The commentator explained it with a simile. When a blacksmith wants to produce fire, he uses the bellows. There are the bellows and there is something at the end of the bellows which is called the spout, and there are the efforts of the blacksmith. Depending on these three things, air is produced to make fire with the bellows, the spout, and the effort of the smith. In the same way, in order to produce breath, you need a physical body, the nasal aperture, and a mind. Depending on these three things, each breath is produced in the body. Without them, there can be no breath. Therefore, these three things are called "origination factors of the breath." When you are practicing meditation on the breath, sometimes the thought may come to you, "because there is a body, because there is a nasal aperture, and there is a mind, there is this breath." When you are contemplating this, you are said to contemplate on the "origination factors" of your breath.

"Dissolution factors" mean the opposite. When there is no physical body, there can be no breath. When there is no nasal aperture, there can be no breath. And when there is no mind, there can be no breath. These three things — breaking up of the body, destruction of the nasal aperture, and the cessation of the mind to function — are called the "dissolution factors of the breath." So, when you contemplate on these three factors, you are said to contemplate on the "dissolution factors" of the breath. And when you are contemplating on all six factors, you are said to contemplate on both, the "origination" and the "dissolution factors" of the breath.

This should not be interpreted that you should deliberately search for these origination and dissolution factors. What is meant is that when, during meditation, the thought of these factors should arise, you should just recognize the origination or dissolution of the breath. These explanations are given in the ancient commentaries.

Mahāsi Sayadaw had something to add. He said that the observing of the arising and disappearing of the breath is also meant in this passage. The Pāli word for "origination factors" is *samudaya dhammas*. It can mean "factors by which something arises," but it can also mean "the state or nature of arising" or just "arising." The same is true for the "dissolution factors." The Pāli word for "dissolution factors" is *vaya dhammas* which can mean "factors by which something dissolves." It can also mean "the state of dissolving" or just "dissolution."

Therefore, in the Venerable's opinion, meditators who closely observe the arising of breath, bit by bit, at every moment and at any place (such as the breath touching the tip of the nose) are said to be contemplating the *samudaya dhammas* of the breath or the arising of the breath. Also, meditators who closely observe the disappearance, bit by bit, at every moment and at any place (such as the breath touching the tip of the nose) can be said to be contemplating the *vaya dhammas* of the breath or the dissolution of the breath.

When you watch the breath, first you see the beginning of the breath; then the breath ends and you watch it disappear. When you watch closely, you observe the arising and disappearance of the breath. It is, therefore, more natural and probable that you will see the arising and disappearance of the breath than that you will see the factors of its arising and disappearing. However, you cannot rule out the seeing of the cause of its arising and disappearing during meditation. Thus, both explanations in this passage are applicable. For a second meaning, the translation could read, "He dwells contemplating the arising nature in the breath body, or he dwells contemplating the dissolving nature in the breath body, or he dwells contemplating both, the arising and the dissolving nature in the breath body."

> *Or his mindfulness is established as "there is only the breath body."*

There are many usages of the word *kāya* in this *sutta*. You have to interpret the meaning, according to its context. Here you have the section on breathing. So, wherever you find the word *kāya*, "body," you must understand that it means the "breath body." Therefore, when practitioners keep themselves mindful of the breath, their mindfulness is established on "there is only the breath body." When you keep your mind on the breath, you see nothing else but breath. There is only breath, no person, no being, no woman, no man, no individual, no I, nothing pertaining to the I, no soul, nothing pertaining the soul, and so on. There is only breath, but no one who is regulating the breath or who is giving orders to the breath, who creates the breath; just the breath. In this way, mindfulness is established.

> *And that mindfulness is established to the extent necessary for further measure of knowledge and mindfulness.*

This means mindfulness that "there is that breath body only" is established for the purpose of further knowledge and mindfulness. When you practice breathing as *vipassanā* meditation, you go from one stage to the other, from a lower stage of knowledge to a higher stage of knowledge and then to the highest knowledge. Mindfulness is established to help you go on to the higher stages of knowledge and concentration. When you don't see that "there is only breath" but see this breath as being permanent or having an owner, a soul, or a self, or any permanent entity, you will not be able to progress on the path of *vipassanā* knowledge. Therefore, mindfulness that "there is only the breath body" is necessary for the development of knowledge.

> *Not depending on (or attached to) anything through craving and wrong views, he dwells.*

When you keep your mind on the breath, watch it, and come to see it as coming and going every moment, you cannot see anything to be attached to. The breath comes and goes, the breath is nothing to be attached to; it is just breath. When you reach the higher stages of *vipassanā* knowledge, you will come to see the arising and disappearing of all phenomena, both the mental and physical ones. You won't find anything to be attached to by way of craving or by way of wrong views. You are sometimes attached to or crave for things. You want something, you like something, and you are attached to it. Sometimes, you have wrong views about these things. When you think that things are permanent, you have wrong views. You think that they will last for ever, that they are lovely or, if it is a person, that there is a permanent entity or soul. When you hold such views, you are said to have wrong views. So, through wrong views or through craving, you become attached to things. However, when you come to see the true nature of the breath as well as the mind and the body, you will not find anything to be attached to or to depend on.

> *Nor does he cling to anything in the world of the five aggregates of clinging.*

"Five aggregates of clinging" mean the five aggregates that are objects of clinging or grasping. They are the aggregate of corporeality, the aggregate of feeling, the aggregate of perception, the aggregate of mental formations, and the aggregate of consciousness. In brief, everything in the world belongs to one or the other of these five aggregates. Seeing the true nature of things, practitioners of *vipassanā* meditation do not cling to anything in the world because there is no longer craving, let alone clinging, to anything.

> *Thus too, bhikkhus, a bhikkhu dwells contemplating the body in the body.*

This indicates that the teachings on breathing meditation have come to an end.

Breathing meditation can be practiced as *samatha* or *vipassanā* meditation. *Samatha* meditation means tranquility meditation which leads to gaining good concentration or *jhāna*. *Vipassanā* meditation leads to eradication of the mental defilements. When you practice *samatha* meditation, you practice differently than when you practice *vipassanā* meditation. When you practice *samatha* meditation on breathing, keep your mind on your breath and count each breath. When you count, neither count below five nor past ten. Counting is to be done from one to five, one to six, up to one to ten, whatever is more appropriate for you For example, "in one, out one; in two, out two; in three, out three; in four, out four; in five, out five," and then again, "in one, out one," etc. Or you may count up to six. Or you may count up to ten.

At first, you should count slowly. The purpose of counting is to help you in keeping your mind on the object; it can be compared to tying the object with a rope. Once you gain concentration through counting and can stay with an object without distraction, you can give up counting and just keep yourself aware of the in-breath and the out-breath. First, you count, and then you practice what we call connecting or collecting the mind and the breath without counting. You just keep your awareness on the breath and it will become more and more subtle.

Sometimes, you may see signs or visions. Different visions come to different people. There are neither a definite number nor definite kinds of visions a person may see. If you ask ten people, you may get ten different answers. Different individuals have different inclinations, dispositions, perceptions, therefore, their visions will vary. In the scriptures, visions are described as appearing "like stars." You may see them "like stars." You may see the sign appear like a star or a cluster of gems or pearls, or it may appear to have a rough touch like that of silk cotton seeds or a peg made of heartwood, or a long braided string or a wreath of flowers or a puff of smoke or a stretched-out cobweb or a cloud or a lotus flower or a chariot wheel or the disk of the moon or the sun. Any of these signs or visions may come to meditators reaching a certain level of concentration. They will then enter the absorptions or *jhānas*, and from the *jhānas* can shift to *vipassanā*.

When you practice breathing as *vipassanā* meditation, you do not count the breaths. You just keep your mindfulness on the breath and practice according to the four stages — breathing long, breathing short, comprehending clearly the entire breath body, and calming the gross breath.

You may not see signs or visions in *vipassanā* meditation. However, if you see them, you just stay aware of them as "seeing, seeing, seeing," and so on. After some time, you will see mind and body clearly, and you will progress more and more, until you reach the stage of realization.

In this *sutta* emphasis is on *vipassanā* and not *samatha* meditation, because contemplating the "origination factors" and the "dissolution factors" is only possible in *vipassanā* meditation. In *samatha* meditation, you do not contemplate on the arising or the disappearing of the objects. You just keep your mind on the objects, just that. When it is said that you contemplate on the origination and the arising or on the dissolution and the falling, you are neither attached to nor clinging to anything. This means *vipassanā* and not *samatha*. In this *sutta*, every object of meditation is directed toward *vipassanā*, although in the early stages, it can be *samatha* meditation. When you practice *vipassanā* meditation, you keep your awareness on the breath and also everything that comes to you through the six sense doors at the present moment. When you see something, you become aware of it. When you hear something, you do the same. When you think of something or there are distractions or stray thoughts, you become aware of them too. This is the difference between *samatha* and *vipassanā* meditation. In the former you keep your awareness only on the meditation object and ignore everything else. In the latter, you keep your awareness on everything that is present, everything that comes to you at the present moment.

In this *sutta*, you know each subject of meditation is directed toward *vipassanā* because at the end of each section you find the passage: "He dwells on contemplating the origination factors...."

THE POSTURES OF THE BODY

The second subsection on the Contemplation of the Body is called "The Postures of the Body." Postures here mean the four deportments of the body: going or walking, standing, sitting, and lying down. Practitioners are to use all four postures in mindfulness meditation.

The Buddha said,

> *And again, bhikkhus, a bhikkhu knows, "I am going,"*
> *when he is going; he knows, "I am standing," when he is*
> *standing; he knows, "I am sitting," when he is sitting; he*
> *knows, "I am lying down," when he is lying down or just*
> *as his body is disposed, so he knows it.*

Here, "a *bhikkhu* knows" means, meditators know thoroughly, they know deeply. It is not just a superficial knowledge, it is a deep knowledge of what is going on. Meditators clearly know the going, standing, sitting and lying down. You must clearly know, "I am going," when going; "I am walking," when walking; "I am standing," when standing; "I am sitting," when sitting, and "I am lying down," when lying down. Mindfulness must be applied to all postures of the body.

The last statement, "just as his body is disposed, so he knows it," allows different interpretations. The commentator interprets this sentence to be a general statement for all four postures, not differing much from the statements made earlier. That means, when meditators are going, they must know "I am going." When they are standing, they must know "I am standing," and so on. The author of the sub-commentary, however, added another interpretation to this statement. According to him, in the statement, "a *bhikkhu* knows, 'I am going,' when he is going," and so on, the different postures are emphasized, but in the last statement, "just as his body is disposed, so he knows it," the body as a whole is emphasized. Therefore, when you know that your body as a whole is going, standing, sitting, or lying down, you may be following the instructions given in the last statement. But when you know, "I am going," when going, and so on, you may be following the instructions given in the previous statement.

Mahāsi Sayadaw had something else to add. He said that the statement covers all the small deportments or postures of the body as well; not only going, standing, sitting and lying down but also the small movements like stretching, bending, or looking forward or sideways. Yogis practicing meditation, especially *vipassanā* meditation, cannot afford to be unmindful of the small movements and deportments. When you fail to make note of these small movements, there may be a tendency to cling to them, by way of craving or wrong views. When practicing *vipassanā* meditation, you must be aware of everything that is present at the moment.

Therefore, in the statement, "just as his body is disposed, so he knows it," all other deportments have to be included. *Vipassanā* must be practiced not only in the four main postures but also in the various small postures. *Vipassanā* must be practiced all the time, not only when you are on a retreat.

There have been some misunderstandings with regard to this statement or instruction. These misunderstandings did not arise recently. They arose before the commentaries were put into writing. The commentary on the division to which this *sutta* belongs, was written down about 2,100 years ago. Even at that time already there were misunderstandings about the meaning of knowing that "'I am going,' when he is going," and so on. Some people did not understand the real meaning of this statement. They ridiculed this type of meditation and said, "Even ordinary people who do not meditate and even animals know, 'I am going,' when they are going. They do not know 'I am going' when they are standing or sitting or lying down. So what is the significance of the instruction that they have to be aware of going, when meditators are going, and so on? When knowing 'I am going,' when somebody is going is to be called meditation or a foundation of mindfulness, then everybody can be said to be meditating all the time. So what is the difference between the knowing of ordinary people who do not meditate and the knowing of meditators?"

The answer is, that the two are diametrically opposed. Let us see how people who do not meditate know "I am going," when they are going. Before going can take place, there has to be the desire or intention to go. When people who do not meditate know, "I am going," when they are going, they do not know at every moment when the going takes place. They may be aware of going superficially at some time, but they are not always aware of it. The intention to go and the going do not occur at the same time. Their knowing is, therefore, superficial and unmindful. When they say, "I am going," when they are going, they do not see the intention which is mental and the body movement which is physical, one separated from the other. They have only a vague idea of what going is. They think that mind and body act together. They do not see the mental and physical aspects of going clearly and do not separate one from the other. Because they do not meditate, they do not pay close attention to what is happening at the present moment. Since their knowledge is superficial, they have no direct knowledge that successive moments of intention are followed by successive movements of the body.

In the twinkle of an eye, it is said, hundreds of thought moments come and go. These moments can cause some material properties to arise. We have four great elements — earth, water, fire and air. In moving, the air element is predominant. The desire or the intention causes the air element to arise in the parts of the body which are going to move. That air element causes the body or parts of the body to move.

When you do not observe the going closely, as is done in meditation, you do not know that going is composed of successive movements caused by intention or desire. You may think that going is caused by someone or some higher authority or some permanent entity. You do not know that the act of going is composed of only the intention and the going, nothing more. You do not know that there is neither an individual nor a being apart from the intention and the going. There is neither an I, nor a man, nor a woman, but just the intention and the going or the body movement occurring together. You do not know it, because you have only a very vague idea of what is going.

Without the close observation of meditation, you do not know that the intention and the going or the body movement do not exist up to the next moment. You think that the intention and the going, which occur at the moment of going, lead to the next moment and from that moment to the next. You see the process of going as one continuous, permanent process. You cannot see that at every moment the intention comes and then goes away. The body movements, and the air element come and go away. Therefore, you cannot say that one moment of intention moves to another moment.

Every moment, they arise and then disappear. This is what meditators experience when practicing meditation, but people who are not meditating, do not perceive it this way.

Their knowledge of walking or going is unmindful. You can stop people walking on the street and ask them what they are thinking about. Most probably, they will be thinking of some other thing than the going itself. They may be thinking of their home or job. Even though they may know, for some moment, that they are walking, their knowing will be superficial.

People think, it is one and the same being, one and the same individual, that has existed in the past, that is existing now, and that will exist in the future. Maybe they have some vague idea of impermanence but they think of one and the same person that has existed, that is existing, and that will exist. Therefore, their knowing cannot shed the belief in a being, while actually, according to the analysis, there is no being at all. Apart from the intention and the movements of the body, there is no person, no individual.

They uphold the belief in the being because they do not see the arising and disappearing of the intention and the movement at any given moment. Their knowing cannot abandon the concept of permanent entity or the concept of soul. They may think that there is something apart from the going, apart from the intention, that administers going, that takes care of going. Therefore, their knowing cannot be called the result of *kammaṭṭhāna*, i.e., meditation.

The Pāli word for meditation, *kammaṭṭhāna*, is defined as a condition for further development. When it is meditation, when it is *kammaṭṭhāna*, it must be a condition to foster development. The knowing of an individual who does not meditate cannot be a condition or a basis for further development, because the knowing is superficial. This individual does not see what going is. It cannot be called *kammaṭṭhāna* meditation.

Since this knowing is without mindfulness, it also cannot be called a Foundation of Mindfulness.

The knowing of people who meditate is very different from the knowing of those who do not meditate. When you meditate while walking, you are aware of the movement. You are taking note of the three stages of one step: lifting, moving, putting down; lifting, moving, putting down. You are watching closely the process of walking. When you are meditating, you know each time when the walking occurs. You are aware each time of the intention and the going itself. You are aware of and will come to observe the intention underlying each voluntary action, as long as you can maintain sufficient concentration.

Some practitioners feel that someone or something is pushing them from behind when they walk, while they are practicing meditation. That is, because they realize that the intention is moving their body. They see the intention and the movement clearly. Each time there is intention and movement, they are aware of them, because they are closely watching the action of walking. While seeing the intention and the movement, they separate one from the other. Going or walking is caused by intention to walk or to go. When there is intention to walk or to go, there will be going or walking. They see these two things separately. This is what meditators observe when they meditate.

They also see that because there are successive moments of desire or intention, there are successive movements of the body. There can be hundreds of thought moments in a twinkle of an eye. So there can be hundreds of moments of moving. These tiny movements appear to you to be one big movement. Meditators come to see this when they apply mindfulness during walking.

Meditators know there are only intentions and going in the act of going and nothing else. You do not see a being or a person or a human or an I who is walking, who is going. You see only these two things in the going.

When you watch the intention and the movements closely, you come to know that these intentions and movements come and go very rapidly. They do not last long. These intentions and movements come and disappear, every moment. You can see this when you achieve real concentration. So, the knowing of those who meditate is thorough, clear and precise.

When you cannot see any being or any person apart from the intention and the going, you do not see going to be a person going, but just the intention and the movement taking place. You do not see any person, any agent in the act of going or walking. When you see the intention and the going arising and disappearing at every moment, you come to realize that what is now going is mind and body, different from those existing a moment ago. At every moment, something new arises, a new mind, new matter or body, and the old ones disappear.

You know that mind and body or the intention and going which exist at one moment, do not exist in the next moment. They just disappear at the moment and at the next moment there are new intentions and new movements. At each moment, they renew themselves or you can say that new intentions and new movements arise.

Meditators come to realize that what is now is not the same as what has been in the past and that it is not the same as it will be in the future. At every moment, present, past or future, everything is always moving, coming and disappearing. When meditators know this, their knowledge enables them to abandon the belief in a person or in an individual. When you see that there are the intention and the movements of the body, you cannot see any person or any being in the act of going. Meditators, who closely observe the actions and who closely observe their state of mind, can abandon the belief in a person or a being, and their knowledge enables them to discard the perception of a permanent entity, a soul, or a self.

Their deep knowing of their going or walking is the basis or the condition for their further development. Meditators will continue to observe the phenomena arising at every moment and they will develop concentration and wisdom further and further, until they reach the final stage of attainment. Your knowing at this stage is the basis or the condition for the further development of concentration and wisdom. Then it really can be called *kammaṭṭhāna* meditation.

When mindfulness is firmly established in the mind of those who practice meditation and watch the going, standing, sitting, and lying down, only this can be called the Foundation of Mindfulness. Therefore, the knowing of people who meditate is both a meditation and the Foundation of Mindfulness. Whatever people who do not meditate do, it neither be called *kammaṭṭhāna* meditation nor the Foundation of Mindfulness.

When meditators know deeply, know clearly and know precisely what constitutes the act of going; when they know that there is only the intention to go, the going itself, and nothing more, their knowledge is said to be thorough, with reference to three questions: Who goes? Whose going is it? And why does going take place? When you ask a meditator, "Who goes?" the answer will be "No living being or person whatsoever," since they see that in the act of going there is just the intention to go and the diffusion of the air element which causes motion or which causes movement. They cannot see any person or any being who goes. So, the answer to "Who goes?" is "No living being or person whatsoever." There is no being or person who goes, apart from the intention to go, the movements of the air element and the consequent movements of the different parts of the body.

Whose going is it? Is there a person or authority who owns the going or who presides over the going? We cannot see anything or anyone like that. Therefore, the answer to the second questions is, "Not the going of any living being or person." Since there is no living being or person, there can be no going belonging to that living being or person, just the intention and the movements. Just that. No person. There is no owner of the going, there is no one, no authority who presides over the act of going. Why does the going take place? On account of the diffusion of the air element, born from mental activity, going takes place. (The four primary elements will be discussed later in this section.) When you want to go, first, there is the desire or intention to go and then, this desire or intention or mind to go causes the air element to arise in the parts of the body which are involved in the going, for example, in the feet, and then that air element causes the body parts to move.

Why is there going or walking? Because there are these three factors: the mind that desires to go, the air element which is caused by the mind, and the movement of the different parts of the body caused by the movement of the air element. Suppose there is a cart and four horses are yoked to it and there is a man, the driver. The man causes the horses to move, and they move, and with their movements, they move the cart. The movements of the body are like the movements of the cart. The body is like the cart. It is to be moved by something. The horses are like the air element, caused by the mind. The mind is like the driver. The mind or the driver causes the horses to move or the air element to arise. With the movement of the air element, the whole body moves. So, the going or walking or moving is composed of these three factors, occurring together: the mind, the air element, and the movements. We call this going.

Meditators knowing the answers to these three questions thoroughly, cannot see any living being, any permanent entity in this act of going and come to realize that the usage, "a person goes," "a person walks," is just for convenience but does not reflect reality. You use such terms or such statements, but actually there is no person or man or woman going, apart from the intention to go and the actual movement of the different parts of the body.

Therefore, people who meditate come to realize this going as it really is and not as it appears to be. This means, meditators achieve the real knowledge or the correct knowledge of going. In the same way, they know the going, standing, sitting or lying down and all the other small deportments of the body. So, this body moves, because there is the mind which causes the air element to arise and this air element causes the body to move. If there were no mind, there would be no movement, because there would be no air element, and if there were no air element, there would be no movement at all.

In the commentary, we find a number of verses which go as follows:

> Just as a ship goes on by winds impelled,
> Just as a shaft goes by the bowstring's force,
> So goes this body in its forward course,
> Fully driven by the vibrant thrust of air.
> As to the puppet's back the threads are tied,
> So to the body-doll the mind is joined
> And pulled by that the body moves, stands, sits.
> Where is the living being that can stand,
> Or walk, by force of its own inner strength,
> Without conditions that give it support?[7]

Without these conditions, without these supporting causes, there can be neither walking, nor sitting, nor standing, nor moving at all.

Thus, you learn to see through meditation. You gain this direct knowledge just by observing closely what is happening at the present moment. You watch what arises at the present moment through the six sense doors. Therefore, the knowing of a person who meditates and the knowing of a person who does not meditate are very different. In fact, their knowing is diametrically opposed. When meditators have developed this knowledge that there is the intention and the going itself, that these are two separate things, where one is caused by the other, they see the intention and the going appearing and disappearing at every moment. Only then, they are said to have the correct knowledge and correct understanding of what is going on.

> *Thus, he dwells contemplating the body in the body internally or he dwells contemplating the body in the body externally or he dwells contemplating the body in the body both internally and externally.*

When meditators watch their own going, standing, sitting, lying down and other small deportments, they are said to be "contemplating the body in the body internally." Sometimes, during meditation, you may think of somebody else who is going, standing, sitting, and lying down, and think, "Just as my going and sitting are impermanent and caused by intentions, so will be the going, sitting down, standing and lying down of other people." Contemplating in this way, you are said to contemplate "the body in the body externally." This does not mean that you deliberately look at other people when they meditate. It is just thinking of other people during your meditation, that "Just as my going or my moving is impermanent, comes and goes, so is the going and coming of other people." When meditators contemplate this way, they are said to be "contemplating the body in the body externally."

Sometimes, meditators contemplate back and forth, on their own going and on other people's going. When contemplating back and forth, they are said to be "contemplating the body in the body, both internally and externally." This also is not deliberately done. It happens when meditators think of some other person during meditation. It is called inferential *vipassanā*.

We have, therefore, two kinds of *vipassanā*, "direct *vipassanā*" and "inferential *vipassanā*." You practice direct *vipassanā* on your own going, sitting, standing and lying down, but when meditating on the going and so on of other people, you practice inferential *vipassanā*. "Just as my going is impermanent, so is the going of other people." By inference, meditators contemplate on the going, sitting, standing, and lying down of other people. (See meditation instructions in Part Three).

> *He dwells contemplating the origination factors in the body or he dwells contemplating the dissolution factors in the body or he dwells contemplating both, the origination and the dissolution factors in the body.*

This passage will be repeated again and again. "Origination factors," as mentioned in the *sutta*, mean the cause of the arising of the body or matter and also the arising itself. There are different causes for matter to arise. When an individual has no knowledge of the *Abhidhamma*, it is difficult to see these causes.

You are here because you have done something in the past. You are here, because of your *kamma*. *Kamma* is the cause of the body to arise. This *kamma* arose because you had some craving for existence (*bhāva*). You have this craving, because you are ignorant. Although you say you know everything about craving, you are actually ignorant and this ignorance causes you to crave for a better life. You accumulate *kamma* and have this good life as human beings.

So, the arising of material properties in this life has different causes, ignorance in the past, craving in the past, *kamma* in the past and food to keep the body alive at present. Food is also one of the causes for the material properties to arise. Sometimes, during meditation, practitioners reflect or contemplate on the causes for arising of the body or the arising of the material properties. The body arises here, because I have *kamma*, or because I have craving, or because I am ignorant.

Furthermore, meditator come to see the arising itself. It is more likely for meditators who have little knowledge of the *Abhidhamma* to see the arising rather than the causes of arising. When meditators are mindful of walking or going, they see the arising of the desire and the arising of the movements. When they see the four causes or the arising itself, they are said to be "contemplating on the origination factors."

"Dissolution factors" are the absence of ignorance, the absence of craving, the absence of *kamma*, and the absence of food. They are the causes of the disappearance or the dissolution of material properties and the dissolution itself. When meditators contemplate on the "dissolution factors," they begin to see, there is desire and they take note of the desire, "desire, desire," and then it goes away. There is movement at one moment and it disappears at the next moment. So, meditators also come to see the dissolution or the disappearing of the different phenomena, when they pay close attention to what is going on. When you recognize one of these factors, then you are said to be seeing the dissolution factors of the body, four causes and one disappearance. For the origination factors, there are also four causes and one arising.

However, when you reach the stage of *vipassanā* knowledge that is called "comprehending the characteristics of the phenomena," you come to see the signs of dissolution clearly. When you reach the stage of knowledge that recognizes the rising and falling, you see the arising and the disappearing clearly and vividly. When you reach the next stage, the knowledge of dissolution of things, the recognition of the rising and disappearing becomes even more vivid. So, when you reach these stages, you see both very clearly.

> *Or his mindfulness is established as "there is the body only." And that mindfulness is established to the extent necessary just for further knowledge and mindfulness.*

When meditators are fully aware of what is going on in their body, they see that there is the body only, neither a person nor a permanent entity. In the early stages, you may not have a clear understanding that there is the body only. But when you progress, your mindfulness will be established as "there is the body only and nothing else."

> *Not depending on (or attached to) anything by way of craving and wrong view, he dwells. Nor does he cling to anything in the world of the five aggregates of clinging.*

When meditators see the arising and the disappearing of the different phenomena, they see no reason to be attached to anything. They see no reason to grasp anything. Then they will have no craving for what is going on. They will not have any craving for themselves or for the action of going. They will not grasp at anything because they see now clearly, by direct knowledge, that everything is impermanent, coming, arising, and vanishing.

When meditators can keep themselves from being attached to anything, from grasping anything, their craving and their grasping are temporarily inhibited or momentarily removed. When you have no craving or grasping for anything, you have removed craving and grasping momentarily with regard to the things you watch, and with regard to the things you do not watch, craving and grasping do not arise for some time. This is called "momentary removal of craving and grasping."

When you can remove craving and grasping for the things you observe, you will also be able to remove craving and grasping for things you do not observe. The ability to remove craving for what is not observed is called "temporary removal." Meditators practice momentary removal for the things they observe and temporary removal for the things they do not observe. Through these two kinds of removal, they won't be attached to anything. This is the result of watching the phenomena as they arise.

> *Thus, too, bhikkhus, a bhikkhu dwells contemplating the body in the body.*

Thus, meditators become mindful of whatever they are doing, walking or standing, sitting or lying down, or whatever small postures they may assume. Thus, they keep themselves mindful of their body and are "contemplating the body in the body."

MINDFULNESS WITH CLEAR COMPREHENSION

The third subsection on the Contemplation of the Body is called "Mindfulness with Clear Comprehension."

When meditation masters give instructions or talk about the practice of meditation, they use different expressions but mean the same thing. "To be aware of the object," "be mindful of it," "watch it," "take note of it," "observe it," "try to see it clearly," "try to know it clearly," all these instructions mean the same thing. They mean "to keep your mind on the object and observe it closely and precisely."

In the text, the Buddha said,

> *In going forward and in going back, a bhikkhu applies clear comprehension.*

What is this clear comprehension that the Buddha says must be applied? Before trying to understand how you should apply clear comprehension, you must first know the meaning of the term "clear comprehension." To know its meaning, you must go back to the commentaries and look at the original Pali word, *sampajañña*.

The word *sampajañña* is derived from the word *sampajāna* which means "one who sees correctly," "one who knows correctly, entirely and equally or evenly." When somebody is called *sampajāna*, his or her state of being is called *sampajañña*. So *sampajañña* means "seeing or knowing or discerning rightly, entirely, and evenly or equally." The syllable *sam*, in the word *sampajañña*, is a prefix which has many meanings. The subcommentary explains three meanings for this word.

Its first meaning is "rightly" or "correctly." Therefore, when meditators try to see or observe the objects of meditation, they must see them clearly and precisely. You must not confuse them with other things. When you are distinguishing mind from matter and matter from mind, you must see mind separate from matter and matter separate from mind. You must not confuse these two with one another. You must see precisely and clearly. This is what is meant by saying, "He must see rightly or correctly."

The second meaning of *sam* is "entirely." When meditators see or discern an object, they must know it in its entirety. In its entirety means, in all aspects of its mental or physical phenomena. You must know the characteristics, functions and manifestations of a given object.

The third meaning of *sam* is "equally" or "evenly." Meditators must know how to evenly apply their mental faculties. When you practice meditation, you put five mental faculties to work. These five mental faculties are confidence, effort, mindfulness, concentration, and wisdom. They must work in harmony and be in balance with each other. Especially important is the balance of energy and concentration. When these faculties are even and equal, there will be concentration and wisdom arisen from concentration. When the faculties are not in balance, concentration is disturbed and scattered and, consequently, penetration into the nature of things cannot arise.

"Clear comprehension" means seeing precisely, seeing everything in its entirety, seeing it by evenly using all mental faculties. Only when there is evenness in the application of the five mental faculties will there be further development of wisdom. When you apply clear comprehension, it means, you observe or take note of the object, paying close attention to it, trying to see it thoroughly, precisely, and with all mental faculties in balance.

There are four kinds of clear comprehension mentioned in the commentaries. One is the "clear comprehension of what is of benefit." The second is the "clear comprehension of what is suitable." The third is the "clear comprehension of the meditator's domain" and the fourth is the "clear comprehension of non-delusion." Meditators have to understand and observe each of the small actions of the body with these four kinds of clear comprehension in mind.

"Having clear comprehension of what is of benefit" means to consider, before doing anything, whether or not it will be a beneficial thing to do. When meditators know it will be beneficial, they will do it. When they know it is not beneficial, they will avoid doing it.

For example, going to shrines or going to a bodhi tree is a beneficial activity for Buddhists. When Buddhists go to such sites and bow in front of them, they are accumulating merit, which means they are cultivating positive mental states. It is a good thing to do and will be beneficial. Giving talks, especially delivering *Dhamma* talks, is also something beneficial to do. This is also true when someone is practicing meditation, contemplating a dead body, and are understanding its nature to be the nature of their own body. These are beneficial activities which are of benefit to those who do them. This is the first clear comprehension, the clear comprehension of what is of benefit.

When meditators know that a certain action is beneficial, they still should not do it right away. The next thing to consider is whether or not it is suitable. Sometimes, although it may be beneficial to do something, it may not be suitable, according to place and time. For example, going to a shrine, a pagoda, or a bodhi tree is beneficial, but when there is a pagoda festival with a lot of people coming from faraway districts, there will be a great crowd. Then, meditators should not go there. When they go there, they will see many people and many things, they will be distracted and their meditation will be disturbed. Therefore, although going to a shrine or going to a bodhi tree is beneficial, it is unsuitable to meditate when there are many people around.

Giving a *Dhamma* talk, for example, is beneficial to do, not only for the listeners but also for the one who gives the talk. However, when there are crowds and when some sort of merry-making is going on, then it is neither a suitable time nor a suitable place to give such a talk. Also, for a monk, it is not suitable to give a *Dhamma* talk in seclusion to a woman, i.e., being alone with her. Examining whether something is suitable or not is the second kind of clear comprehension, the "clear comprehension of what is suitable."

Furthermore, the "clear comprehension of what is suitable" in looking at a corpse and applying its nature to your own body may be beneficial, but it is not suitable for meditators to look at a corpse with lustful thoughts. Thus, it is not a suitable action and a suitable object of meditation.

These two kinds of clear comprehension can be applied to any ordinary daily activities. When meditators apply these two clear comprehensions to what they are doing, they will not do anything wrong. They will prosper.

The "domain of the meditator" is the third clear comprehension. The domain of the meditator means meditating in seclusion. It is said when people stay in their own domain or in their own territory, they will not come to any harm. Nobody can harass them. But when they leave their domain, they may be harassed. Therefore, the Buddha advises *bhikkhus* to live in their own territory, their own domain which are the Four Foundations of Mindfulness. The practice of the Four Foundations of Mindfulness is said to be the territory or the domain of meditators. Here, the "clear comprehension of the domain" means just the practice of the Four Foundations of Mindfulness. Whether going forward or going back, whether looking forward or back, or looking sideways, meditation must be practiced. By always practicing meditation, meditators are said to be living in the domain, in their own territory. The "clear comprehension of domain" means just practicing meditation.

With regard to the "clear comprehension of the domain" and how meditation should be practiced, the commentaries mention four kinds of *bhikkhus*. The first is a *bhikkhu* who carries meditation to a village when going for alms but does not carry meditation back to the monastery. The second is a *bhikkhu* who goes to the village without meditation but comes back from the village with meditation. The third is the worst. It is a *bhikkhu* who neither carries meditation to the village nor returns with meditation from the village to the monastery. He does not meditate at all. The fourth *bhikkhu* takes meditation to the village and brings it back to the monastery intact.

So, the first *bhikkhu* who carries meditation to the village but does not bring it back to the monastery can be a person who is meditating. He meditates the whole day, walking and sitting. He also meditates during the night, that is, during two watches of the night. *bhikkhus* divide the night into three watches. During the first and the third watch, *bhikkhus* practice meditation; only during the second, the midnight watch, do they rest. This is the way *bhikkhus* practice meditation: during the whole day and two watches of the night.

This *bhikkhu* practices meditation the whole day and during two watches of the night. Getting up early in the morning, he does whatever has to be done with regard to his monastery, that is, he cleans his quarters, sweeps the monastery and brings water, and so on. He does all this with mindfulness and then, after sitting for some time, he goes to the village for alms. When he goes to the village, he carries meditation with him. It means, he practices mindfulness meditation as "walking, walking, walking," or "making one step, making another step," or "right, left; right, left." When he reaches the village, he may be asked to accept food in a house. He eats his food there or he may carry it in his bowl to the monastery. On his way, back from the village, he may meet some young *bhikkhus* or novices and they will ask him questions about the person who offered the food. "Was he a relative?" and so on. The *bhikkhu* has to talk to them. He has to speak well about the persons who offered food to him. When he goes back to the monastery, he is not able to take meditation with him. He has to give it up in order to talk to the young *bhikkhus* and novices. However, after he has reached the monastery, he again practices meditation. He is a person who carries forth meditation to the village but does not carry it back to the monastery.

The second *bhikkhu* is one who goes to the village without meditation, but comes back with meditation. He is also a meditator who practices meditation the whole day and during two watches of the night. He gets up early in the morning and does what has to be done in the monastery. Then, he sits in meditation for some time, and, after he has finished his meditation, he goes to the village for alms. He has very good digestion. In the morning, his stomach is empty and so the digestive fire or the digestive juices attack the lining of his stomach. When he feels some heat or some burning in his stomach, he is not able to practice meditation. He cannot keep his mind on the object, because there is a burning in his stomach and he may be sweating or he may be feeling dizzy. So, when he is going to the village to collect alms, he is not able to practice meditation. He just gives up meditation and, perhaps, goes quickly to the village.

After he has received some food, some kind of rice gruel, he may approach a *bhikkhus'* sitting hall in the village and eat some of the food. Having eaten, his digestive juices are now attacking the food instead of the lining of his stomach. He achieves tranquility and can practice meditation. When he eats some food, he is eating it with mindfulness, just like you do during a retreat, noting all the activities involved in the act of eating. He eats with meditation and goes back to the monastery with meditation because now he is quite satisfied with regard to his stomach and can concentrate more easily on the object of meditation.

It is said in the commentaries that many *bhikkhus* experienced enlightenment while eating; they kept their meditation while consuming food. Therefore, during a retreat, mealtime is also a time for meditation. Instructions are given to practice mindfulness even while eating. This instruction is found in the commentaries.

The third kind of *bhikkhu*, mentioned in the commentaries, lives heedlessly. He has neither desire for nor interest in meditation. He does not even know that there is such a thing as meditation practice. He just eats and talks and mingles with lay people. He does not practice meditation at all. Such a *bhikkhu* goes to the village without meditation, collects alms, and then comes back to the monastery without meditation. The whole day and the whole night he does not practice at all. He is a *bhikkhu* who either has forsaken responsibility for the practice of meditation or has given up interest in the practice of meditation. No *bhikkhu* should act this way.

The fourth kind is the best *bhikkhu*. He carries meditation to the village and returns from the village with meditation. He has cultivated in his mind the ability to meditate. He arises early and sits in meditation for some time. Then, he goes to the village with meditation, collects alms with meditation, and returns to the monastery with meditation. He practices meditation the whole day and two watches of the night. Such a *bhikkhu* is the best among the four kinds of *bhikkhus* mentioned in the commentaries. He is one who carries meditation to the village and back again to the monastery. He meditates all the time. When you are on a retreat, you should be like this *bhikkhu*, practicing meditation all the time. Sustain meditation diligently through all the moments from arising early in the morning till falling into sleep at night.

In past centuries, there were *bhikkhus* who practiced meditation carrying it both to the village and back to the monastery. Sometimes, there were thirty, forty or more *bhikkhus* living together and meditating. When they met, they agreed to practice meditation seriously. They admonished themselves, "We became *bhikkhus* not because we were troubled by creditors or afraid of some punishment by the king, also not because we could not earn our living. We became *bhikkhus* because we wanted to escape from this round of rebirths, from this mass of suffering. Therefore, we must practice meditation diligently."

They decided to practice meditation and made up their minds to get rid of mental defilements the moment they arose. For example, when a mental defilement arose in them while they were walking, they tried to get rid of it just in the process of walking and did not allow it to carry over to the other postures. These *bhikkhus* practiced this kind of observance. When *bhikkhus* recognized an unwholesome thought or defilement in their mind, they tried to get rid of it by walking. When they could not achieve it, they stopped. When they stopped, the other *bhikkhus* behind them also stopped.

When *bhikkhus* stopped, they said to themselves, "The other monks now know that I have a defilement. This is not becoming for me. Try to get rid of this defilement." And so they tried to get rid of the defilement, standing. When they were successful in getting rid of the defilement while standing, they proceeded forward. But, when they could not take care of the defilement, then they would sit down and try to get rid of it sitting down. And all the other *bhikkhus* sat down also. Then, they admonished themselves that they should be able to get rid of the defilement and be able to achieve attainment. *Bhikkhus* should practice meditation all the time, keeping meditation always with them, even when they go to the village and they should keep meditation with them when they return.

There are some stories with regard to the fourth kind of *bhikkhus*. For example, there was an elder named Mahā Phussadeva, the Veranda Dweller. That means, he lived in the courtyard. This elder practiced the observance of carrying meditation back and forth. It means, he meditated when going to the village and when returning to the monastery. He practiced for nineteen years. Going to the village or returning, when he had performed some activities or had walked without mindfulness, he would go back to that place and start all over again. When he had gone four or five steps without mindfulness, he would go back to the place of the first step and start to practice again.

When the villagers who were working in the fields saw him, they thought he might have lost his way or dropped something. The elder, however, did not pay any attention to them. He just practiced as he was supposed to practice. In his twentieth year, he attained arahathood. He practiced meditation all the time. He carried his meditation to the village and brought it back to the monastery.

When *bhikkhus* go to the village, they don't speak. But when they are asked something, about the *Dhamma* or casual questions, they have to answer. Only then they talk; at other times, they don't talk.

There was another elder named Mahā Nagathera who lived in the Black Creeper Pavilion. This is the name of a monastery. He focused his attention on the Buddha's struggle to become enlightened. The Buddha had spent six years practicing severe asceticism to become enlightened. To emulate the Buddha, the elder practiced the observance of carrying meditation to the village and back for seven years. During these seven years, he practiced only the postures of standing, that means, he did not lie down.

After seven years, he continued to practice this observance for sixteen more years, twenty-three years in all. At the end of the twenty-third year, he attained arahathood. To achieve this, he had done one thing. When he went to the village for alms, he kept some water in his mouth in order not to talk. When lay people pay homage to a *bhikkhu*, the *bhikkhu* must say something. "May you live long," or "May you be happy," and so on. He did not even want to say these words, because they would distract him from the object of meditation. Therefore, not to talk heedlessly, he kept some water in his mouth and went to the village. When somebody asked a question, he answered after swallowing the water. Thus, he could keep his observance of carrying meditation to and from the village and, at the end of the twenty-third year, he was able to attain arahathood.

At another time, there were five hundred *bhikkhus* living in a monastery which was called Kalamba Landing. They practiced the same kind of observance. They kept water in their mouths when they entered the village. When no one had asked them any questions, they spat the water on the ground at the entrance of the village. The people would know how many *bhikkhus* had come to the village, just by looking at the puddles of water on the ground, saying, "Today, five *bhikkhus* have come" or "Today, ten Venerables have come." These *bhikkhus* attained arahathood in only three months. They had gone to the monastery to spend the rainy season which lasts three months and, at the end of the three months or during the three months, they attained arahathood.

This is how *bhikkhus*, during earlier centuries, applied the "clear comprehension of the domain," i.e., the clear comprehension of practicing meditation. They lived always in the domain. They did not leave the domain, even when they were going to the village to collect alms and when they were returning to the monastery. When keeping inside the domain, they also practiced the observance of carrying meditation back and forth.

There was a *bhikkhu* named Mahā Thera who practiced the observance of carrying meditation back and forth. One day, while he was in the monastery, the other *bhikkhus* came to him and asked questions. He had to talk to them. In the course of talking, he made a movement without mindfulness. He moved his body, perhaps he stretched or bent. When he did that, he remembered to be mindful and stopped, just putting the limb back to the former place and then he moved slowly again. When the other *bhikkhus* asked him what he was doing, he said, "Ever since I began to practice meditation, I have never made a move without mindfulness. Now, because I had to talk to you, I moved without mindfulness. So I took the limb back to the place and started all over again, to keep up my meditation." The other *bhikkhus* were pleased with him. "Well done, Sir. Every truly meditating *bhikkhu* should act like you." This *bhikkhu* also reached enlightenment.

In this way, during earlier centuries, *bhikkhus* practiced the observance of carrying meditation back and forth. They carried meditation to the village and then they carried it back to the monastery. Carrying meditation back and forth to the monastery is the most difficult time for a *bhikkhu* to keep his meditation intact. When you are in a monastery, in your house, or in a meditation center, there are not so many distractions. Therefore, it is easy to keep your meditation in these places. But when you are going to the village for alms and you come back, you are walking and while you are walking, you have to be careful of the road, of animals, and so on. It is difficult. Even at difficult times, *bhikkhus* must maintain their meditation. These stories are told to show the importance of the third clear comprehension, "clear comprehension of the domain."

The last kind is "clear comprehension of non-delusion." This means not confusing the different acts when going forth and when returning. You must recognize them and know the differences clearly. When you comprehend them clearly, when you see them distinctly, then you are said to apply "clear comprehension of non-delusion." Now, this "clear comprehension of non-delusion" will come when you thoroughly apply "clear comprehension of the domain." You don't have to worry about the "clear comprehension of non-delusion." It will arise by itself, when the "clear comprehension of the domain" or simply the practice of meditation has been brought to maturity. So, when practicing meditation, the "clear comprehension of the domain" is important. It means that you apply comprehension to whatever you are doing, whether going forward or returning.

The Buddha said in this section,

And again, bhikkhus, a bhikkhu, in going forward and in going back, applies clear comprehension.

All four kinds of clear comprehension can be applied here. Before going out or before returning, meditators must consider whether or not it is "beneficial" to go out or to return. Meditators must also consider whether or not it is "suitable" to go out or to return. When it is not suitable, they won't do it. While going out or returning, you should also apply the "clear comprehension of the domain." That means applying clear comprehension in going out, taking note, "going out, going out, going out" or just "going, going, going." When you return, you say, "returning, returning, returning." So, meditators keep themselves mindful of going out and returning.

When you keep noting or when you keep being mindful of going out and going back, a time will come when you will see clearly the nature of going out and going back. You won't find any permanent entity who does the going. You won't find any soul or any self which does the going out or returning. You will see that there is nobody who commits the act of going out or returning. You just see the mere phenomena, the intention and the going caused by intention. When you come to see clearly that there are just these two things happening at the moment, then you are said to have "clear comprehension of non-delusion." Your comprehension or your knowing is not deluded. Your knowing is precise, thorough, and to the point.

> *In looking straight on and in looking away from the front,*
> *[he] applies clear comprehension.*

That means, when meditators look straight ahead or to the side, they must note, "looking, looking, looking," so that they can have clear comprehension of what they are doing. When looking straight ahead or when looking to one side, they also apply the four kinds of clear comprehension. Only when it is beneficial and suitable to look straight ahead, do they look straight ahead. When it is not beneficial and not suitable, they do not look straight ahead.

When meditators keep mindfulness in any way they look, looking straight ahead or looking away, they are applying the "clear comprehension of the domain." When their meditation has reached maturity, they will come to see that there are only two things in looking straight ahead and in looking away: the mind and the body, the intention to see and the act of seeing which belong to the mind, and the body which is seen. There are only these two things and no other permanent entity.

Whether meditators are looking up or looking down or looking back, they must apply clear comprehension, although it is not so likely that somebody who is meditating will look up or look down or look back. That is why these actions are not specifically mentioned in the *sutta*. However, you must understand that, when you should look up or down or back, you must apply clear comprehension.

> *In bending his limbs and in stretching his limbs [he] also applies clear comprehension.*

Meditators bend or stretch only when it is beneficial and when it is suitable to do so. When they bend at a wrong moment or at a wrong place, they may get hurt or lose mindfulness. In the old days, there was a *bhikkhu* who stretched at an unsuitable place and was bitten by a snake. Another *bhikkhu* was burnt when he put his foot into the fire, and so on. Meditators have to look before bending or stretching, whether or not it is beneficial and suitable to do so. When you apply "clear comprehension of the domain," that is taking note, "bending, bending, bending," or "stretching, stretching, stretching," you will come to see that when there is intention, there is bending. There is only intention and then bending. There is no person and no self.

> *In wearing the double robe and other robes, and in carrying the bowl, [he] applies clear comprehension.*

These instructions are meant for *bhikkhus* whose robes and bowl should be suitable. For a *bhikkhu* who is sensitive to cold, thick robes are suitable, and for a *bhikkhu* who is sensitive to heat, thin robes are suitable, and so on. Also, bowls are made of iron and may be heavy. Therefore, for a *bhikkhu* who is weak, a heavy bowl is not suitable. For lay people, it means, "in wearing different clothes and in using or taking hold of bowls, cups, plates," and so on. Meditators should wear loosely fitting clothes; weak meditators should not wear burdensome clothes; their clothing should be suitable. When you become aware of these activities, noting "wearing, wearing, wearing," "changing, changing, changing," or "carrying, carrying, carrying," you apply "clear comprehension of the domain." When you have brought your clear comprehension to maturity, you will see that there are only these two things, mind and matter, just doing these things, and no entity or being.

*In eating, drinking, chewing, and savoring, [he] applies
clear comprehension.*

Eating means "consuming solid food," rice, bread, and so
on.   Drinking means "drinking liquids."   Chewing means
"eating cakes" or eating candy, eating desserts, and savoring
(*sāyana*, in Pāli) means "licking," as when you eat honey.
When meditators do these things, they must apply clear comprehension.   When eating, you must eat suitable food.   You
must not eat food that is not good for you.   When you keep
applying clear comprehension to what you are eating, the
"clear comprehension of non-delusion" will arise.   You will
see that there is only this body eating and this mind that wants
to eat.   Nothing more.

*In obeying the calls of nature, [he] applies clear com-
prehension.*

In *vipassanā* no activity should be ignored, because
meditators take note of every action.   You must be mindful of
all your actions, whether it is a major or a minor activity.   They
are all included in the meditation.   When you go to the toilet
and use the toilet, you have also to be mindful of your activities.   You have to go to the toilet at a suitable time.   You
have to empty your bowels at a suitable time.

*In walking, standing, sitting, falling asleep, waking,
speaking, keeping silent, [he] applies clear comprehension.*

So, when meditators walk, they walk with clear comprehension, with meditation.   They stand with meditation.   They sit
with mindfulness.   Falling asleep is not just about preparing
to sleep.   They continue to meditate falling asleep and when
they are sleeping.   When you lie down, you take note of the
breath and when sleepiness arises, you just note, "sleepiness,
sleepiness, sleepiness," and let sleep come to you.   With regard
to waking, it is very difficult to be aware of the very first
moment of waking up.   Try it.   Try to see the first moment of
waking up.   As soon as you wake up, say, "I am waking up,
waking up, waking up."   In waking up, you also apply clear
comprehension.   When you are speaking, take note, "speaking, speaking, speaking."   When you stop speaking and keep
silent, you apply clear comprehension to being silent.   When

you keep "clear comprehension of the domain," the "clear comprehension of non-delusion" will automatically come to you. In these actions, there is only mind and body; only the intention to do these things and the doing of these things are present, neither a being nor a permanent entity.

Instructions given at a retreat are based on the Buddha's teachings, especially on this section and the last two subsections.

> *Thus he dwells contemplating on the body in the body internally... [these are repetitions]*

> *Nor does he cling to anything in the world of the five aggregates of clinging. Thus, too, bhikkhus, a bhikkhu dwells on contemplating the body in the body.*

When meditators contemplate this way, they do not grasp for anything. Through the "clear comprehension of non-delusion," you come to see the true nature of things and do not find anything to cling to. There is no clinging to anything in the world of the five aggregates of clinging. Thus, "a *bhikkhu* dwells on contemplating the body in the body."

This is the end of the third sub-subsection which is called, "Mindfulness with Clear Comprehension."

In the commentaries, you find three durations of postures mentioned: postures of long duration, postures of middle duration, and postures of short duration. The previous section dealt with the postures of long duration, going, standing, sitting, and lying down. The postures in this section, going forward and back, looking straight ahead and away, bending and stretching are said to be postures of middle duration which are maintained neither too long nor too short. Walking, standing, sitting, falling asleep, waking up, speaking, and keeping silent are postures of short duration. It should be understood that walking for a long time belongs to the first section, while walking for a short time belongs to this section. The same applies for the postures of standing and sitting. Therefore, three durations of postures have been covered in these two sections.

Whatever posture you assume, you should apply clear comprehension. You should carry out all activities of the body with clear comprehension and with mindfulness. Sometimes, you say "clear comprehension," sometimes you say "knowing," sometimes you say "watching." These are all the same attitudes. When you try to keep your mind on an object, you need effort, mindfulness, concentration, and understanding. You must maintain these four qualities or states as much as you can. When you practice in this way, you are said to apply clear comprehension. Therefore, clearly comprehending or knowing thoroughly or knowing clearly or seeing clearly all mean the same thing.

When you practice meditation, try to pay close attention to the objects and do not look at other things. Don't bother about penetrating the nature of things. When you are mindful of everything that is present, insight will come to you by itself. When you take note of everything that exists at the present moment, this insight will arise by itself.

REFLECTION ON THE REPULSIVENESS OF THE BODY

The fourth section on the Contemplation of the Body deals with the "Reflection on the Repulsiveness of the Body." It also deals with the different parts of the body. According to the *sutta*, there are thirty-two body parts. Meditators are instructed to contemplate on the repulsiveness of these thirty-two parts. This is the same meditation on the body which is described in the *Visuddhimagga, The Path of Purification*.

In the *sutta*, the Buddha said,

> And again, bhikkhus, a bhikkhu reflects on this body, upward from the soles of his feet, downward from the tips of his hair, enclosed by the skin and full of diverse impurities, thus: "There are in this body

> | | |
> |---|---|
> | head hair, body hair, nails, teeth, skin; | 5 |
> | flesh, sinews, bones, marrow, kidneys; | 5 |
> | heart, liver, intestines, spleen, lungs; | 5 |
> | bowels, stomach, undigested food, feces, brain; | 5 |
> | bile, phlegm, pus, blood, sweat, fat; | 6 |
> | tears, lymph, saliva, nasal mucus, oil of the joints [synovial fluid], urine." | 6 |

Meditators survey their own body, look at it mentally, see the thirty-two parts of the body, and contemplate repulsiveness with respect to these parts.

For many Westerners the meditation on the repulsiveness of the body is difficult to understand and to accept. This difficulty should be a reminder to look at this kind of meditation with an open mind. With an open mind and a firm dedication to freedom from suffering, you may come to understand why this meditation was praised by the Buddha, who said,

> Bhikkhus, when one thing is developed, repeatedly practiced, it leads to a supreme sense of urgency, to supreme benefit, to supreme surcease of bondage, to supreme mindfulness and full awareness, to acquisition of knowledge and vision, to a happy life here and now, to realization of the fruit of clear vision and deliverance. What is that one thing? It is mindfulness occupied with the body.[8]

And again, the Buddha said,

> Bhikkhus, meditators experience the deathless who cultivate mindfulness occupied with the body; they do not experience the deathless who do not cultivate mindfulness occupied with the body.[9]

It does not mean, however, that only this type of meditation will lead to the realization of truth; it is one of the many types of meditation that lead to realization. Anyone who wants to practice this kind of meditation, must first learn, preferably from a teacher, what should be known about it.

The Sevenfold Skill of Learning

To practice this meditation, first meditators must know the "sevenfold skill of learning." The first thing to start with is oral recitation. This means knowing the thirty-two parts of the body by heart and reciting the names of the body parts for quite some time, i.e., throughout the day, during all waking hours. It is said in the scriptures that even though meditators are well-versed in the *Tipiṭaka*, i.e., the Buddhist scriptures, they must first recite the names of the thirty-two body parts. The recitation of the thirty-two parts of the body should be practiced diligently for 165 days. You should do it in the following way.

For convenience, the thirty-two parts of the body are divided into six groups. The first group is called the "skin pentad," i.e., five body parts ending with "skin." The next group is the "kidney pentad," the five parts ending with "kidneys." Similarly there are the "lungs pentad," "brain pentad," "fat sextad," and "urine sextad," the last two groups consisting of six parts each. Thus, there are four groups of five parts and two groups of six parts.

It will take meditators fifteen days to complete the recitation of the first group. They must recite these five body parts in forward order for five days, in backward order for five days, and in forward and backward order for another five days. Meditators should recite them like this:

"Head hair, body hair, nails, teeth, skin; head hair, body hair, nails, teeth, skin," and so on (forward for five days).

"Skin, teeth, nails, body hair, head hair; skin, teeth, nails, body hair, head hair," and so on (backward for five days).

"Head hair, body hair, nails, teeth, skin; skin, teeth, nails, body hair, head hair; head hair, body hair," and so on (forward and backward for five days).

The recitation of the next group, the "kidney pentad," will take thirty days, because it must be recited like the "skin pentad" for fifteen days, and then together with the "skin pentad" for another fifteen days. These body parts should be recited like this:

"Flesh, sinews, bones, marrow, kidneys; flesh, sinews, bones, marrow, kidneys," and so on (forward for five days).

"Kidneys, marrow, bones, sinews, flesh; kidneys, marrow, bones, sinews, flesh," and so on (backward for five days).

"Flesh, sinews, bones, marrow, kidneys; kidneys, marrow, bones, sinews, flesh; flesh, sinews," and so on (forward and backward for five days).

"Head hair, body hair, nails, teeth, skin; flesh, sinews, bones, marrow, kidneys; head hair, body hair," and so on (forward for five days).

"Kidneys, marrow, bones, sinews, flesh; skin, teeth, nails, body hair, head hair; kidneys, marrow, bones, sinews, flesh," and so on (backward for five days).

"Head hair, body hair, nails, teeth, skin; flesh, sinews, bones, marrow, kidneys; kidneys, marrow, bones, sinews, flesh; skin, teeth, nails, body hair, head hair; head hair, body hair," and so on (forward and backward for five days).

The recitation of each of the remaining groups will also take thirty days: fifteen days each group alone and fifteen days together with the previous two, three, four, and five groups, respectively.

Thus, it will take meditators 165 days, or nearly half a year, to complete the oral recitation.

After the oral recitation comes the mental recitation in the same manner for the same number of days. This is the second skill in learning.

After the oral and the mental recitations, meditators must learn the color, shape, direction, location, and delimitation of each body part. "Direction" here means whether a particular part is in the upper portion of the body or in the lower portion. "Location" means the place where it is located. There are two kinds of delimitations, namely, "delimitation of the similar" and that "of the dissimilar." The first means knowing that a particular part is bounded above, below and around by something, and the second means knowing that one part is not another part, and vice versa. Thus, you learn the sevenfold skills, namely, oral recitation, mental recitation, color, shape, direction, location, and delimitation of each part of the body.

To show how further contemplation should be practiced, let us take the hair of the head as the subject of meditation.

The hair of the head may be black in "color." In the east, hair is generally black, but in the west, it may be brown, blond or brunette.

The "shape" of the head hair may be like a long measuring rod, sometimes like small sticks.

Its "direction" is the upper part of the body.

Its "location" is the wet inner skin that envelops the skull, bounded on both sides by the ears, in front by the forehead, and behind by the nape of the neck.

With respect to "delimitation of the similar," it is bounded below by the surface of its own roots; to the amount of the tip of a rice grain, fixed by entering into the inner skin that envelops the head. It is bounded above by space, and all around by other hair. There are no two hairs together in one space.

With respect to "delimitation of the dissimilar," the head hair is also not body hair, and body hair is not head hair. It is, furthermore, not intermixed with the remaining thirty-one parts, the head hair is a separate part of the body.

In this way, meditators contemplate on the thirty-two parts of the body, one by one.

The Tenfold Skill of Paying Attention

After learning this, they must study the "tenfold skill of paying attention." This is very involved. First, they must learn to repeat and to contemplate in "following the prescribed order." They must follow the sequence without skipping a part. Second, they should "not recite or contemplate too quickly." If they should do so, they might get confused. Third, they should "not recite or contemplate too slowly." If they recite too slowly, they might forget the different parts. The fourth skill to learn is "warding off distraction." Meditators should not follow the temptation to discontinue meditation and let the mind be distracted by external objects. Meditators should keep their mind on the parts of the body and not let it be distracted by any other object.

The fifth skill is "going beyond the concept." When meditators say, "head hair, body hair," and so on, they are repeating concepts of names, i.e., the name of the parts. You must go beyond these concepts. You must not concentrate on the concepts of the parts when you recite, but try to establish your mind on the aspect of repulsiveness of the parts. That is necessary because the aim of this meditation is to establish in the mind of meditators the repulsiveness of the different parts of the body so that they can become detached from it.

The repulsiveness should be viewed in five ways or aspects: by color, shape, odor, habitat, and location.

For example, the "color" or the appearance of the hair is repulsive. When you see it through a concept, it is one thing, but taken away from that concept it is another. When you see a hair or something resembling a hair in your food, you are disgusted and say, "Take this food away." When you are eating and you feel something which you suspect is a hair you become disgusted. The "shape" is also repulsive. The natural "odor" of the head hair is not pleasant. When it is not washed, dressed with scented oil, or decorated with flowers, it becomes smelly. The odor of the head hair is repulsive, too.

"Habitat" means the origin or the source. Where does this part of the body come from? The hair grows on your body and the body itself is the combination of all other parts: blood, pus, phlegm, urine, and so on. The hair grows out of these repulsive things. So, hair is also repulsive by habitat. "Location" means where the body part is found. With regard to hair, it is the place where it grows. It grows on the body which is the meeting place of all unpleasant things. In this way, the repulsiveness of each and every part of the body must be viewed by color, shape, odor, habitat, and location.

The sixth skill is that of "successive leaving." When meditators recite the parts of the body, some will appear to their mind clearly but others may not. When this happens, meditators should leave out the part which does not appear to them clearly and recite only those parts that are clear, until one of them appears very clearly. You eliminate the different parts one by one, until you come to the one part of the body that appear to you most clearly. You should keep this object of meditation with you and contemplate on this part again and again until you reach absorption of the *jhāna* stage.

The seventh skill is "paying attention to absorption," i.e., meditators must understand that absorption (*uppanā*) can arise in each one of the body parts.

The three other skills are collectively mentioned in three *suttas* and can be achieved by reading these *suttas*.

Aṅguttara, i.256-8, deals with paying attention to three things when contemplating or meditating. Meditators, intent on reaching higher consciousness, should pay attention to these three things: concentration, exertion, and equanimity. Paying attention to concentration only, there is the possibility of becoming indolent. Paying attention to exertion only, there will be agitation. Paying attention to equanimity only, there will be no proper concentration. So all these three things — concentration, exertion, and equanimity — should be paid attention to. All three must be in proper balance.

Aṅguttara, iii.435, teaches *bhikkhus* to achieve six things when they want to realize supreme coolness. These six things are: restraining the mind when it should be restrained, exerting the mind when it should be exerted, encouraging the mind when it should be encouraged, looking at everything with equanimity, resolving to attain superior states, and taking delight in *nibbāna*.

The third *sutta*, *Saṁyutta*, v.113, explains when a certain factor of enlightenment should be developed. There are seven factors of enlightenment and each of these factors should be developed at a specific time. The seven factors will be discussed in the section on the Contemplation on the *Dhammas*.

These three *suttas* should be read by meditators and the advice in them should be followed. Thus meditators learn these "ten skills in paying attention."

Advancing the Practice

When meditators have learned the ten skills, they go to a suitable place and recite the different body parts first orally and then mentally, and so on. You contemplate the thirty-two parts of the body again and again until one part becomes clearest to you and you then dwell on it. You continue to contemplate this part until you achieve absorption or reach the stage of *jhāna*.

This meditation was taught by the Buddha so that meditators may become less attached to their own body as well as to the bodies of others. It can be practiced as *samatha* meditation leading to the attainment of the first *jhāna*, or it can be practiced as *vipassanā* meditation. In the latter case, meditators attain the first *jhāna* and then shift to *vipassanā* by contemplating on the *jhāna* itself or by contemplating the object of that *jhāna*, in this case, one of the thirty-two parts of the body. You try to see the arising and fading away of the *jhāna* or the object of that *jhāna*, until you reach the higher stages in *vipassanā*. Alternatively, without developing *jhāna* you view the body parts as elements and develop *vipassanā* on these parts. Either way you will ultimately realize *nibbāna*.

That *samatha* alone is not the goal will become clear by studying the passages in the *sutta*.

> *Thus, he dwells contemplating the body in the body internally, or...externally, or...both internally and externally.*
>
> *He dwells contemplating the origination factors in the body, or...dissolution factors in the body, or...both the origination and dissolution factors in the body.*
>
> *Not depending on (or attached to) anything by way of craving and wrong view, he dwells.*
>
> *Nor does he cling to anything in the world of the Gfive aggregates of clinging.*

> *Thus too, bhikkhus, a bhikkhu dwells contemplating the*
> *body in the body.*

Seeing the arising and fading away of things can be achieved only through *vipassanā* and not through *samatha*. When you find the contemplation on the origination and the dissolution factors mentioned, you know that *vipassanā* is meant. *Samatha* meditation is, therefore, subordinate to *vipassanā* meditation.

When meditators try to contemplate on the "repulsiveness of the parts of the body," and really see how repulsive they are, there cannot be any attachment or wrong view left; in other words, there cannot be any clinging to these body parts. So, meditators do not cling to anything in the world of the five aggregates.

The benefits to be enjoyed when practicing this kind of meditation are many. People are often not happy when they are in secluded places, but those who have practiced this meditation can "conquer boredom in secluded places" with their meditation. They can delight in such places. They can also "conquer delight in sensual pleasures." People are used to indulging in sensual pleasures, but when they have practiced this meditation, they can overcome those desires. They will see not the attractiveness of different parts of the body but rather they will be indifferent to them.

The other benefit is "conquering fear and dread." Meditators who practice this kind of meditation have no concept of a being and of the attractiveness of different parts of the body. When dangers arise, you experience neither fear nor dread. You will also be able to bear cold, heat, hunger, etc. You will have more patience with the climate, food, and different situations.

Meditators can reach the four *jhānas* basing meditation on the color aspect of head hair, and so on. When they practice only repulsiveness meditation, they can reach only the first *jhāna*. It will not help them to reach the second, third and fourth *jhānas* because they need the *jhāna* factor of initial application (*vitakka*) to support their consciousness on the gross object, which is the repulsive aspect of the body. Only the first *jhāna* is accompanied by that *jhāna* factor. When you contemplate on the color aspect of the head hair and so on, it will become a color meditation for you. (There are color *kasinas* — blue, yellow, white, and red). When it becomes a color meditation, you can develop *jhāna* on these objects, and that *jhāna* can be the first, second or third or fourth. Thus, you can attain all four *jhānas* basing meditation on the color aspect of the hair on the head, and so on.

After reaching the fourth *jhāna*, meditators can go on to develop it further so that they acquire the ability to see things that are far away, or perform something unusual, and so on. This is called the "penetration of six kinds of 'supernormal knowledge' (*abhiññas*)." These are the benefits to be gained from the practice of this kind of meditation.

When meditators practice meditation on the parts of the body, they do not need to bother about the clinical accuracy of the body parts and whether some are to be called parts at all. For example, undigested food, feces and urine are not constituent parts of the body. They are mentioned here just for the sake of meditation. There are, of course, more than thirty-two body parts but these thirty-two parts suffice. As you have seen, when meditators practice meditation on the first part alone, they can reach the *jhāna* stage, then change to *vipassanā* and attain the Realization of Truth.

There have been different translations for some body parts, but you need not concern yourself with them either. You cannot see everyone of these parts, though you may go to a hospital or to a place where autopsies are performed. There are also books which show pictures of different parts of the body. So you can look at the pictures in the book and select a part as an object of your meditation. When you have the chance to see one or more of these body parts in reality, it will be much better. Then you can meditate on something you have actually seen.

You should note that in the *sutta* as well as in numerous texts, "brain" is not mentioned among the body parts. But commentators said that it is mentioned in the *Patisambhidamagga* and so where it is not mentioned, it must be understood as included under "marrow." Thus this meditation has "the meditation subject consisting of the thirty-two-fold aspects of the body."

REFLECTION ON THE MATERIAL ELEMENTS

> *And again, bhikkhus, a bhikkhu reflects upon this very*
> *body just as it is placed or disposed, with regard to its*

primary elements: There are in this body the earth ele-
ment, the water element, the fire element, and the air
element.

As a skillful butcher or his apprentice, having slaughtered
a cow and divided it into portions, were sitting at the
junction of four highways, just so, monks, a monk reflects
upon this very body just as it is placed or disposed, with
regard to its primary elements: "There are in this body
the earth element, the water element, the fire element, and
the air element."

This section in the *sutta* talks about these material elements
and how meditators should reflect on their body whatever
position they might be assuming, whether they are sitting or
walking, standing or lying down. They will reflect on their
body with respect to these four primary elements.

Traditionally, there are four material elements: the earth
element, the water element, the fire element, the air element.
Meditation on these four elements is mentioned only briefly
in this *sutta*. It is meant for meditators with quick understanding, i.e., for people of quick intelligence. Elsewhere, in
the *Mahāhatthipadopama Sutta,* the *Rāhulovāda Sutta* and the
Dhātuvibhaṅga Sutta, this meditation is explained in more
detail. These *suttas* are for people who are not so quick in
understanding. Whenever the Buddha delivered a sermon, he
looked at the likes and dislikes of his listeners, and also
whether or not their minds were mature. Only after investigating this, did he deliver his sermon or discourse according
to the situation. So, in some *suttas*, he went into more detail.
In this *sutta*, the *Mahāsatipaṭṭhāna Sutta*, the topic is treated
very briefly. The purpose of this kind of meditation is to
remove the concept of a being or seeing yourself and others as
beings. To remove this concept, you need to practice the
meditation of mentally dividing the body into four parts and
seeing them separately, each as one of the four elements which
are called "great elements."

The "earth element" does not mean the earth as you know
it. It means something that is inherent in the earth, (and, of
course, in other things as well), the state of being of the earth,
or the "quality of stiffness, hardness or softness" which are the
characteristics of the earth element. It is stated in the scrip-

tures that these four elements are found everywhere in sentient beings as well as in plants and inanimate objects. The characteristics of stiffness or hardness or softness are what here is called the earth element. When you touch the water, you feel some kind of softness and that softness is the earth element. When you feel the wind blowing in your face, you feel some kind of hardness or softness, and that is the earth element. You find this earth element everywhere. Its function is to act as a foundation, something on which something else is resting or exists. To practitioners of *vipassanā* who meditate on the earth element, it manifests itself as receiving or accepting. Therefore, you must understand the earth element, according to its characteristics, or function or manifestations. To repeat, its characteristics are hardness or softness, its function is to act as "foundation," and its manifestations are "receiving or accepting something."

Next, you have the "water element." Water element here means not the water as you know it, but its characteristics, which are "trickling" or "cohesion" or "fluidity." Trickling or cohesion or fluidity indicate the presence of the water element. It is present in everything. There is cohesion in the earth or wood or bricks, and so on. This cohesion which holds things together is one characteristic of the water element. Its function is to "intensify." It intensifies everything which comes into contact with it. It manifests to meditators as "holding things together." When you add water to flour, for example, you get dough. The water holds the flour particles together. This holding together is a manifestation of the water element. When you meditate, this manifestation will sometimes come to you. You will see or know it, sometimes by its characteristics, sometimes by its function and sometimes by its manifestations.

Next, you have the "fire element." This is not the fire as you know it, but the state of being of the fire, the quality of fire, i.e., heat. Heat or fire "mature and age" things. By heat, we mean cold also. Heat, cold or "temperature" is the characteristic of the fire element. When you feel hot or cold, you feel the fire element. And when the body becomes mature or when it ages, this is the work of the fire element. Its functions are to "mature" things, to "cool" or to "heat" things. Its manifestation is "continued supply of softness." For example, when you cook something, what is cooked will soften. In the same way, the heat in your body softens it, so that your body ages. These are the characteristics, the functions, and the manifestations of the fire element.

There are four kinds of fire elements. One is that by which somebody or something is "warmed." You feel warmth in your body and when you are sick you have a temperature. The second kind of fire element is that by which things "age." The third is that by which somebody or something is "burnt up," i.e., excessive heat. When you have high fever, you experience excessive body heat. The fourth is the "digestive heat" by which everything eaten, drunk, chewed, or savored is digested. When there is good digestive heat, or good stomach fire, as we Burmese call it, you can digest whatever you eat. When you don't have good digestive heat, you will have stomach trouble. These are the four kinds of fire element.

The last element is the "air element." The characteristics of the air element are "extension, expanding or distending." When you blow air into a balloon, it becomes extended. The fact that you can sit or stand upright and do not fall down is also the work of the air element which "supports you from all sides." Its function is to "cause motion." When you move, your motions are caused by the air element. Its manifestation is "conveying."

There are six kinds of air element:

1. Up-going, which causes vomiting or hiccups, etc.;
2. Down-going, which carries feces and urine out of the body;
3. Wind in the belly outside the bowels;
4. Wind in the bowels;
5. Wind that runs through all limbs;
6. Breath, i.e., the in- and out-breath.

It is the air element which causes movements in the body. When you walk or stretch or bend, the element of air is working, caused by your intention or consciousness.

Meditators contemplate these four elements during their practice. Let us now see how you can observe these four elements when you are walking. When you walk, first you lift your foot. The upward movement manifests the lightness in the foot. That lightness is caused by the fire element. When you raise your foot, there is movement. That movement is caused by the air element. When you push your foot forward, this movement is also caused by the air element. When you put your foot down, it becomes heavier which indicates the presence of the water element. When you touch the ground or the floor with your foot, you feel hardness or softness both in the floor and in the foot. That hardness or softness is the characteristic of the earth element. In making one step, you can distinguish these four elements. In lifting the foot, the fire and the air elements are evident, in pushing the foot forward, you recognize the air element, in putting the foot down, the water element, and in touching the ground or the floor, the earth element. Thus, meditators observe the four elements which are present in a single step, although, at first, they may not notice the presence of all four elements.

When meditators see the elements clearly, they lose the concept of a being; they see now that there are just these four elements; four elements going, four elements standing, and so on. When you see only these four elements going, and so on, you cannot see a person, and lose the concept of a being.

The observation of the four elements is explained in the *sutta* with a simile. The commentary explains it as follows. When a butcher is feeding a cow or is nourishing it, and then takes it to the slaughtering place, ties it to a post, and kills it, he still has the notion that it is a being, a cow. If someone would ask him what he is doing, he would say, "I am feeding the cow" or "I am killing the cow." Even after having killed it, before he cuts it up into pieces, he still maintains the notion that it is a cow. But when, after cutting the slaughtered cow into pieces, he takes and puts the pieces on a table at the crossroad, from that point on, he loses the notion of a cow. If someone would ask him what he is selling, he would not say, "I am selling a cow." So, after cutting the cow into pieces, he loses the concept of a cow. In the same way, when meditators "cut" themselves into four elements — whatever they have, whatever is in their body, are just four elements — then they will lose the concept of a being, a person. This meditation was taught by the Buddha to eliminate the concept of "there is a being." The simile, given above, should not lead to the conclusion that meditators must conceptualize the elements. The elements, taught in Buddhism, are in fact not concepts but are part of what is called "ultimate reality" which consists of consciousness, mental factors, matter and *nibbāna*. They are considered to be the real things in contrast to things in "conventional reality."

Meditators will gain many benefits from practicing this kind of meditation. In *The Path of Purification*, Buddhaghosa said,

> This monk who is devoted to the defining of the four elements immerses himself in voidness and eliminates the perception of living beings. Since he does not entertain false notions about wild beasts, spirits, ogres, etc., because he has abolished the perception of living beings, he conquers fear and dread and conquers delight and aversion (boredom), he is not exhilarated or depressed by agreeable or disagreeable things, and, as one of great understanding, he either ends in the deathless realm or he is bound for a happy destiny.[10]

When people practice *vipassanā* meditation, this will not lead to the attainment of *jhānas* like in *kamaṭṭhāna* meditation, it leads to the attainment of proximate *samādhi* or access concentration. When people practice meditation according to the *vipassanā* teachings, they try to see the four elements in every movement, i.e., in everything. They will see these four elements as well as their mind appearing and disappearing. When they recognize the rising and fading away of things, they are said to have achieved the basic *vipassanā* knowledge. From then on, they will reach higher levels until they reach the end of *vipassanā* and attain realization. There is the rising and fading away of the elements and of the mind which dwells on the elements. When meditators have reached this stage of seeing the rising and fading away of phenomena, they can be sure to achieve higher stages of *vipassanā* knowledge, until they reach the realization stage.

> *Thus he dwells contemplating the body in the body internally, or...externally, or...both internally and externally.*

When you contemplate the elements in other people, you are said to be "contemplating externally." When you contemplate your own and other people's elements back and forth, you are said to be "contemplating both internally and externally."

When you see that there are only these four elements and no person or being, you do not find anything to cling to. So,

> *he does not cling to anything in the world of the five aggregates of clinging.*

When there is no clinging, no *kamma* can form. When there are no *kamma* formations, there will be no becoming and no rebirth. You will have reached the end of the round of rebirths.

THE NINE CEMETERY CONTEMPLATIONS

The Buddha described the Contemplation of the Body in fourteen different ways. This means, there are altogether fourteen topics for the Contemplation of the Body. We have finished five subsections. The Nine Cemetery Contemplations are designed to cultivate the concept of repulsiveness of the body. This is used to develop detachment from the body. You are attached to your body and to the bodies of others. As long as there is any attachment, there will be suffering. In order to get rid of suffering, you should have no attachments to your body and the bodies of others. The cemetery contemplations will help you to get rid of these attachments.

The nine kinds of cemetery contemplations dwell on the different stages of decay of a corpse.

The first contemplation is on a "festering body." The Buddha said,

> *and again, bhikkhus, when a bhikkhu sees a body one day or two days, or three days dead, swollen, blue, and festering, discarded on the charnel ground, he then applies this perception to his own body: "Truly, this body too is of the same nature, it will become like that and will not go beyond that nature."*

This is the first topic of the cemetery contemplations. It is said, "when a bhikkhu sees a dead body." People who practice *satipaṭṭhāna vipassanā* meditation, need not always go to a cemetery. They may still have visions of a dead body during *vipassanā* meditation. This may be the result of either deliberately thinking of corpses or alternatively the concept of corpses may come to them for no apparent reason. Whether the visions come to you on their own without any apparent reason or come to you due to deliberate meditation on their part, you must investigate these visions and consider them repulsive, noting, "repulsive, repulsive, repulsive," or just, "seeing, seeing, seeing," until they disappear. When practicing *vipassanā*, it is important to be aware of what comes to the attention of meditators, to their mind or to the other five sense doors (see glossary). When meditators have a vision, they just become aware of it, mindful of it, mentally noting, "seeing, seeing, seeing," until the vision goes away. The cemetery meditations, given in this *sutta*, are designed for the purpose of achieving awareness of the foulness or loathsomeness or repulsiveness of the body.

Meditation, in this *sutta*, is directed toward *vipassanā*, which attempts to see the rising and fading away of phenomena. But you can practice this meditation as *samatha*, a tranquility meditation, which will lead you to attain *jhāna*. People who want to practice this kind of meditation must first approach a teacher and get instructions. The teacher must show them how to acquire the perception of foulness and then how to characterize the surrounding things, that means, how to take note of the things found around the corpse.

Then, the teacher has to explain how to apprehend foulness in six ways, and, when this is not enough, in five additional ways. Furthermore, the teacher must instruct meditators how to investigate and take note of the path to and from the corpse. Only after having learned these techniques from a teacher, should meditators practice this kind of meditation and go to a place where a corpse has been left.

After having learned all these necessities from their teacher, meditators should "not leave immediately" upon hearing that a corpse can be found in such and such a place, because there may be wild beasts or non-human beings near the corpse.

Generally, men should not look at the corpse of a woman and women should not look at the corpse of a man, because feelings of excitement may arise in them. However, even contemplating on a corpse of the same sex can cause lustful thoughts to arise, so meditators should not contemplate on any corpse that may cause such thoughts.

The road to the place where the corpse lies may lead through a village or may lead alongside a beach or through fields, where meditators may see people who might become the cause for lustful thoughts. Meditators must take care of all these considerations.

When *bhikkhus* go to such a place, they must "tell the senior *bhikkhu* or a well-known *bhikkhu*" in the monastery where they are residing of their intention to go to the cemetery. Lay meditators must tell their meditation teacher. This is necessary because if they get into trouble at the cemetery, the other *bhikkhus* or fellow meditators can take care of them or their belongings or help them at the cemetery. A cemetery is generally a deserted place where robbers and thieves feel safe. They may go there, when followed by the owners of the stolen property. They may drop the stolen goods and other people, coming there, will see the goods near meditators and might think, they are the thieves, and may accuse them of stealing. When they have informed others that they are going to the cemetery, then the senior *bhikkhu* and the other *bhikkhus* or fellow meditators can help them. It is, therefore, essential that *bhikkhus* inform the senior elder or a well-known *bhikkhu* of their monastery that they are going to practice this kind of meditation at a cemetery or when they are laymen that they tell their meditation teacher.

Meditators must go alone to the cemetery, without a companion. They must go with unremitting mindfulness, that is, they must go with mindfulness established in them. They must go with the sense-faculties turned inward and not outward. They must not look in this direction or that direction. They must keep their mind to themselves, turned inward and not outward. Thus, they should go to the place where a corpse has been left.

On the way, they "review the characteristics of the path." The reason for this review will become clear below. It means, when they go along the way, they must take note, saying, for example, "I am going in such a direction through such a gate. This path leads toward the eastern or the western direction, the southern or the northern direction or it leads to an intermediate direction." Also, when they go to the cemetery, they must notice what is on the left and on the right of the path. They must notice whether there is an anthill or a tree or a creeper. They must take note of all the things along their path.

After having done this, meditators will "approach the place where the corpse lies." When they go toward the corpse, they must approach it from upwind, because the odor of the corpse might make them dizzy or might make them want to turn around. They must sit neither too close nor too far from the corpse, but sit on one side of it, in a place convenient for them to look at it. When they go too close to the corpse, they might get frightened. When they stop too far from it, they will be unable to recognize clearly its foulness. They must not sit right at its feet or head. If they do, they won't be able to see properly the signs of foulness of the corpse. They must also take note of the surroundings, the place where the corpse has been left. Are there any stones or anthills or trees, bushes or creepers, particular signs in relation to the corpse? For example, there may be a rock near the corpse and this rock is high or low, or this rock is large or small, or this rock is brown or black or white, long or round. They must take note of all these details. In relation to the corpse, they must note that "In this place, there is a rock, this is the sign of foulness." Sign of foulness means the corpse. Such reflections like, "This is the sign of foulness, this is a rock," are necessary to clarify the confusion and the delusion in their mind.

Sometimes, when meditators look at a corpse, the corpse may appear to them as if it is moving, as if it is getting up and assaulting or frightening them. So when the corpse appears to be moving, they can avoid confusion by thinking of the things noted before, "There is a rock near the corpse and the rock does not come to me, it cannot come to me. When the rock cannot come to me, the corpse also cannot come to me. The corpse is lifeless and cannot move. It can only be a delusion, an error in perception." After they have selected the object for meditation, they can now meditate. When they try to meditate and things appear or visions arise, they can prevent confusion. Meditators have, therefore, to note everything which can be seen around the corpse.

After standing and sitting near the corpse, meditators should look at the corpse and try to apprehend its foulness in six ways. First, they apprehend it by distinguishing its "color." "This is a body which has a black or a yellow skin," whatever color it might have. Meditators also distinguish the corpse by its "mark." By its mark does not mean its being a man or a woman, but its age. Age means, that this is the body of someone who was in the first, middle or last phase of his or her life. Generally, the life of a person is divided into three phases or periods — each extending approximately thirty years. These contemplations serve to apprehend the foulness of a corpse.

When meditators look at the "shape" of the corpse, they notice "this is the shape of its head. This is the shape of its neck. This is the shape of its hands, its chest, its hips, its thighs, its calf, its feet, its whole body." Meditators have to look at the whole body to comprehend the concept of foulness.

Meditators also look toward the "four directions." Directions here mean the upper part and the lower part of the corpse. The lower part of the body is the part down from the navel and the upper part that up from the navel. So, they know, "This is the upper part and this is the lower part of the corpse." Meditators should also observe, "I am standing in this direction, the sign of foulness (i.e., the corpse) is in that direction. I am here, say, in the south and the corpse is over there, in the north, and so on."

Meditators should also note the "location." Location means here, "The hand is in this location, the foot is in that location, the middle of the body is in this location, and so on." Or, "I am in this location, the sign of foulness is in that location."

Meditators should also note the "delimitations." "This body is delimited below by the soles of its feet and above by the tips of its hair and all around by the skin. The space is so delimited, i.e., it is filled up by the thirty-two parts of the body." In this way, meditators must recognize the limitations of the body. "These are the delimitations of its hands, its feet, of his head, of the middle part of the body, or this part of the body is bloated, and so on." The corpse must be one which does not cause lustful thoughts to arise, for even though it is a dead body, lustful thoughts may arise in meditators. Only when meditators are sure that lustful thoughts will not arise, even when meditating on a corpse, may they sit in meditation near that corpse.

Meditators should develop the sense of foulness, with respect to a corpse in these six ways.

When meditators can see the corpse with their eyes closed, they are said to have obtained the "learning." They develop it so that it becomes a "counterpart sign."

If they cannot get the sign by contemplating on the corpse in the above-mentioned six ways, then they must continue to comprehend foulness in five additional ways. Foulness is first comprehended by its joints. Joints means here fourteen major joints. Three are in the right and three in the left arm, three in the right and three in the left leg. There are also one head and one waist joint. The observation of these joints will lead to the understanding of the loathsomeness of the body.

Then, meditators should observe "openings." Openings here mean the hollows between the arms and the sides, the hollow between the legs, the hollow of the stomach, the hollow of the ear, or the open and closed states of the eyes and the mouth.

They must, furthermore, define the corpse by "concavities," such as the eye sockets, or the inside of the mouth or the base of his neck. Meditators must also observe, "I am standing in a concave place, the corpse is lying in a concave place."

Next, they consider "convexities," that means, any raised place such as the knee or the chest or the forehead. They define them, e.g., "I am standing in a convex place, the corpse is lying in a concave place."[11]

Lastly, meditators must "observe everything around," i.e., the entire corpse and the area around it. After having considered all these things, they establish their mind on "bloated, bloated, bloated," as if it is a bloated body.

Contemplating on the corpse in these six and then these five different ways, meditators surely will get the sign of foulness. They contemplate and think about foulness again and again, ten times or ten thousand times, until they get the sign. "They get the sign" means they can see the bloated corpse with their eyes closed.

If *bhikkhus* get this sign but cannot reach the end of this meditation at the cemetery, they should go back to the monastery, because *bhikkhus* cannot be at a cemetery all the time. When they go back, they take note of everything on the path back to the monastery. They note the direction, whether they are going to the east or the west, to the north or to the south. They note also what they see, the stones, shrubs, and trees. The taking note of everything on the path to and from the corpse is to keep the mind of practitioners on the track of meditation. Back at the monastery, they may be asked questions. When asked, they must not avoid the question; they must give an answer. If they are asked about something concerning the *Dhamma,* they must answer. When they arrive at the monastery, they might have some duties toward other *bhikkhus.* When they answer questions or fulfill duties toward senior *bhikkhus*, they may lose the sign be unable to recall it, because they are distracted. When lay people return from the cemetery, they also will have to answer questions and there will be duties waiting to be performed.

When meditators have lost the sign and cannot go back to the cemetery, they may sit and mentally go to the cemetery where the corpse is lying and then return again. In this way, they may be able to retrieve the sign. The method of having noted the things along the path, going to and coming from the corpse, will be helpful. *Bhikkhus* will review the stone, the rock, one item here and another item there, until they have reviewed all items on the way. They recall in their mind all the details of going and the signs of foulness. When they get the sign, which is called the "learning sign" again, it appears to them as really frightful and repulsive. They dwell on it again and again, noting, "repulsive, repulsive, repulsive," or "bloated, bloated, bloated," until the mental picture becomes clearly defined. It will now appear to them as not being very disgusting but as a very fat man having eaten his fill.

This sign is called the "counterpart sign." After that, the hindrances will be inhibited and meditators will reach the state of *jhāna* or absorption. This is the way *bhikkhus* or lay people should practice this meditation.

Concerning the meditation on the body, there are "ten kinds of foulness" described in *The Path of Purification*. In this *sutta*, there are only nine stages mentioned. After going through this process, meditators may reach the *jhāna stage*. Having gained the *jhāna* stage, they can make this *jhāna* the object of *vipassanā* meditation. They can review the factors of the *jhāna*, watching the factors of the *jhāna* come and go, arise and disappear. They see them rising and fading away. From that stage, they go on to the different *vipassanā* stages, until they reach the end of the *vipassanā* process, the attainment of *nibbāna*. Therefore, this kind of meditation can be practiced first as *samattha* meditation and then as *vipassanā* meditation. It can be practiced as it is described in the *sutta*, for the perception of foulness and the perception that one is in danger or in fault. When this perception arises in the mind of practitioners, they see the perception arise and go away. They see also the mind that perceives the object arise and go away. They see the rising and fading away of the mind and the mental object which is the corpse, i.e., the dead body. Thus, they practice *satipaṭṭhāna* meditation until they reach the stage of sainthood.

When meditators practice *satipaṭṭhāna* meditation using these cemetery meditations, they need not go to a cemetery, because what is important in *vipassanā* meditation is the application of the repulsiveness or the foulness of the dead body to their own body. "Just as the dead body is repulsive and foul, so is this body. This, my body, cannot go beyond this nature." So, they meditate on these contemplations.

In Western countries, it is very difficult to go to a cemetery and practice meditation on the foulness of body, because you won't see a corpse in a cemetery. In America, a dead body is made to look like a sleeping man or woman, and will look beautiful. In the United States, you may not get the sense of repulsiveness by looking at a dead body. You can get some pictures of corpses, but photographs do not suffice, because, even when such photos can be found, the dead body will neither be bloated nor be festering nor cut up, and so on. Even in Eastern countries, it is nowadays difficult to see a corpse in different stages of decay.

The second to eighth stages of decay of the dead body, mentioned in the *sutta*, are

> *devoured by crows, by hawks, by vultures, by herons, by dogs, by leopards, by tigers, by jackals, being devoured by various kinds of worms,*
>
> *reduced to a skeleton, held by the tendons, with some flesh adhering to it,*
>
> *reduced to a skeleton, held by the tendons, blood-smeared, fleshless,*
>
> *reduced to a skeleton, held by the tendons, without flesh and blood,*
>
> *reduced to loose bones, scattered in all directions, here bones of the hand, here bones of the foot, shin bones, thigh bones, pelvis, spine, and skull,*
>
> *reduced to bleached bones of shell-like color,*
>
> *reduced to bones more than a year old, lying in a heap.*

The ninth stage is

> *when a bhikkhu sees a body, discarded in the charnel-ground, reduced to rotten bones, crumbling to dust, he then applies this perception to his own body, saying, "Truly this body too has the same nature, it will become like that body and won't go beyond that nature."*

So, we come down to rotten and crumbled bones. There is another meditation on foulness, called "skeleton meditation." Some people take a skeleton or bones as objects of meditation. When meditators have practiced this kind of meditation for a long time, they will see only the bones. Although somebody may be still alive, meditators will see only his or her skeleton.

There is the story of a *bhikkhu* who was called Elder Mahā Tissa. When he was on his way to the village to make his alms round, he met a woman. She had quarreled with her husband and was returning to her parents' house. When the woman saw the *bhikkhu,* she laughed. The *bhikkhu* saw only the teeth of this woman and perceived only a skeleton. He had been practicing this meditation. He achieved the perception of repulsiveness of the body and saw only a skeleton. He immediately practiced *vipassanā* meditation and became an *arahat.* The husband, following this woman, met the *bhikkhu* and asked him whether he had seen a woman on the road. The *bhikkhu* replied, "I saw neither a man nor a woman going down this road. What I saw was a skeleton going down this road." This is the result of practicing the meditation on the foulness or repulsiveness of the body using the cemetery meditation.

We have come to the end of the Contemplations on the Body. There are fourteen topics of meditation or contemplations on the body — mindfulness of breathing, mindful postures of the body, mindfulness with clear comprehension, reflections on the repulsiveness of the body, reflections on the material elements, and the nine cemetery contemplations.

2 Contemplation of Feelings

We have many kinds of feelings — pleasant, unpleasant or neutral. Feelings here must be understood to be mental. When you have pain, you feel the pain and that mental feeling is called, in Pāli, *vedanā*. Whenever you say *vedanā*, you mean feeling pain, feeling pleasure or indifference. Meditators who contemplate or note the pleasantness, unpleasantness or neutrality of feelings are said to be practicing the Contemplation on Feelings.

The Buddha said,

> *And how, bhikkhus, does a bhikkhu dwell on contemplating the feelings in the feelings?*
>
> *Herein, bhikkhus, when experiencing a pleasant feeling, the bhikkhu knows, "I experience a pleasant feeling"; when experiencing a painful feeling, he knows, "I experience a painful feeling."*

Whatever feeling they experience, meditators must take note of it and observe it. These are the instructions given by the Buddha about the practice of *vipassanā* meditation. When you have painful feelings in the body, pain or numbness or stiffness, you focus your mind on the place of pain and take note of the pain by saying, "pain, pain, pain." When you have a good feeling, a pleasant feeling, then you just say, "pleasant, pleasant, pleasant," or "good, good, good," or "happy, happy, happy."

What meditators know about different feelings is very different from what people who do not meditate know. When you are feeling good, you know that you are feeling good. And when you are feeling bad, you know that you are feeling

bad, but, this is not meditation. This is not *vipassanā* meditation. Practitioners of *vipassanā* meditation see and observe the
feeling just as feeling not as the feeling of a person, not as a
personal feeling and not as a permanent or lasting feeling. Just
as in the practice of knowing, "going, going, going," when you
are going, so meditators should here also understand, "feeling, feeling, feeling."   The knowledge of meditators is
diametrically opposed to the knowledge of ordinary people
who do not meditate. The mind of ordinary people who do
not meditate cannot remove the concept of being and cannot
do away with the notion of self. Therefore, it cannot be insight
meditation. However, the mind of meditators can see that
there is just feeling. There are just pleasant or unpleasant
feelings. There is no one who feels, apart from the feeling
itself. This feeling cannot be said to belong to any person or
being.

You also know that this feeling does not last. When you
have a painful feeling and you keep noting this feeling as being
"pain, pain, pain," it may take ten or fifteen minutes until you
come to see that this pain is not constant. It is not one solid
pain. There are different stages of pain and different moments
of pain. One pain comes and goes, then the next pain comes
and goes. You see pain is not one continuous thing. When
you can see through the continuity, you come to see the
impermanence of things, because the illusion of continuity
cannot cover or hide reality. When you think of continuity,
you think of things being permanent as lasting for a long time.
When continuity is removed, you come to see the rising and
fading away, the appearing and disappearing of things. Thus,
the knowledge or understanding of meditators is much
deeper than that of ordinary people.

There are different feelings. First, there are pleasant or
unpleasant feelings, and then there are neutral feelings. You
may have pleasant worldly feelings which are connected with
things you come across in your life: sights, sounds, smells,
tastes, odors, thoughts, and things you think you possess such
as a husband, a wife, children. This pleasant feeling depends
upon worldly things, so it is called "pleasant worldly feeling."
When you have such feeling, you must be aware of it and take
note of it as "pleasant." Sometimes, you may have unpleasant
feelings. You feel sad. You may be depressed. Or sometimes
there is something you possess, something of value which has

disappeared or has been taken away from you. Then you get angry or you become sad and you feel sorry. These are unpleasant feelings concerned with worldly things. It can happen to meditators too when they think of something bad which has happened to them. When such a feeling arises in them, they must be mindful of this and think, "sorry, sorry, sorry," or "angry, angry, angry," about whatever it is.

Neutral feelings are neither pleasant nor unpleasant. Sometimes, when meditators who are practicing *vipassanā* come across sense objects, they feel neither pleasure nor displeasure, nor can they give up the object. Here neutral feelings accompanied by attachment arise in meditators. Such feelings are called "worldly neutral feelings." This is also called "indifference depending on worldly things" or "indifference accompanied by delusion or ignorance" (*aññānupekkhā*, literally, "not-knowing indifference").

You may also have unworldly feelings. "Pleasant, unpleasant or neutral unworldly feelings" mean feelings which arise during meditation. When you meditate, you may have good concentration or you may see the rising and fading away of things. Then you feel happy. You feel so happy at that time that you just want to get up and tell other people about it. You can hardly contain or suppress this feeling. Such a feeling may come to meditators especially when they have reached the stage where they see the rising and fading away of phenomena. Meditators should not experience that feeling with attachment. They must be aware and mindful of that feeling. If they are attached to this feeling, they will stay in this stage and won't be able to make progress.

What are "unpleasant unworldly feelings?" Sometimes, you cannot meditate as much as you try and your mind does not stay on the object. You become discouraged or depressed. That is an unworldly unpleasant feeling. Sometimes, meditators have reached the stage of *jhāna* and then have fallen from it and experience some sadness or sorrow. Such a feeling must be noted, "sad, sad, sad," or "sorry, sorry, sorry," and overcome.

There is a story of an elder who was very learned. It is said that he taught eighteen groups of students. He was a really great teacher and especially learned in the scriptures. As many as thirty thousand *bhikkhus* attained arahathood just following his advice. One of those pupils, one day, reviewed the good qualities in himself and thought of his teacher and then he reviewed his teacher. He found that his teacher was still a worldling and had not yet attained arahathood. So he went to teach his teacher a lesson. When he had come to the teacher, the teacher asked him, "What do you come for?" and he said, "I want to hear a Dhamma talk from you." The teacher said, "I have no time. I am very busy." Then the pupil said, "I will ask you when you go to the village for alms." "Oh no, there will be many people who will ask questions at that time." The student kept asking for an appointment but every time the teacher was too busy for him. At the end, the pupil told the teacher, "Sir, don't you have time for, at least, two or three sittings? If you don't have any time, you won't even have time to die. You are always busy, you are like the back of a chair. You are relied upon by other people, but you cannot rely on yourself. I don't want anything more from you." The student went away. The teacher was moved and decided to meditate on this event. He thought he would become an *arahat* in two or three days. He did not tell anybody about it. However, he could not attain arahathood. He passed through one rainy season (*vassa*) and, at the end of the rainy season, he still could not attain anything. He felt sorry, so he wept. He wept and wept and wept and practiced for twenty-nine years. In the thirtieth year, at the end of the rainy season, he was still a worldling and had not attained anything. He became very sorry and wept aloud. At that time, a deity approached him and wept too. So he asked, "Who is weeping here?" "I am a deity." "Why are you weeping?" "Oh, I saw you weeping and I thought I might get one or two attainments just by crying." The *bhikkhu* was deeply moved and said to himself, "Now even the deity is making jokes about me. It is not proper for me to be depressed or sorry." So he removed his sorrow, continued to practice and, finally, became an *arahat*. Although he was well-versed in the *Tipiṭaka*, it took him thirty years to become an *arahat*. His obsession with this sorrowful feeling with respect to non-worldly things, during meditation, had been an obstacle to his attainment.

The neutral feelings during meditation which are called "mindful non-worldly feelings" occur when meditators reach higher stages of *vipassanā* knowledge and experience the feeling of neutrality. They do not have to put in much effort in contemplating the object, it just comes to them by itself. So, at this time, they have this feeling of neutrality, the feeling of equanimity. Such feelings are called "neutral non-worldly feelings." When they arise in you, you must be mindful of them, and note them, "neutral feeling, neutral feeling, neutral feeling." In this way, meditators will be able to be aware of the rising and fading away of whatever feelings they are experiencing. They will then reach higher and higher stages of *vipassanā* knowledge until they reach the level of attainment.

Feelings have to be noted. When meditators take note of them when they arise, they will come to see their rising and fading away; they will also come to see that because there is pain there are painful feelings; because there is comfort, there are pleasant feelings, and so on. Thus, meditators recognize the "origination factors" of the feeling, the "dissolution factors" of the feeling or both the origination and the dissolution factors of the feelings. They may contemplate internally on their own feelings or, by inference, externally, on other people's feelings or both, internally and externally. This is the way feelings should be dealt with during meditation, by being aware of them, by being mindful of them, by taking note of them. When meditators see the arising and fading away of feelings, they won't cling to them. Without clinging, they can achieve the "Realization of Truth." This is the Contemplation of Feeling in the Feelings.

3 Contemplation of Consciousness

Consciousness is a part of the mind. In the teachings of the Buddha, there are two component parts of the mind — consciousness and mental factors. "Consciousness" is that which is aware of an object. It is the bare awareness of an object. "Mental factors" are what colors consciousness. They arise together with the consciousness and modify the consciousness. Greed is a mental factor. Hatred or anger are mental factors. Delusion is a mental factor. Faith is a mental factor. Wisdom is a mental factor. When these mental factors arise, they arise together with certain kinds of consciousness. Though consciousness is emphasized in this section, consciousness and mental factors cannot be separated. When you observe consciousness, you also observe the mental factors. When you have anger in your mind, and note it, "angry, angry, angry," you practice the contemplation of this consciousness. "Angry" means, your mind is angry, or "I have a consciousness which is accompanied by anger." So when you note, "angry, angry, angry," you are practicing this kind of meditation, the Contemplation of Consciousness.

Other types of consciousness should be noted also. Different kinds of consciousness are mentioned in the *sutta*: with lust, without lust; with hate, without hate; with delusion, without delusion.

"Constricted consciousness" refers to a type of consciousness you have when you are oppressed by sloth and torpor. When you are sleepy, then your consciousness is constricted. "Scattered consciousness" refers to a type of consciousness you have when you are restless. "The mind has become great," means "*jhāna* consciousness." "The mind that has not become great," means the other types of consciousness pertaining to the sense sphere.

"Surpassable consciousness" means types of consciousness pertaining to the sense-sphere and the form-sphere. "Unsurpassable consciousness" means types of consciousness pertaining to the formless sphere.

"Concentrated consciousness" is one with access concentration and absorption concentration. "Unconcentrated consciousness" means consciousness which is scattered and unfocused.

"Freed consciousness" is one which is free from defilements momentarily or temporarily. It is *vipassanā* consciousness or *jhāna* consciousness. "Unfreed consciousness" means consciousness which is not free from defilements.

You need to know the *Abhidhamma* to understand all these different kinds of consciousness. However, it is not necessary to be able to differentiate the various kinds of consciousness by their respective names. It is sufficient that you are aware when you are sleepy, and say, "sleepy, sleepy, sleepy." When you are distracted, you note, "distracted, distracted, distracted."

These types of consciousness have to be noted whenever they arise in your mind. During the Contemplation of Consciousness, one consciousness is the object of another. They cannot arise at the same moment. The consciousness which is the object of meditation arose just a little bit earlier and the noting consciousness arises just a little bit later. But you can call them present, because there is a very small difference in time when you contemplate on consciousness. When different kinds of consciousness arise and fade away, you take note of these specific types when they arise.

When you observe consciousness in this way, you will come to see that there is consciousness only and no person or being that is its agent. You will also recognize that since it arises and fades away every moment, it is impermanent. When you see its impermanence, you won't cling to it through craving or wrong view. When there is no clinging there can be no formation of *kamma* and you will be able to achieve freedom from suffering.

This is the Contemplation of Consciousness.

4 Contemplation of the Dhammas

We have studied so far three of the Four Foundations of Mindfulness: the Contemplation of the Body, the Contemplation of Feelings, and the Contemplation of Consciousness. Now, we are going to study the Fourth Foundation of Mindfulness, i.e., the Contemplation of the *Dhammas*.

The Contemplation of the Body is the contemplation of the physical or material body. The Contemplation of Feelings is the contemplation of what is the mental experience " pleasant, unpleasant or neutral " of physical sensation. The Contemplation of Consciousness is also a contemplation of mental things, the mental factors or mind states. The Contemplation of the *Dhammas* is a contemplation of material as well as mental things.

The first contemplation is the contemplation of material aggregates, meditation on the aggregate of corporeality. During the second contemplation, the Contemplation of Feelings, practitioners meditate on the aggregate of feeling. The third is the contemplation of the aggregate of consciousness. The fourth contemplation is the Contemplation of the *Dhammas,* i.e., on the aggregate of mental formations. The word *dhammas* is left untranslated, because it is difficult to find an English word which covers the full meaning of the word *dhammas*. The word *dhammas* is usually translated "mental objects." This is neither accurate nor concise, because the objects of meditation mentioned in this section belong to both groups, the mental as well as the material group. When "mental objects" mean the objects of the mind, then the body is also an object of the mind and feelings and consciousness are also objects of the mind. When "objects of the mind" mean objects which are mental, then you have also material things among these objects of contemplation. Therefore, it is better to leave the word *dhammas* untranslated and try to understand what *dhammas* mean in this *sutta*.

This section discusses the "five hindrances," the "five objects of clinging," the "six internal and the six external sense-bases," the "seven factors of enlightenment" and the Four Noble Truths. The "five hindrances" are mental. The "five objects of clinging" are material and mental. The "six internal and the six external sense-bases" are material and mental. The "seven factors of enlightenment" are mental and the Four Noble Truths consist of both material and mental things.

THE FIVE HINDRANCES

We will now study the first subsection of the Contemplation on the *dhammas*, namely, the "five hindrances." Whatever you are doing, you will find that you have some kind of obstacles or hindrances to overcome. Hindrances are negative factors of meditation. They hinder or obstruct the gaining of concentration. With regard to the hindrances, the Buddha said,

> *Herein, bhikkhus, a bhikkhu dwells contemplating the Dhamma in the dhammas in the five hindrances.*

How shall we understand that "a *bhikkhu* dwells on the contemplation of the *Dhamma* in the *dhammas* in the five hindrances?" What are the five hindrances?

Sense-desire

> *Herein, bhikkhus, when sense-desire is present in him, the bhikkhu knows, "There is sense-desire in me," or when sense-desire is absent in him, he knows, "There is no sense-desire in me." He also knows the reason by which the arising of non-arisen sense-desire comes to be; he also knows the reason why the abandoning of arisen sense-desire comes to be; and he also knows the reason by which non-arising of the abandoned sense-desire in the future comes to be.*

With these words, the Buddha instructs us how to deal with sense-desire. Sense-desire is the first of the mental hindrances, mentioned in this section. "Sense-desire" means the desire for sensual objects — desire, attachment, craving, longing, lust. It means the desire for visible objects, audible objects, smells, odors, tastes, tangible and mental objects. Desire for anything is called sense-desire in this section. When sense-desire is present in practitioners, they know, "There is sense-desire in me." When, during meditation, you have thoughts of desire, thoughts of lust or craving, or thoughts of attachment, then you should be aware of the presence of sense-desire in you. You will know that there is sense-desire present in you. You must mentally note "desire, desire, desire"; or "attachment, attachment, attachment"; or "craving, craving, craving." "Present" means that something exists because it occurs repeatedly. Good thoughts or bad thoughts, *kusala* (wholesome) or *akusala* (unwholesome) thoughts cannot coexist. These thoughts are not really "present" at the moment meditators come to know them, because these thoughts cannot coexist with the knowing of them. But since these thoughts arise in meditators again and again, they are said to be "existent." At the moment of observing them, at the moment of observing the hindrances, they are already gone. They last, maybe, a fraction of a second. "Present" means something which has occurred that very moment. You have to recognize what is present, existent, or occurs repeatedly. When a desire is present, meditators know, "There is such and such a desire in me." And when sense-desire is absent in meditators, they know, "There is no sense-desire in me."

"Absent" here means two things. First, it means not existing because it does not occur or it has been abandoned. Second, it means it is absent simply because it does not arise. Or, it first arises in meditators, they observe it, and then it disappears. When it disappears, it will be absent. Sometimes meditators notice the absence of desire. It just does not arise in them. Sometimes, meditators feel desire and they take note of this desire. Then, it disappears and they notice the disappearance of desire in them. So, whatever is the case, you must be mindful of the absence of sense-desire when it is absent.

He also knows the reason by which the arising of non-arisen sense-desire comes to be.

There are causes of the arising of good thoughts or of bad thoughts. Generally speaking, there are two kinds of what we

call "reflections." We call them" attitudes" or "viewing." They
are "unwise reflections" and "wise reflections."   Unwise
reflections lead to *akusala* thoughts and wise reflections to
kusala thoughts. "Unwise reflections" means inexpedient
reflections, reflections on the wrong track, so we call them
"wrong reflections." They are the kinds of reflection which
take the impermanent to be permanent, the unsatisfactory to
be satisfactory, that which is soulless to have a soul, and the
ugly to be beautiful. So, when you take things to be permanent, satisfactory, substantial, beautiful, something to be
attached to, then you have this kind of unwise reflection.
These reflections are unwise because they cause *akusala*
thoughts to arise. So, unwise reflections are the general cause
of the arising of *akusala* thoughts.

Reflections of the opposite kind are "wise reflections." They
are expedient reflections, reflections which are on the right
track. These are the kinds of reflection which take the impermanent to be impermanent, the unsatisfactory to be unsatisfactory, soullessness to be without soul, the ugly not to be
beautiful, and the undesirable to be undesirable. This is the
correct way of viewing things. The Buddha said that everything is impermanent, unsatisfactory and insubstantial. You
are not to be attached to anything. When you see things in this
way, you are said to have this kind of wise reflection which is
a right and correct reflection or view of things.

Sense-desire arises in you because you have "unwise reflections." There are objects which are conditions for sensuality,
conditions for sense-desire to arise. You see things which you
consider to be beautiful, which you think are desirable, and
then you develop a kind of attachment to all these things and
experience a sort of craving. This craving or attachment arises,
because you have a wrong attitude. You reflect incorrectly on
these things. So, when sense-desire arises in meditators, they
may notice that this desire arises in them, because they are
reflecting unwisely. They have viewed the objects of sensual
desire in a wrong way, in a way which made them think they
are lasting, satisfying, substantial and beautiful. In meditation, you can notice this and become aware of it. "Because I
have unwise reflections, this sense-desire arises in me."

> He also knows the reason why the abandoning of the
> arisen sense-desire comes to be.

The abandoning of sense-desire can be achieved in two ways, i.e., by observing it and by cultivating wise reflections on the object as having the nature of foulness. Meditators may attain *jhāna* contemplating on the concept of foulness.

The Buddha said the body is not desirable, not beautiful and not auspicious. Wise reflections on this object can cause the abandonment of sense-desire. Or, when practitioners have reached *jhāna,* depending on or taking the concept of foulness as the object of meditation, they may be able to get rid of sense-desire. In *vipassanā* meditation, just by being mindful, this sense-desire is removed or abandoned. When you are aware of its absence, you know the cause of the disappearance of this sense-desire: "Because I have this wise reflection, the correct attitude or the correct view towards this object, the sense-desire will disappear."

Sometimes, meditators notice the cause of the disappearance of sense-desire. Then, they also know why this abandoned sense-desire won't arise again in the future. That means, when meditators become *arahats,* the sense-desire, once abandoned, will never return to them. They "know the reason by which non-arising of the abandoned sense-desire comes to be." They know that by attainment of path-consciousness, by reason of path-consciousness, the sense-desire which has been abandoned will never return. By attaining path consciousness, sense-desire is completely eradicated. This happens, when meditators attain arahathood. It pertains to the attainment state, the attainment of path consciousness, the attainment of sainthood. So, when meditators have sense-desire, they have come to know why sense-desire arises. They know why sense-desire disappears and they know why sense-desire is abandoned, momentarily or temporarily.

What can you do, when sense-desire arises? You make this sense-desire the object of your meditation. You dwell on it. You take note of this desire. Just by being noted, the desire will disappear. The commentator pointed out six things practitioners can do to abandon sense-desire. They can be done when the practitioners are out of *vipassanā* meditation.

First, meditators can take up "meditation on the foulness of the body," looking at a corpse or dwelling on the thirty-two parts of the body. Practitioners learn this kind of meditation and then their practice will help them to abandon sense-desire.

The second way is the practice of "meditation on foulness so that they reach the *jhāna* stage." when meditators reach the *jhāna* stage, they will be able to abandon sense-desire.

The third way is " controlling the faculties of the senses." That means, meditators control their senses, their eyes, their ears, their nose, and so on, so that no *akusala* thoughts can arise in them through one of the six sense doors.

The fourth way is "practicing moderation with respect to food." Eating moderately will help to abandon sense-desire. When you eat too much, you will have more sense-desire. You will also have more desire for food. Therefore, meditators are advised not to eat all the food in front of them when they are eating. They should leave four or five lumps uneaten. In Asia, *bhikkhus* eat with their hands and one handful is called a lump. When *bhikkhus* come close to finishing the food in front of them, they should not eat everything and should leave four or five lumps uneaten. They drink water instead. That means, when eating, *bhikkhus* should not fill their stomach to the rim. They leave room for water. This is enough for the comfort of *bhikkhus* who have set their mind toward reaching *nibbāna*. It is enough for the comfort of anybody whose mind is set toward reaching the state of *nibbāna*. This section tells you how to eat comfortably. Moderation in food means just eating and avoiding filling your stomach to the rim.

The fifth way is "having a good friend." This is really a *kalyāna mitta*, a friend firmly on the path or, as we say in the West, a "spiritual friend." To have a good friend is very essential. When you have a good friend, you can have good advice. You can learn from your friend and take him or her as an example. So, a good friend who has no sense-desire can help meditators to abandon sense-desire.

The sixth way is "practicing suitable talk." To abandon sense-desire, meditators should talk about the foulness of the body. They should talk about the bad results of attachment, and so on. These six things lead to the abandonment of sense-desire.

Ill Will

The second hindrance, discussed in this section, is ill will. Ill will here means resentment, anger, hatred and also fear, anxiety, tension, frustration, and impatience.

When ill will is present in him, he knows, "There is ill will in me," or when ill will is absent in him, he knows, "There is no ill will in me."

Here again, we have two kinds of reflections. When you have unwise reflections, you will have ill will. When you have wise reflections, you will experience the absence of ill will.

During meditation, anger or resentment may often arise in practitioners. They may be angry with themselves or they may be upset because somebody makes a noise. They cannot concentrate. Soon they will be restless or become angry. When such anger or ill will arises, sometimes you will think of someone with whom you have quarreled and towards whom you feel resentment. So, when these different kinds of emotions arise in meditators, they must become aware of the presence of anger and note, "I have anger," or just note, "anger, anger, anger." When you notice resentment and ill will, you then note, "ill will, ill will, ill will." You may notice hatred and, sometimes, fear, then you note, "fear, fear, fear." Because you are noticing anger and you are noticing it three or four times, the anger or the ill will disappears. When it has disappeared, meditators must be aware of its disappearance and note, "There is no anger in me anymore," and so on.

He also knows the reason by which the arising of non-arisen ill will comes to be.

Here practitioners exercise wise reflections. Everything is impermanent. The objects of ill will are also impermanent and when meditators wisely reflects on their impermanence, they cannot be angry about them. But when they reflect unwisely, then they will experience ill will and anger toward these objects. Therefore, sometimes, during meditation, you may notice, "I have this ill will because I reflect wrongly. I have an unwise attitude towards things. I have wrong views of things." When you are aware of this, you are said to be aware of the cause of the arising of ill will.

He also knows why the abandoning of arisen ill will comes to be.

When you experience ill will and take note of it you will also observe it disappear. When it has disappeared, you become aware of its disappearance. You know that it has disappeared because you took note of ill will. Also, when you reflect wisely, especially on *mettā* (loving kindness), ill will will leave you. So, wise reflections are the cause of the disappearance of ill will.

Outside of *vipassanā*, there are also six ways meditators can practice to abandon ill will.

The first to learn is "taking up loving kindness meditation," sending out thoughts of love, thoughts of good will, toward all beings. The second is to "practice loving kindness meditation" until you reach the *jhāna* stage. When meditators reach the state of *jhāna*, they will be able to abandon ill will. The third is to reflect on "*kamma* as your own property." To reflect on your *kamma* as your own property is important for many reasons. When you are angry, you can say to yourself, "Who am I angry with?" You are reborn on this earth as result of the *kamma* you have accumulated in the past. You will also be reborn hereafter, according to the *kamma* you accumulate in this life. So, beings are born and die according to their *kamma* and, since it is according to their *kamma* that beings are reborn and die, there is no reason for you to be angry with anybody. A person who is angry is like a person who wants to strike somebody else. Such persons want to take up a red-hot iron to strike or pick up filth to throw at somebody else. But they hurt themselves first, before they can harm somebody else. So, meditators should reflect on their own *kamma* as being their responsibility. We all shape our own life according to our own *kamma*.

The fourth way is "extensive contemplation on good things about *mettā* and bad things about ill will." This means trying to see the advantages of loving kindness and the disadvantages of anger, ill will, and hatred. By recognizing what is good and seeing the advantages of loving kindness as well as the disadvantages of ill will, meditators will be able to abandon hatred, ill will, and anger.

The fifth way is "having a good friend," a *kalyāna mitta*. A good friend is always a condition or cause for abandoning *akusala* thoughts which, in this case, are ill will. People who are full of love can influence other people to be full of love, too. So, when you associate with a friend, with a person that has abundant loving kindness, then you will be able to abandon ill will and anger, taking the friend as example.

The sixth way is "suitable talk," talk about loving kindness meditation, talk about the advantages of loving kindness and the disadvantages of ill will. This will help to abandon ill will.

> *He also knows why the abandoning of arisen ill will comes*
> *to be, and he also knows the reason by which non-arising,*
> *in the future, of abandoned ill will comes to be.*

This statement also pertains to the moment when meditators attain path consciousness. When meditators reach the third stage of sainthood, they abandon ill will altogether.

Sloth And Torpor

The next hindrance is "sloth and torpor" which is, simply, sleepiness. This sleepiness may come to meditators every now and then. We all have experienced this sloth and torpor during meditation.

> *When sloth and torpor are present in him, he knows,*
> *"There are sloth and torpor in me," or when sloth and*
> *torpor are absent in him, he knows, "There are no sloth*
> *and torpor left in me."*

When meditators feel sleepy, they must be alerted to their sleepiness and take note of it. Often, just by taking note, they are able to abandon or drive away sleepiness, sloth and torpor. When they disappear, you are also aware of their disappearance. You know then that "There is no sloth and torpor left in me. They have disappeared."

> *He also knows the reason by which the arising of non-*
> *arisen sloth and torpor comes to be.*

Here again, the unwise reflections on the states of boredom, languidness, lethargy, and sluggishness of the mind are the causes of sloth and torpor. "Unwise reflections" mean thinking that there is no harm in boredom, languidness, lethargy, and sluggishness, and so on. However, by wise reflections and through correct attitudes towards the exertion of effort, meditators can abandon sloth, torpor, and sleepiness altogether. Therefore, when you are sleepy, you can do two things, one is to take note of your sleepiness, "sleepy, sleepy,

sleepy." The other is to step up energy, to put in more effort or to pay more attention to the objects of meditation. By way of effort, sloth and torpor can be abandoned. When sloth and torpor are abandoned, when they are absent, meditators know that they are absent or that they have been abandoned.

> *He also knows the reason by which the arising of non-arisen sloth and torpor comes to be. He also knows the reason why the abandoning of arisen sloth and torpor comes to be, and he also knows the reason by which non-arising, in the future, of the abandoned sloth and torpor comes to be.*

Sloth and torpor are eradicated altogether in attaining the final stage of sainthood. When practitioners become *arahats,* only then they will abandon sloth and torpor altogether. They are aware that sloth and torpor have been eradicated, because they have truly attained the last stage of sainthood.

There are also six ways which lead to the temporary abandoning of sloth and torpor.

One is "seeing the cause of sloth and torpor in eating too much." That means, you must know that when you eat too much, you will feel sleepy. When the stomach is full, it needs more blood and the blood, which would have gone to the brain, will go to the stomach. You will feel dizzy or you will feel sleepy. When you know this, you will practice moderation in eating, and then you may be able to abandon sloth and torpor.

The second way is "changing your posture." When you feel sleepy while you are sitting, you may change that posture. You may stand up and practice standing meditation or you may walk up and down. So, when you change your posture, you will drive away sloth, torpor and sleepiness.

The third way is "reflecting on the perception of light." You try to see light in your mind, the light of the sun, the light of the moon, star light or electric light, and so on. Reflecting on the perception of light helps you to abandon sleepiness. You just close your eyes and try to see light and think of things that are bright. This way you may be able to abandon sloth and torpor.

The fourth way is "staying in the open." You may feel sleepy while being in a house, then you may go outside and sit under a tree or you may sit somewhere outside. Then you will be able to abandon sleepiness.

The fifth way is "having a good friend," a friend who is not fond of sleeping, a friend who is not given to too much sleepiness. When you associate with a person who is energetic, who does not feel sleepy all the time, then you may be able to abandon sloth, torpor and sleepiness.

The sixth way is "using suitable talk." You recognize the disadvantages of sleepiness and the advantages of keeping yourself awake.

In the *suttas,* you find more references and more advice to counter sleepiness. Have you heard of the Venerable Moggallāna? He was one of the two chief disciples of the Buddha. He was the most developed in the field of psychic powers. Before he reached arahathood, while he was practicing meditation, he was overcome by sleepiness. He just nodded and nodded. He could not keep his mind on the object of his meditation. The Buddha knew this through his supernatural powers. He showed himself to Moggallāna and advised him how to fight sleepiness. This is mentioned in a *sutta* of the *Aṅguttara Nikāya, The Book of the Gradual Sayings*:

> "Are you nodding, Moggallāna, are you nodding?"
> the Buddha asked and Moggallāna said, " Yes, I am
> sleepy." Then, the Buddha said, "Well, Moggallāna,
> whatever thoughts of drowsiness befall you, you
> should not pay any attention to such thoughts. You
> should not dwell on such thoughts. By doing so, it
> will be possible that your drowsiness will vanish."

So, when you think of something that causes sleepiness, you should "avoid this thought." This is advice number one. The second is:

> If, by doing so drowsiness does not vanish, then you
> should reflect upon the teaching that you have heard
> and learned. You should ponder over these teach-
> ings and examine them closely in your mind. By
> doing so, it is possible that your drowsiness may
> vanish. That means, you should think of the *Dhamma*
> you have learned and think of the *Dhamma* you have
> heard about. That means, you develop some kind of

curiosity about the *Dhamma* or have some reflections on the *Dhamma*. And when you ponder over the *Dhamma,* examine it closely in your mind, you will become alert again and you will be able to drive away sleepiness or drowsiness.[12]

When by doing so, drowsiness won't vanish, the third way is to "repeat, in detail, the teachings you have heard and learned." That means, you will recite them. When you have learned something by heart, you recite it. Through the recitation of whatever you have learned, you may be able to drive away sleepiness.

When by doing so, your drowsiness does not vanish, the fourth way of removing it is to "pull both ear lobes" with your hands and to "rub your limbs" with your hands. You pull your ears and rub your limbs to become alert. By doing so, it is possible that drowsiness may vanish.

When by doing so drowsiness still does not vanish, the fifth way is to "get up from your seat and wash your eyes with water," with cold water. You should look around in all directions. By doing so, it is possible that your drowsiness may vanish.

When by doing so drowsiness does not vanish, the sixth way is to "pay attention to the perception of light," the perception of daylight, and as by day so by night, as by night so by day. That means, even when it is night, you think of it as by day and think of it as light. By doing so you may be able to drive away sleepiness. Thus, with your mind clear and unclouded, you can cultivate your mind and fill it with brightness. By doing so, it is possible that your drowsiness will vanish.

When by doing so, drowsiness does not vanish and when your senses are turned inward, and your mind not straying outward, the seventh way is to "walk up and down." So, when you feel sleepy, you get up and do walking meditation. Being aware of going back and forth, you take note of your steps and the different stages of the steps. By walking up and down, and being aware of going back and forth, you can drive away sleepiness. It is possible that your drowsiness may vanish.

When by doing the above, drowsiness still does not vanish, you may lie down, lion-like. This means on your right side, placing one foot on the other, clearly aware of what you are doing and keeping in mind the thought of rising. You say, "I will wake up at such and such a time in the morning." So, when you want to wake up in the morning without an alarm, you make a decision, before you go to sleep, "I will wake up in the morning early." When you have something to do in the morning which is really important, you will wake up at the right time, because you have made up your mind that you will wake up at that time. You really do wake up at that time. "Keeping in mind the thought of rising" means making up your mind to wake up in the morning at a certain time. When waking up, you should get up quickly. No snooze alarm. The moment you hear the alarm, you must get up, thinking, "I must not indulge in the comfort of resting and reclining, i.e., the pleasure of sleeping." Thus, you may be able to drive away drowsiness and sleepiness.

So, there are eight methods to deal with sleepiness and one of these methods will be the right one for you.

Restlessness and Remorse

The next hindrance is "restlessness and remorse." Restlessness means the inability of the mind to stay with one object. The Pāli word for "restlessness" is *uddhacca*. This means, "shaking above." The mind cannot rest on the object but stays above it. "Remorse" means feeling some guilt for the bad or the wrong things you have done and for the good things you have not done. Causes for arising of remorse are unwise reflections on mental agitation, like thinking, "This mental agitation cannot do me any harm," and so on. Causes for abandoning remorse are wise reflections on mental tranquility. When you have wise reflections on mental tranquility, you will be able to abandon restlessness and remorse. So when you experience restlessness and remorse, you know that they are present. When they have disappeared, you know that they are absent. That means, when you experience restlessness, you make it the object of your meditation, noting, "restlessness, restlessness, restlessness." Or when you experience remorse, you just note, "remorse, remorse, remorse." After you have taken note of them, remorse and restlessness will disappear. When they have disappeared, you become aware of their disappearing. Then you can note, "disappearing, disappearing, disappearing."

Remorse can be abandoned completely by attaining the third stage of sainthood and restlessness can be abandoned completely by attaining the fourth stage of sainthood. When practitioners have reached the third stage of sainthood, they become aware of the complete abandonment of remorse. When they have attained the fourth stage, they become aware of the complete abandonment of restlessness.

There are six things which lead to the abandonment of remorse and restlessness.

One is "reaching the state of being learned in the teachings of the Buddha." Practitioners try to have a good knowledge of the teachings of the Buddha.

The second is "inquiring about what is permissible and what is not." When you do something wrong, you will feel remorse. To not do wrong, you must know what is permissible for you. When somebody is a *bhikkhu*, he must know what is permissible and what to avoid. To know what is permissible and what is not permissible will help meditators to avoid doing wrong things. Then they won't experience remorse.

The third way is "understanding the disciplinary rules." This is for *bhikkhus* who are expected to have a good knowledge of the disciplinary rules. When *bhikkhus* know the disciplinary rules thoroughly, they won't do anything wrong, so they will not experience either remorse or restlessness.

The fourth way is "associating with more experienced and older persons" in the practice of virtues like *sīla* (discipline).

The fifth way is "having a good friend." A good friend can help you to abandon restlessness and remorse.

The sixth way is "using suitable talk," talking about the disadvantages of restlessness and remorse and the advantages of tranquility.

Practicing these six ways, you may be able to drive away restlessness and remorse.

Doubt

The last hindrance is "doubt."

> *When doubt is present in him, he knows, "There is doubt in me," or when doubt is absent in him, he knows, "There is no doubt in me."*

There may be doubt about the Buddha, about the *Dhamma*, about the *Sangha*, about the practice, about the topic of meditation. All these things can become subject to doubt. Causes for arising of doubt are unwise reflections on things which can cause doubt or doubt itself. Causes for abandoning of doubt are wise reflections on things which are wholesome and healthy. With wrong reflections, you may have doubts about the Buddha, the *Sangha,* and the teachings. When you have wise reflections, you won't have these doubts. So when doubts arise in you, you must be aware of them, noting, "doubts, doubts, doubts." When you take note of them, after three or four times of noting, they will disappear. When they disappear, you note their disappearance, saying to yourself, "disappearing, disappearing, disappearing."

When meditators reach the first stage of sainthood, doubt is altogether eradicated and they know that they have eradicated doubt altogether.

There are six ways outside of *vipassanā* which lead to the "abandonment of doubt."

The first is "becoming learned in the Buddha's teachings." Try to become knowledgeable of the Buddha's teachings.

The second is "inquiring about the Buddha, the *Dhamma,* and the *Sangha.*" Ask questions about the Triple Gems when you have doubt. The people in this country ask so many questions. You will be doing the right thing by asking many questions. When you have doubt, you ask questions and remove the doubt.

The third way is "understanding the disciplinary rules." This way is for *bhikkhus.* When you understand the rules, then you know what to do and what not to do. So, you have no doubt.

The fourth way is "being decided about the truth of the Triple Gems." It means developing *saddhā* (faith), well-founded on understanding of the Buddha, the *Dhamma,* and the *Sangha.*

The fifth way is "having a good friend." Have a good friend who has this kind of confidence or faith in the Triple Gems.

The sixth way is "using suitable talk." Talk about the disadvantages of doubt and talk about the advantages of the disappearance of doubt. When you practice meditation and doubts come to you, and they may come to anyone, just make these doubts the object of meditation. Note, "doubt, doubt, doubt," especially when you doubt the efficacy of this method. When doubts come up, just make them the object of your meditation, noting, "doubt, doubt, doubt," until they disappear.

You may have noticed that "sloth and torpor" are taken as one hindrance here. They are actually two fetters, two different mental factors. They are taken as a pair because they have the same function, the same cause, and the same opposites. Sloth and torpor have the function of "sluggishness." Both have, therefore, the same function. There is sluggishness of the mind, the sluggishness of the mental factors and the sluggishness of the body. Both have the same cause, "indolence or laziness." Both have the same opposite, "effort or energy." Since they have the same function, the same cause, and the same opposite, they are here grouped together as one hindrance.

"Restlessness and remorse," though two fetters, are also taken as one hindrance. "Non-tranquility" is their function. When there are restlessness or remorse in your mind, you become agitated, you are no longer tranquil. Agitation or non-tranquility is, therefore, the function of both restlessness and remorse. Their cause is "thinking of relatives, thinking of this or that." When you think of so many things, you will become restless. When you think of things you have done wrong in the past and good things you have not done in the past, you will feel remorse. Thinking of relatives and other things is the cause both of restlessness and remorse. Both have the same opposite, "tranquility." They have the same function, the same cause, and the same opposite. This is the reason why they are grouped together here as one hindrance.

How many hindrances have we? One, two, three, four, five, six, seven hindrances? And these are not all, there are more hindrances but they are not named "hindrances" in the scriptures. Some of them are thoughts, "wandering thoughts." When your mind wanders, you do not have concentration. These wandering thoughts really do not belong to the category of hindrances, but they are also hindrances which obstruct the achievement of concentration. Generally, you speak of five or seven hindrances but there are also wandering thoughts which should be eliminated just by being mindful of them, just by taking note of them.

After you have abandoned, at least momentarily, these five hindrances, you will become concentrated and, with concentration, you will be able to realize and penetrate the nature of mind and body. When meditators dwell upon these hindrances in themselves, they are said to be "contemplating internally" and when they are thinking of the hindrances of other people, "Just as these hindrances are in me and they are impermanent, so will be the hindrances of other people," they are said to "contemplate externally." Sometimes, you may think of your hindrances and then of the hindrances of other people and so on, back and forth, back and forth, this is called "contemplating internally and externally." When meditators try to be aware of the hindrances and see the common nature of them, they will recognize that there is nothing to grasp and be attached to. So, they dwell,

> *not attached to anything in the world of the five aggregates of clinging.*

This is the way meditators should contemplate the *dhammas* in the *Dhamma* in the five mental hindrances.

This is the end of the subsection on the "five hindrances."

THE FIVE AGGREGATES OF CLINGING

The second sub-section on the Contemplation on the Dhammas includes the "five aggregates of clinging" and the "twelve sense-bases."

When the Buddha described the world, the animate as well as the inanimate one, he described it sometimes in terms of the "five aggregates," sometimes in terms of the "twelve sense-bases," sometimes in terms of the "twenty-two faculties," and sometimes in terms of the Four Noble Truths. He did so according to needs and degree of understanding of his listeners. Some had the disposition of preferring the five aggregates, others preferred the twelve sense-bases. When the Buddha described the world in terms of the five aggregates, he spoke about the five aggregates of clinging. Therefore, you have to understand the two words "aggregates" (*khandas*) and "clinging" (*upadāna*).

"Clinging" here means intense craving, intense desire. There are two levels of desire. The milder form of desire is called "attachment and craving." The more intense level is called "clinging or grasping." Clinging or grasping is the translation of the Pāli word *upadāna*, which means "taking hold firmly." It has to be understood as a figure of speech because no physical grasping is meant. What is meant is mental grasping, mentally clinging to different objects. There are two kinds of clinging: craving or upholding wrong views. You see a certain object and it appears to you to be desirable. It is beautiful. You like it, you become attached to it. You want to have it. Then you will mentally cling to this object because you are attached to it, because you crave it, because you desire it. Sometimes, you may have wrong views about things. The Buddha said, "All things are impermanent and subject to suffering." Sometimes, you see things as being permanent, sometimes you think they are good enough to be owned, and so on. So, through wrong views, you cling to different things and you grasp the different things with which you come into contact. Therefore, when you use the terminology of the Buddha's teachings, clinging and grasping are said to be two mental factors.

When the Buddha talks about "aggregates," aggregate means a "group or heap." There are five aggregates: the aggregate of matter (*rūpa*) or corporeality; the aggregate of feeling (*vedanā*); the aggregate of perception (*saññā*); the aggregate of mental formations (*saṅkhāra*); and the aggregate of consciousness (*viññaṇa*). The whole world is composed of these five aggregates. This includes all physical and mental phenomena. Aggregate also means "something that is divided into past, present, and future; internal and external; gross and subtle," and so on. When a thing can be seen as being in the past, present, or future, internal or external, then it is seen as being composed of "five aggregates."

Of each of the five aggregates, there can only be one aggregate present at one time. Therefore, with regard to the aggregate of feeling, there can be only one feeling which has the characteristic of experiencing an object. This one feeling is called "aggregate of feeling" or "group of feeling" or "heap of feeling," because feeling can be divided into belonging to the past, the present, or the future, and so on. The same is true for the other aggregates.

Let us look at the first of the five aggregates, the aggregate of matter or corporeality or material properties. Without the mind, your body is matter. The whole outside world, mountains and trees, lakes and roads, houses and cars, all belong to the aggregate of matter or corporeality.

The second aggregate is the aggregate of feeling. You may have different sensations in the body and you may have different sensations of different objects. However, when you see an object, you will experience some feeling. It may be a good or a bad or a neutral feeling. When you recognize pain, you will experience a painful feeling. When you recognize something pleasant, you will experience a pleasant feeling. There may also be neutral feelings, feelings of indifference. This feeling is mental not physical. Pain is physical and the feeling of that pain is mental. A certain sensation is physical and the feeling of those sensations as pain is mental. The same is true for pleasure. The sensation of pleasure may be physical but the feeling of pleasure is mental, it occurs in the mind. Feeling means the "mental property" or the "mental state of experiencing an object." It may be pain, it may be pleasure, or it may be neither a pleasant nor an unpleasant mental state. Sometimes, you experience mental objects which become the objects of feeling. When you are sorry for something or when you are happy about something, you experience one mental state which is the object of another mental state. This is the aggregate of feeling.

The next aggregate is the aggregate of perception. This is the translation of the Pāli word *saññā*. Perception has the characteristic of perceiving things. Its function is to make mentally a mark or a sign as a condition for perceiving again or perceiving later that, "This is the same thing, this is it." So, making a mental mark or sign to remember or recognize when you come across something later is called "perception" or *saññā* in the *sutta* or in the five divisions of the aggregates. It is compared to carpenters drawing marks or signs on timber. Carpenters draw marks or signs on timber so that they may know later which part should be used, which should be cut off, and what should go where. The perception can be wrong or it can be right and correct. When a blind man, for example, meets an elephant, he wants to know what an elephant is. If he touches the elephant at only one spot, the elephant will appear to him to be like a post or a wall, depending on the part of the elephant he is touching. This perception manifests to meditators as the action of interpreting by means of the apprehended sign. This can be compared to the perception of a deer when it sees a scarecrow. When people want to scare the deer away from their fields, they may put up a scarecrow. When a deer sees this scarecrow, it reacts as if this were a human being. The scarecrow is the proximate cause for the deer perceiving the scarecrow to be human. So, *saññā* manifests to meditators as the action of interpreting by means of the apprehended sign. Its proximate cause is the objective field in whatever way it appears. It is, in fact, the object understood as being correct. So, perception draws a mark or a sign so that it may remember or recognize the object later on. There can be only one mental factor that is called "perception" present at one time. It is called an "aggregate," because it can belong only to the past, the present or the future or it can either be internal or external, subtle or gross, and so on. One object can never belong to the past, present and the future at the same time, nor can it be internal and external or subtle and gross at the same time. Therefore, perception is called an "aggregate."

The next aggregate is the aggregate of mental formations. These are different states or factors of the mind. Volition leads the mental states which are called "mental formations" or, in Pāli, *saṅkhāra*. We have fifty kinds of mental formations. Greed is a mental formation; craving is a mental formation; hatred is a mental formation; delusion is a mental formation; faith is a mental formation; mindfulness is a mental formation; wisdom or *paññā* is also a mental formation. They form something and are, therefore, called "formations." Since they belong to the mind, they are called "mental formations."

The last, *viññaṇa*, is the aggregate of consciousness. In the teachings of the Buddha, the mind is divided into two parts. One is consciousness and the other is composed of the mental states or mental factors. Consciousness is just the bare awareness of an object. It is not the same as awareness, a term which we use in describing mindfulness. It is just the bare awareness of an object and not the perception whether it is good or bad or whether it is blue or red, and so on. It is just the awareness of an object; that means, meditators recognize that it is just an object. This is called "consciousness." Consciousness and mental factors always arise together.

There are altogether eighty-nine or one hundred twenty-one kinds of consciousness described in the *Abhidhamma Pitaka*. When meditators know or are aware of consciousness then they are said to experience the "aggregate of consciousness." There are different kinds of consciousness. You have studied them in the section on the Contemplation on Consciousness, e.g., consciousness arising with lust, consciousness arising without lust, and so on.

Among these five aggregates, one belongs to the material and four belong to the mental realm. The first one is material and the other four — feeling, perception, mental formations, and consciousness — are mental. You perceive two things in a human being — mind and matter. You see matter as matter, and feeling, perception, mental formations, and consciousness as mental and belonging to the mind. According to the teachings of the *Abhidhamma*, the mind is divided into two parts, namely, consciousness and mental factors. In terms of the five aggregates, the three aggregates of feeling, perception and mental formations belong to the mental factors.

What is meant by "aggregates of clinging?" These are aggregates that are the objects of clinging. They are the objects of grasping. Some of these aggregates belong to mundane states and some belong to supramundane states. There are also eighty-nine types of consciousness. Among them, eighty-one belong to mundane states and eight belong to supramundane states. Among these eight kinds of supramundane consciousness, you have feeling, perception, and some mental formations. So, some feelings, some perceptions, and some mental formations belong to supramundane states and other feelings belong to mundane states.

Only those which belong to mundane states can be objects of clinging. You cannot cling to the supramundane kinds of consciousness by craving or wrong views. When you use the term "aggregates of clinging," this means aggregates that are objects of clinging and these are aggregates which belong to mundane states alone. In brief, practically everything in the world belongs to the five aggregates of clinging. When people practice *satipaṭṭhāna* meditation, they become aware of these aggregates and recognize the presence of these aggregates.

> *And again, bhikkhus, a bhikkhu knows, "This is material form, this is the arising or cause of arising of material form, this is the passing away or cause of passing away of material form."*

This is the way meditators will recognize the aggregate of matter or material form. Meditators, for example, watch their breath and take note of their breathing, in and out, in and out. Breathing belongs to the aggregate of matter or the aggregate of material form. Meditators know that this belongs to matter or this is a material form. When you see an object, you know this is an object, this is a physical, visible object, this is a material form. When you hear a sound or noise, you know this is material, this has material properties, this is matter. In this way, *bhikkhus* or meditators learn what a material form is and what the aggregate of matter or the aggregate of corporeality is. "This is material form," means in the this *sutta,* "This is material form and nothing else." "This is the arising of material form" means, meditators observe and recognize the arising of material form or coming up of material form, such as in the arising of the breath. The in-breath and the out-breath come and go. So, when there is in-breath, there can be no out-breath. When there is out-breath, there can be no in-breath. The in-breath comes after the out-breath and the out-breath comes after the in-breath. So meditators recognize the arising of this material form, of this matter, which is breath

When meditators have knowledge of the *Dhamma,* they may know the cause of material form. "This material form which is breath belongs to the body and I have this body now, because I was ignorant and craving in the past. I may have accumulated some good *kamma* in the past, that is why I have this body and this material form." So, meditators know or see the cause for the material form. When meditators closely observe their breath, they will recognize its disappearance. The in-breath disappears and then the out-breath will appear. The out-breath disappears and, then the in-breath will arise. Thus, meditators recognize the disappearance of the material form and also the cause of fading away of the material form. If you would not have been ignorant of craving in the past, you would not have accumulated bad *kamma* in the past, and so you would not have this material form in this life.

Recognizing the cause of arising and fading away of material forms is called "inferential *vipassanā.*" We have two kinds of *vipassanā,* "direct *vipassanā*" and "inferential *vipassanā.*" When practitioners recognize the cause of arising and fading away of material forms, it may be "inferential *vipassanā.*" The same is true for the other aggregates.

> *This is feeling, this is the arising or cause of feeling, and this is the fading away or cause of fading away of feeling.*

With regard to feeling, meditators know that it is just feeling and nothing more. When you know, "This is a pleasant feeling," or "This is an unpleasant feeling," you are said to be contemplating on feelings and not on the *dhammas*. But when you know, "This is just feeling and nothing else," then you are said to be contemplating on the *dhammas*.

When there is pain, meditators know that there is pain, or they have the feeling of pain. They also know that because there is pain, there is the feeling of pain. The same is true for other feelings. So, meditators see the arising of feeling as well as the cause for the arising of feeling, when they observe the feeling closely.

When pain disappears, meditators know that pain has faded away. They also know that because there is no pain, there is no feeling of pain. The same is true for other feelings. So they recognize the fading away of feeling as well as the cause for the fading away of feeling when they watch feeling closely.

Feelings will be very evident during meditation. After sitting for some minutes, sensations will arise and will cause the feeling of numbness, pain or stiffness. When such a feeling arises, meditators know this is feeling, just "feeling, feeling, feeling." They also recognize the arising of this feeling and the disappearance of this feeling, the cause of the arising of this feeling and the cause of the disappearance of this feeling.

> *This is perception, this is the arising or cause for arising of perception, this is the fading away of perception or this is the cause for fading away of perception.*

Meditators should also be aware of their perceptions. They are not as evident as material forms or feelings. Sometimes, meditators have knowledge of the *Abhidhamma* and of the five aggregates. Then, they will notice that these are perceptions, that, "There is now perception in me." This, making notes and marks is perception. Perception is understanding, recognition and assimilation. It is the mental process of assigning meaning to sensations that come through all the sense doors. You know that perception arises because there is an object. Perceptions occur during your entire life. Since you were ignorant craving in the past, you accumulated *kamma* and had perceptions. Meditators know the fading away of perception and the cause of the fading away of perception. This perception may arise in them just for a moment. When the moment has passed away, the perception disappears. Meditators come to see also the cause of fading away of perception. When there are no objects of perception, perceptions will disappear altogether. When there is no ignorance, no craving, no *kamma* anymore, perceptions can no longer arise.

> *These are mental formations, this is the arising or cause of arising of mental formations. This is the fading away or cause of fading away of mental formations.*

When meditators experience mental formations, they recognizes them. When practicing meditation, you may, sometimes, experience anger or sloth and torpor or boredom. Sometimes, you may experience just good thoughts. When these thoughts appear in your mind, you recognize them as being mental formations. "This is the arising or cause of mental formations." Since there is an object, there are mental formations. Since you have been ignorant in the past, since you have craved in the past, you have accumulated *kamma* in the past. You experience now these mental formations. With respect to the disappearance of mental formations, when meditators, for example, are aware of anger and say, "anger, anger, anger," after some moments, the anger will disappear. This is experiencing the disappearance of anger. The same is true for the other mental formations. If you would not have been ignorant in the past, if you would not have experienced clinging in the past, you would not have accumulated any *kamma* in the past. Then, there would not be any mental formation in this life. When meditators contemplate on the mental formations, they will readily recognize the process.

> *This is consciousness, this is the arising or cause of consciousness, this is the fading away or cause of fading away of consciousness.*

With regard to consciousness, meditators recognize it as just "consciousness," not consciousness with lust, consciousness without lust, and so on. If you see it the latter way, you are said to be contemplating on consciousness, but if you see it just as consciousness, then you are said to be contemplating on the *dhammas* as five aggregates. You know the arising of consciousness. There are different kinds of consciousness.

When you see something, you experience "seeing conscious-ness." When you hear something, the seeing consciousness disappears and the "hearing consciousness" will arise. Thus, meditators know how the different kinds of consciousness come into being and also how the different kinds of conscious-ness disappear. When you see the arising and the disappear-ing of consciousness, you are contemplating on the *dhammas*.

The Buddha does not mean that meditators should deliberately dwell on the five aggregates. They should not search for these five aggregates; they just happen to notice them and become aware of them during meditation. You take note of whatever arises in you. The object of your recognition may be material properties or matter. Sometimes, it may be feelings, sometimes mental formations, and sometimes con-sciousness. Thus, meditators come to know the five aggregates.

When meditators watch the five aggregates, they are said to be contemplating the *Dhamma* in the *dhammas* internally, but they may also be contemplating the *dhammas* of other people, i.e., "Just as this aggregate is in me, so it will be in other people." When you contemplate in this way, you are con-templating externally, and when you contemplate back and forth on the five aggregates in yourself and on the five ag-gregates of others, you are said to be contemplating both internally and externally. So when you practice this con-templation, you recognize the arising and fading away of the five aggregates and won't find anything to cling to, anything to grasp. You dwell on the awareness of the five aggregates, without grasping and without clinging to anything.

THE SIX INTERNAL AND SIX EXTERNAL SENSE-BASES

Next we have the "twelve sense-bases." Sometimes, the Bud-dha described the world in terms of the five aggregates, some-times in terms of the twelve sense-bases. They are called bases or, in Pāli, *ayātanas,* because they are the abode of other things, the place where other things are. Here, they are the place of consciousness and of some mental factors. There are six inter-nal and six external sense-bases.

The six internal sense-bases are the eyes, the ears, the nose, the tongue, the body, and the mind. They are called "inter-nal," because they are most beneficial to beings. They are the innermost bases of the body.

The six external sense-bases are visible objects, sounds, smells, tastes, tangible objects, and the *dhammas*. *Dhammas* here mean the "mental factors," some subtle forms of matter, and *nibbāna*. As noted before, the word *dhammas* has different meanings at different places and in different contexts.

The six internal sense-bases correspond to the six external sense-bases or the six external sense-bases correspond to the six internal sense-bases.

The first is the eyes and the visible forms. The eyes are called a sense-base because, depending on the eyes, eye-consciousness arises. If you would not have eyes, you would not have eye-consciousness. The eyes are the base of eye-consciousness or the place of the eye-consciousness. Visible forms or visible objects are also conditions for eye-consciousness or seeing-consciousness. If there would not be any visible form, there could not be any seeing-consciousness. A blind person does not see anything. When there is nothing to see, when there is no visible object, there cannot be any seeing-consciousness. The same is true for sound and other things.

You have ears or rather ear sensitivity. When you say "ears," you do not mean the external ears but the internal ears or ear-sensitivity. Because you have ear sensitivity, you have hearing consciousness or just ear-consciousness. Because there are noises and sounds, you have ear-consciousness or hearing consciousness. Hearing consciousness depends on the ears as well as on sounds and noises. The same is true for smells, for tactile objects, flavors, and the *dhammas*.

Consciousness depends always on two sense-bases — on the eyes and visible objects, on the ears and sounds, on the nose and smells, on the tongue and tastes, on the body and tactile objects, or on the mind and the *dhammas*. That is why they are called "sense-bases." Altogether, you have twelve sense-bases. How do meditators know these sense-bases?

> *Herein, bhikkhus, a bhikkhu knows the eye, knows the*
> *visible forms and knows the fetter that arises dependent*
> *on both.*

When you know the sense-bases thoroughly, you do not only know the sense-bases, you know also the fetters that arise dependent on both. That means, when there is a desirable visible object, a beautiful object, and you see it, there arises in you seeing-consciousness. Because it is a desirable object, you may have attachments, thoughts of attachment. When the object is ugly and undesirable, you may feel anger or you may feel resentment and aversion. So, depending on these two, the eyes and the visible object, sense-desire can arise, anger can arise, and so on. Meditators know that the anger arises dependent on the eyes and the visible forms, and so on.

These sense-desires, ill will and so on, are called "fetters." They are like ropes. They bind you to the round of rebirths, to *samsara*. There are altogether ten kinds of fetters which are described in the *Abhidhamma.*[13]

The first is sense-desire. When you see (hear, taste, etc.) something, you may experience sense-desire.

The second is ill will or anger. Ill will arises when you see something which you don't want to see or when you hear something which you don't want to hear.

The third fetter is pride or conceit. When meditators think, "Only a person like me can see these things," they are experiencing pride and conceit.

The fourth fetter is false view. Meditators can have false views about what they see or hear. They might think that certain things are permanent or that these things are good to have, that they are desirable, and so on. When you are holding these false views, they will become fetters. They become ropes that tie you to the round of rebirths.

The fifth fetter is doubt. Doubt can arise when meditators see or hear something. If such doubt arises, ask yourself, "Is this a living being?" Or, "Is this the property of a living being?" When you experience such doubts, they can become fetters and ropes.

The sixth fetter is belief in rites and ceremonies. The Pāli word for it is *sīlabbata-parāmāsa.* What is actually meant is that some rites and ceremonies, some kind of practices, are based on the wrong belief that such practices will lead to the eradication of defilements and the attainment and realization of truth. In the time of the Buddha, there were people who adopted very strange practices believing those practices would lead to their liberation. They accepted as true that there was joy or suffering in their life on account of the *kamma* they had accumulated. In order to escape from the effects of *kamma,* they believed they had to do something to their body so that the effects of *kamma* would be used up. They acted like dogs, lived like dogs, ate like dogs, in order to get rid of mental defilements. Other people lived like cows, ate like cows, slept like cows, in order to eradicate defilements, craving and desire. Believing that such practices lead to getting rid of mental defilements is what is meant here by belief in rites and ceremonies. Of course, you can find rather strange beliefs and practices in our time. This kind of belief can arise in you through contact with different objects and different sense-bases.

The seventh fetter is desire for existence. You have two kinds of desire. One is the desire for sense objects, the desire for sensual pleasures and the other is desire for existence, the desire for a good or better existence. This means that when you believe you will be reborn in the future, you want to be reborn into a better existence. You are attached to a better existence. You have this desire for existence.

The eighth fetter is envy or jealousy, being jealous of the property and possessions or the prosperity of others. The function of this fetter is to "become dissatisfied with what other people own." It also means, when people experience envy, they do not want other people to own certain things. They do not like the idea that other people have certain things. It manifests as "being adverse toward other people's property and the belongings of other people." The proximate cause of envy is, indeed, the "property of other people." So, the object of envy or the proximate cause of envy is other people's property. When you see something good, something desirable which belongs to other people, you may feel jealous, and then you will experience this fetter. You may also feel envious of other people's intangible property like happiness and health. In such cases, you may want to cultivate *muditā* (altruistic joy) instead.

The ninth fetter can be translated as "avarice." It is difficult to find a word in English that correctly translates the Pāli word, *macchariya*. It has the characteristics of "hiding one's own property." When you are avaricious, you don't like to share your possessions with other people. You don't like that other people use your things. For instance, I have this tape recorder. If I do not like other people using it, I have this kind of avarice. It is intolerance of seeing my things being used by other people. It manifests as "shrinking" or "meanness." Its proximate cause is "your own property." Envy and avarice have different objects. You can experience envy about another person's property and avarice about your own property. These experiences are akin to stinginess but really are not the same. Stinginess comes from *lobha,* "greed," "attachment," but envy and avarice are concomitant with *dosa,* "resentment" or "anger." When somebody uses your things, you become angry. This is caused by avarice. Not giving everything away, when asked to do so, is not *macchariya,* "avarice." When someone asks something from you and you don't want to give it to him or her, that is not necessarily "avarice" or *macchariya.* Even *arahats* may have these experiences.

At the time of the Buddha, there was a *bhikkhu* who went to a nun asking her to give him her undergarment. He had ulterior motives; he wanted to see the nun change clothes. But the nun refused, saying, "I cannot give you this garment. It is my only and last garment." The *bhikkhu,* however, persisted and so, in the end, the nun had to give him the garment. The nun, however, was foremost among the nuns who had supranatural powers. She used her magic power and gave the monk her garment without showing any part of her body. Her initial refusal to give the garment does not mean that she was avaricious. She was an *arahat* and so she had no avarice or any other mental defilements. Therefore, not giving anything that is asked for is not necessarily "avarice" or *macchariya.* Nor was it stinginess as it was the only garment she had.

The tenth fetter is "ignorance." Ignorance appears always together with the other fetters. When there is sense-desire, there always will be ignorance. Ignorance is concomitant with every unwholesome mental state.

These are the ten fetters. They can be eradicated by the four kinds of attainment, attainment of the first, the second, the third, and the fourth stages of arahathood.

When meditators reach the first stage of attainment, they eradicate the fourth, fifth, sixth, eighth, and ninth fetters.

The second stage of attainment eradicates the first and the second fetters which are gross: gross sense-desire and gross ill will.

When meditators reach the third stage of attainment, they eradicate the subtle first and second fetters. And when they have reached the fourth stage, the third, seventh, and tenth fetters will have been eradicated.

Thus,

a bhikkhu knows the eyes, knows the visible forms and also knows the fetters that arise dependent on both. He also knows the reason by which the arising of non-arisen fetters comes to be.

Meditators achieve this because they cultivate wise reflections.

He also knows the reason why the abandoning of the arisen fetters comes to be.

Meditators achieve this because they cultivate wise reflections.

And he also knows the reason by which non-arising, in the future, of abandoned fetters come to be.

Meditators abandon the fetters by attainment of *magga*, path consciousness. Once eradicated, at the moment of path consciousness, these fetters will never again arise in them. They know this also when they have attained the stage of sainthood.

When you are contemplating, you observe things at the present moment, and you come to see these sense-bases and also the fetters that arise dependent on them. You also see the arising and disappearing of these fetters and their sense-bases. When you see their arising and disappearing, you won't find anything to cling to, nothing to grasp in the world of the five aggregates of clinging.

Thus, a bhikkhu dwells contemplating the Dhamma in the dhammas on the six internal and the six external sense bases.

When you see them clearly, you are said to contemplate on the sense-bases, internally and externally.

THE SEVEN FACTORS OF ENLIGHTENMENT

When you practice meditation, you have to deal with factors that are unfriendly, that are impediments. You also experience factors that are positive, that are constructive. We are now going to study the Seven Factors of Enlightenment which are positive factors of meditation.

The Pali word *sambojjhanga* is a combination of two words, *sambodhi* and *anga*. *Sambodhi* normally means "enlightenment," the realization of truth, but, in this context, it also means the thorough knowledge of the *dhammas*, the thorough knowledge of the objects of meditation, which are *nāma* and *rūpa*, mind and matter, or mentality and materiality. The Pali word *anga* means "limb" or component or part. Here it is translated as "factor." So, the Factors of Enlightenment mean limbs or components or parts or members of the thorough knowledge of the *dhammas* or mind and matter. This knowledge begins with discerning the rising and fading away of phenomena and can be met through all the different stages of *vipassanā* knowledge, leading to the moment of attainment or realization of truth.

Mindfulness

The first of these factors is mindfulness. The Buddha explained it as follows:

> *Herein, bhikkhus, when the enlightenment factor of mindfulness is present in him, the bhikkhu knows, "There is the enlightenment factor of mindfulness in me," or when the enlightenment factor of mindfulness is absent in him, he knows, "There is no enlightenment factor of mindfulness in me."*

Mindfulness is a mental factor by which you remember things. Its characteristic is not wavering, not floating on the surface, going deep into the object or being thoroughly aware of the object. Its function is to remember. When you practice mindfulness meditation, you remember to note things or objects that come to you at the present moment. Mindfulness manifests to meditators as guarding, something like a guard preventing meditators from falling into heedlessness. Its proximate cause is the fourfold foundation of mindfulness. So, when you want to develop mindfulness, you practice the Four Foundations of Mindfulness.

When mindfulness arises in meditators, they know that there is mindfulness in them. This means you have mindfulness and take note of it, saying to yourself, "mindful, mindful, mindful" or "mindfulness, mindfulness, mindfulness." The cause for the arising of this mindfulness is wise reflection. As noted above, the cause for the arising of hindrances and unwholesome states is unwise reflection, for example, taking something impermanent for permanent, suffering for happiness or pleasure, soullessness for soul, and so on. Wise reflections means the opposite. Wise reflections mean reflecting that, "I will be mindful. I will gain knowledge, I will experience joy," and so on. The previous moments of mindfulness are the causes of succeeding moments of mindfulness. So, wise reflection here means reflecting, "I will be mindful," "I will gain knowledge," or "I will experience joy."

When this factor of enlightenment, this mindfulness, is present in meditators, because they have attained mindfulness or it is just present in them, they know, "There is mindfulness in me." When it is not present because they have not attained it, they know, "Mindfulness is not present in me." This mindfulness is brought to perfection by cultivating the mind. When meditators have attained arahathood, they have brought this mindfulness to perfection. Then

> *he also knows the reason by which the perfection through cultivation of the enlightenment factor of mindfulness comes to be.*

Meditators who attain arahathood know that by attaining arahathood they have brought this mindfulness to perfection. It should be understood similarly with regard to the passages on the other factors.

There are four things which lead to the arising of and cultivating mindfulness:

1. *Mindfulness with clear comprehension:* You must try to be mindful of whatever you are doing, your postures, your going back and forth, and so on. Review again the section on Clear Comprehension. Mindfulness can be cultivated by following the advice given in that section.

2. *Avoiding people with confused minds:* By avoiding people whose minds are confused, you can cultivate mindfulness.

3. *Associating with people who have mindfulness:* When you associate with people who have mindfulness, you tend to become mindful too. There is a saying in Burmese, "When you stay near a hunter, you will become a hunter. When you stay

near a fisherman, you will become a fisherman." When you associate with people whose minds are confused, you may also become confused and lose mindfulness; but when you associate with people who are mindful, you too tend to become mindful.

4. *Inclination towards mindfulness:* This means that in all postures, whatever you are doing, you should try to be mindful. Your mind should always be inclined toward the attainment of mindfulness, so that you can develop the tendency toward mindfulness and prepare yourself for clear comprehension.

Investigation

The Second Factor of Enlightenment is *dhamma vicaya*. This Pāli phrase is translated "investigation of the *dhammas*." The word *dhamma* can have different meanings in different contexts. Here, *dhammas* means just mind and matter or mentality and materiality, which are the objects of *vipassanā* meditation. Investigation of the *dhammas* here does not mean that meditators deliberately investigate the *dhammas*, i.e., *nāma* and *rūpa*, mind and matter. It is just knowing or discerning. "This is mind, this is matter; this is arising, this is fading away. This is impermanent, and so on."

When noting and investigating the *dhammas*, this knowing of the *dhammas* is present in meditators at every moment. When you take note of the breath, the breath is matter and the consciousness which notes the breath is mind. Thus, you see or discern the objects clearly, "This is mind, this is matter. This is arising of breath and this is the disappearing of the breath," and so on. So, when you see clearly, whatever you are noting, you are said to have this *dhamma vicaya* or that you are investigating the *dhammas*.

Actually, investigation of the *dhammas* is synonymous with "knowledge" or "wisdom." In the Eightfold Path, it is called *sammā diṭṭhi*, "right view." In the Seven Factors of Enlightenment, it is called *dhamma vicaya*, "investigation of the *dhammas*." Both mean the same thing, the correct discerning of *nāma* and *rūpa*, mind and matter.

Its characteristic is penetrating things according to their individual essence. This means seeing *nāma* and *rūpa*, for example, as, "This is *rūpa* because it does not cognize; this is *nāma* because it is bent or inclined toward objects." When the investigation of the *dhammas* penetrates, it penetrates surely and correctly the object, so its penetration is accurate and stable. Its function is to illuminate the objective field like a lamp. When there is no light in the room, you cannot see things. When the light is turned on, everything in the room is illuminated so you can see things clearly. In the same way, when you investigate the *dhammas*, which is knowledge (*paññā*), you can see the objects of meditation, mind and matter, clearly.

It manifests in meditators as "non-bewilderment." When meditators are investigating the *dhammas*, they are not bewildered. Therefore, penetration can be compared with a lamp lighting a room. The meditators are no longer bewildered. When they have *paññā* and are investigating the *dhammas*, they can no longer be bewildered, because they see clearly what an object is. They know when the object comes into being and they know when it goes away. This can also be compared with a guide in the forest. Though people may get lost in the forest, a guide can lead them through the forest without getting lost. So, the investigation of the *dhammas* manifests as non-bewilderment.

There are seven ways which lead to the arising of *dhamma vicaya* or the investigation of the *dhammas*:

1. *Inquiring about the teachings of the Buddha, the five aggregates, the twelve sense-bases, the elements or the Four Noble Truths:* By inquiring, you get answers. You will know more and more about the objects of meditation and can develop this knowledge of the *dhammas*.

2. *Purification of the basis:* "Purification of the basis" means internal and external cleanliness. Internal cleanliness refers to bodily cleanliness. When you want to develop this enlightenment factor, you have to keep your body clean. When your body is not clean, your mind cannot be clean. When the mind is not clean, the investigation of the *dhammas*, which is one of the components of the mind, cannot be clean. So, internal cleanliness or bodily cleanliness is necessary for the development of "knowledge," *paññā*. External cleanliness means keeping your house, your room, your clothes and so on clean. When they are dirty, you should wash them. When meditators see a neat meditation hall, they tend to have more concentration and wisdom. When a room is messy, the

meditator's mind will also be messy. Messiness is not conducive to attaining concentration and wisdom. Internal and
external cleanliness will lead to the development of the investigation of the *dhammas* or *paññā*.

3. Balancing the faculties (indriyas): Meditators can also develop
paññā by keeping their mental faculties in balance. There are
five mental faculties present when you meditate: faith (or
confidence), energy, mindfulness, concentration, and
knowledge. Faith and knowledge should be in balance, as
should concentration and energy. It is important to keep
energy and concentration in balance. You have to equalize
these two faculties. When meditators put forth more energy
than needed, they will become agitated and restless, but when
they use less energy than needed, they will become sleepy.
Meditators have to navigate between these extremes, excess
of energy and excess of concentration, excess of faith and
excess of knowledge. Mindfulness balances these two pairs
of faculties. Mindfulness is always needed. Buddha said
that mindfulness is to be desired everywhere. There cannot be
any excess of mindfulness. It has to be present all the time.
It is like a seasoning used in every dish. In the East, for
example, they put salt into every dish. Mindfulness is also
compared to the prime minister who attends to all the
king's affairs. Among all faculties, mindfulness is the most
needed one.

4. Avoiding ignorant people: You can develop the investigation
of the *dhammas* by avoiding those who are ignorant, ignorant
of the Teachings, of the five aggregates, of the twelve sense-
bases, of the elements, and so on.

5. Associating with wise people: Associating with people who
are well-informed with respect to the aggregates and so on,
will help you to develop this factor of enlightenment.

6. Reflecting profoundly: First, you inquire about the Teachings
of the Buddha, the aggregates, and so on, and then you reflect
on them profoundly. You call to mind again and again what
you have studied and learned. By reflecting profoundly on
the aggregates and so on, you will be able to develop the
investigation of the *dhammas*.

7. Inclination towards investigation: Your mind should always be bent towards gaining knowledge, whether you are sitting or standing, lying down or whatever you are doing. So keep your mind turned towards the investigation of the *dhammas*, towards knowledge, so that knowledge will become yours.

Energy

The third enlightenment factor is *vīriya*, "effort" or "energy." It is the mental effort which is present at every moment of noting. It should neither be too much nor too little. When meditators keep their mind on the object, it involves mental effort. When they do not make any mental effort, they cannot keep their mind on the object. So mental effort is necessary to keep the mind on the object. Mental effort has to be present during any moment of mental activity, during any moment of noting. However, meditators should not make too much or too little effort. Too much effort leads to restlessness, and too little effort leads to sleepiness.

The characteristic of energy is driving towards something. Its function is to consolidate mental states which arise together with the mental effort. It supports and helps the investigation of the *dhammas*. It manifests to meditators as non-sinking, non-collapsing. When meditators put forth effort, they do not sink or collapse. It is said in the commentaries, that when rightly initiated, effort should be regarded as the root of all attainments. No attainment can be reached without making an effort or using energy.[14]

Eleven practices lead to the arising of energy:

1. Reflection on woeful states (apāya): " If I do not have energy, if I do not put forth some effort in practicing meditation and accumulate wholesome actions or *kamma,* I will surely be reborn in woeful states and will suffer much." Reflecting on the fearfulness of woeful states, you will not dare to neglect your practice but want to make effort.

2. Reflecting on the benefits of energy: You can reflect this way, "By putting forth more energy and making more effort, many meditators have attained arahathood. Arahathood cannot be attained by meditators who are slothful and indolent. So I must make effort."

3. *Reflecting on the Path*: This path of meditation, of *vipassanā*, has been trodden by the Buddha, the *Pacceka* Buddhas, and the great disciples who were energetic. When you are going along this path, it is not fit for you to be lazy.

4. *Honoring the alms*: This is meant for *bhikkhus* who are supported by lay people and also applies to yogis on retreat who are taken care of by volunteers. They should always be conscious of this support. Lay people offer food and other requisites to *bhikkhus* and yogis, with the expectation that this will support energetic practice. Only by practicing meditation energetically can yogis honor their supporters. The Buddha allowed *bhikkhus* to receive alms and other requisites not for leading a lazy life but for the practice of meditation and for the cultivation of virtues to attain arahathood. Therefore, in order to honor the custom of almsgiving, yogis must put forth effort.

5. *Reflecting on the heritage:* Here, "heritage" means the heritage of the Buddha. Meditators should reflect thus, "Great, indeed, is the heritage of the Buddha, namely, the *Dhamma* treasures. They are not attained by the slothful. An indolent person is like a child disowned by his parents. There is no inheritance when the parents pass away. So, too, it is with the treasures of the *Dhamma*. Only an energetic practitioner will gain from them."

6. *Reflecting on the Master:* It means recalling the great events in the life of the Buddha and admonishing yourself thus, "It does not befit me to be lazy after having heard such a teacher."

7. *Reflecting on the race :* "Race" here means birth as a *bhikkhu*, because, by becoming a *bhikkhu*, a person gets a new birth as a spiritual child of the Buddha. It is not proper for such a person to be lazy.

8. *Reflecting on other followers of the Dhamma:* Meditators should admonish themselves thus: "Sāriputta, Moggallāna, and the great disciples penetrated the supramundane *Dhamma*. Am I following their way of life?"

9. *Avoiding lazy people:* By avoiding people who are lazy and indolent, you can become energetic.

10. *Associating with energetic people:* Energy arises by associating with people who put forth effort to acquire wholesome *kamma* and who practice meditation.

11. *Inclining toward energy:* Directing your mind towards putting forth energy in every posture and in whatever you are doing leads to more energy.

Joy

The next factor of enlightenment is *pīti*. This Pāli word is usually translated "joy," "happiness," "zest," "rapture," and "pleasurable interests." There are many translations possible for this word. *Pīti* means mainly contentment about getting a desirable object. We must, therefore, differentiate *pīti* from *sukkha* which also is translated "happiness" or "bliss." *Sukkha* refers to the actual experience of the object obtained. *Pīti* is the contentment that you will get a desirable object. *Pīti* belongs to the Aggregate of Mental Formations while *sukkha* belongs to the Aggregate of Feeling. So when you learn that you will experience something desirable, you have *pīti*, but when you actually experience it, you have *sukkha*.

The characteristic of *pīti* is to render co-nascent states more endearing. Its function is to refresh body and mind and to pervade them. *Pīti* manifests to meditators as elation.

There are five kinds of *pīti*:

1. *Minor pīti:* It raises the hair on the body. When you practice meditation, you sometimes have goose bumps or your hair stands on end. You are experiencing *pīti*.

2. *Momentary pīti:* It appears like a flash of lightning. You experience this kind of *pīti* in your body like a flash of lightning, once in a while. You feel very good and there is coolness in your body. Coolness is a welcome quality in the East where the climate is mostly hot.

3. *Wavelike pīti:* This kind of *pīti* comes over your body again and again, like waves on the sea shore.

4. *Uplifting pīti:* It levitates the body and can even make it jump into the air. There are stories of people who levitated on account of this kind of *pīti*.[15] When practitioners in our days experience this kind of *pīti*, their body may be lifted up a little

or move to another place, without disturbing their posture. Sometimes, they may even feel, they are lifted up into the air. These are manifestations of uplifting *pīti*.

5. *Pervading pīti:* It completely pervades the whole body. It is compared to oil pervading a piece of cotton. When it arises in meditators, their whole body is, so to say, soaked with this kind of *pīti*.

One, two, three, four or all these five kinds of *pīti* will be experienced by meditators in the course of their meditation. Venerable Mahāsi Sayadaw described *pīti* thus:

> There arises also *rapture* in its five grades, beginning with minor rapture. When purification of mind is gained, that rapture begins to appear by causing "goose flesh," tremor in the limbs, etc.; and now it produces a sublime feeling of happiness and ex-hilaration, filling the whole body with an exceedingly sweet and subtle thrill. Under its influence, he feels as if the whole body has risen up and remained in the air without touching the ground, or as if it were seated on an air cushion, or as if it were floating up and down.[16]

There are eleven practices which lead to the arising of *pīti*:

1. *Reflecting on the qualities of the Buddha:* Pīti can be developed by reflecting on the qualities of the Buddha, recollecting, "The Buddha is the one whose mind is totally pure. The Buddha is the one who knows all that is to be known."

2. *Reflecting on the qualities of the Dhamma:* This can be done by reflecting, "The *Dhamma* has been well proclaimed by the Buddha. The *Dhamma* is visible here and now."

3. *Reflecting on the qualities of the Sangha:* This can be done by reflecting on the qualities of the community of noble ones, "The community of the Blessed One's disciples has entered the good way. The community of the Blessed One's disciples has entered the straight way."

4. *Reflecting on your own virtue (sīla)*: When you have been virtuous and your moral conduct has remained pure, then you can reflect on your purity of conduct and experience *pīti*.

5. *Reflecting on your own generosity (cāga)*: When you donate something to a charitable purpose or give something to someone, you can reflect on your generosity and experience joy or *pīti*.

6. *Reflecting on deities*: Sometimes, meditators compare their qualities with the qualities of those who are born in the celestial worlds by saying, "There are people who possessed good qualities. After their death, they were reborn as deities in the celestial worlds. These qualities are present in me, too." Reflecting this way, you experience *pīti*.

7. *Reflecting on peace*: "Peace" here means subsidence of mental defilements. *Pīti* can be experienced by reflecting, "The mental defilements, abandoned by the attainments, do not occur for sixty or seventy years." The *Visuddhimagga*, however, explains that "peace" here means *nibbāna*, or the stilling of all suffering. According to it, *pīti* can be experienced by reflecting on the special qualities of *nibbāna*, such as being the best of all *dhammas*, disillusionment of vanity, elimination of thirst, abolition of reliance, termination of the round, destruction of craving, fading away, cessation.[17]

8. *Avoiding coarse people*: You can develop *pīti* by avoiding people who are coarse or rough in their actions.

9. *Associating with refined people*: You can develop *pīti* by associating with people who are refined in their attitudes and actions, who have much confidence in the Buddha, and who are gentle of mind.

10. *Reflecting on discourses which inspire confidence*: Discourses which illumine the qualities of and inspire confidence in the Buddha are discourses which inspire confidence. By reflecting on them, you will be able to develop *pīti*.

Tranquility

The next factor is *passaddhi*, "calmness" or "tranquility." It occurs when feelings of tiredness or other unpleasant feelings subside without any special effort. When meditators have reached a certain level of *samādhi*, this *passaddhi* is experienced. You won't feel tired or have unpleasant feelings in your body. Without any special effort, you experience this *passaddhi*.

Its characteristic is quieting disturbances of consciousness and mental factors. Its function is to eliminate disturbances. It manifests to meditators as inactivity or coolness of consciousness and mental factors.

Seven practices lead to the arising of *passaddhi*:

1. *Resorting to fine food:* "Fine food" means suitable food, neither gourmet nor lavish, but sufficient to satisfy and nourish you.

2. *Resorting to comfortable weather:* Comfortable weather allows you to practice meditation in tranquility.

3. *Resorting to a comfortable posture:* Assuming a stable comfortable posture allows you to practice without too much discomfort.

This does not mean that meditators should fuss about food, weather or posture. Dedicated meditators will bear with inconveniences in practice. The commentator said, "But he who has the nature of a good man is patient about all kinds of weather and postures."

The Sub-commentator also said,

> Resorting to this threefold suitability brings about well-being of mind by way of the basis of bodily well-being and so is the cause of twofold tranquility.[19]

4. *Reflecting on beings who have kamma as their property:* It is called "judgement according to the Middle Way." Taking pain and happiness as they are experienced by beings to be causeless is one extreme, and taking them to be a creation of an overlord and others is another extreme. Avoiding these two extremes, you should know that suffering and happiness are the result of your own *kamma*. All beings suffer or are happy because of the *kamma* they have accumulated in the past. By reflecting thusly, meditators can develop tranquility.

5. *Avoiding physically restless people:* Avoiding people who harass others will help you to develop tranquility. If you should associate with such people, you would also become restless and this is the opposite of tranquility.

6. *Associating with physically calm people:* Those are people who are "restrained of hand and foot" and who are restrained in their actions.

7. *Inclining towards calmness:* Inclining or directing the mind towards calmness in all postures will help to attain the desired qualities.

Concentration

The next factor is *samādhi*, "concentration." It is the ability of the mind to stay with one object, to be stuck to it, as it were. Its characteristic is non-wandering or non-distraction. Its function is to integrate mental states, to keep them together. *Samādhi* manifests as peace and peacefulness. Its proximate cause usually is happiness or comfort. So, when meditators experience *sukkha*, happiness or comfort, concentration will follow.

There are eleven practices leading to the arising of concentration: The first two have been explained above.

1. *Purification of the bases*

2. *Balancing to the faculties*

3. *Skill in the sign:* This means skill in meditating on the *kasina* sign or any other signs which will cause the arising of *jhānas.*

4. *Inciting the mind:* When the mind is sluggish, due to excessive lack of energy, it should be incited or encouraged by bringing into being the enlightenment factors of *dhamma vicaya, pīti* and *passaddhi* (investigation of the *dhammas,* rapture and tranquility).

5. *Restraining the mind:* When the mind is restless or too active, due to excessive energy, it should be checked by bringing into being the enlightenment factors of *passaddhi, samādhi,* and *upekkhā* (tranquility, concentration and equanimity).

6. *Gladdening the mind:* When meditators cannot get concentration, due to weak application of wisdom or non-attainment of peacefulness, they tend to become discouraged. At such a time, they should gladden their mind, for example, by contemplating on the qualities of the Buddha.

7. *Reflecting with equanimity:* When meditation is going well, when meditators do not experience sloth and torpor, restlessness and discouragement, they should not disturb their meditation by inciting, restraining, and gladdening their mind. They should just continue to practice with equanimity, like a charioteer looks forward, without interfering, when the horses are running well.

8. *Avoiding people who don't have a collected mind:* This means avoiding people who are distracted and lack concentration.

9. *Associating with people whose mind is collected*: People whose mind is collected are those who have either access concentration or absorption concentration.

10. *Inclining towards concentration:* Directing your mind towards concentration in all postures leads to attaining the desired qualities.

Equanimity

The last and seventh factor is *upekkhā*, "equanimity" or "neutrality." Its characteristic is conveying consciousness and its concomitants evenly. Because of this factor, consciousness and other mental factors do their respective functions properly, without being deficient or excessive. Therefore, it has the function of preventing deficiency or excess, because it keeps the concomitants neither too slack nor too energetic and restless. Since it prevents deficiency or excess, it is not partial to any of the concomitants. Therefore, its function is also to inhibit partiality. It manifests as neutrality.

There are ten kinds of *upekkhā* mentioned in the commentaries. It is important to know which *upekkhā* is meant in a given context[20] This enlightenment factor of equanimity, *upekkhā*, is not the *upekkhā* which is a neutral or indifferent feeling. When you have a neutral feeling, you have one kind of *upekkhā*, and when you have equanimity, you have another kind of *upekkhā*.

There are five practices which lead to the arising of *upekkhā*.

1. *Detached attitude toward beings:* When you are attached or partial to beings or persons, you do not have equanimity or neutrality. To develop equanimity, you need to have a detached attitude toward all beings. This is brought about by reflecting on beings as the possessors of their own deeds, thinking, "I am reborn here on account of my own *kamma* which I have accumulated in the past and I will depart from here on account of my own *kamma*. Who then is the being I am attached to?" You can also reflect on beings in the highest sense, "In reality no living being exists. To whom then can I be attached?"

 2. *Detached attitude toward things:* When you realize that you are attached to a thing, you can develop equanimity by reflecting on the ownerlessness and temporariness of things. Ownerlessness may be reflected on in this way, "This thing will get old, decay and one day be thrown away." To think "This thing cannot last long, it will decay in a short time," is reflecting on the temporariness of things.

3. *Avoiding people who are egotistical toward other living beings:* Such people cherish their sons, daughters, and so on, when they are lay people, and pupils, teachers and the like, when they are recluses. They are so attached to them that they attend to their needs and cannot let them do any work or use them to do any work. When somebody comes and asks them to send a son or a pupil to have some work done, they will say, "They are not made to do even their own work; if they were made to do this work, they would get tired." People, egotistical in this way, are to be avoided.

4. *Avoiding people who are egotistical with regard to things:* When they are asked to loan something, such people will say, "Even I myself do not use it, how can I loan it to you?"

5. *Inclining towards equanimity:* Inclining and bending your mind towards having equanimity in all postures will help to achieve these qualities.

When these Seven Factors of Enlightenment are present, meditators will know that they are present and when they are absent, will know they are absent. You will also know the causes for the arising of these factors, which are wise reflections and the reasons by which the perfection of the enlightenment factors comes to be. That means, by the attainment of arahathood, all these seven factors reach perfection. So when meditators have attained arahathood, they know that the factors have been brought to perfection by the attainment of arahathood. They dwell contemplating on these factors when they arise, internally, i.e., in their mind. Sometimes they reflect on the factors that arise in other persons, i.e., externally, and sometimes, they may contemplate, both internally and externally. They will come to see that there are these factors only, not a being, not a person. Meditators, seeing this way, live independently and do not cling to anything in the world.

> *And again, bhikkhus, a bhikkhu dwells on contemplating the Dhamma in the dhammas in the Seven Factors of Enlightenment.*

In practicing the contemplation of the *Dhamma* in the *dhammas*, you contemplate first on the five aggregates, then on the five hindrances, then on the twelve sense-bases, and then on the seven factors of enlightenment.

THE FOUR NOBLE TRUTHS

"Noble Truth" is the English translation of the Pāli term *ariyasacca*. *Ariya* means " noble" and *sacca* "truth". There are Four Noble Truths. They are called "Noble Truths" because they are perceived and penetrated by the Noble Ones. The Noble Ones are those who have seen these truths and whose minds are free from defilements. This is the first explanation of the term. The second explanation is that they are called "noble," because they were discovered by the "Noble One." The "Noble One" here means the Buddha who is the noblest of the nobles. These four truths were neither created nor produced by the Buddha, they were just discovered by Him. They are always there, but may be hidden under the cover of ignorance. When there is no Buddha in the world, the Noble Truths are forgotten.

There have been many Buddhas in the past and, only at the time of a Buddha are these Four Noble Truths discovered and revealed to the world. With the passing away of a Buddha and his immediate disciples, his Teachings gradually disappear and these Four Noble Truths become hidden again. After a long period of time, another Buddha will appear, discover the Four Noble Truths and reveal them again to the world.

Another explanation mentions that they are called Noble Truths because those who penetrate them become noble. One who penetrates or realizes these truths becomes a person whose mind is free from defilements. The penetration or the realization of these truths implies nobleness in a person, and they can be called Noble Truths or Noble-Making Truths.

The fourth explanation is that the truths themselves are noble and, therefore, can be called Noble Truths. "Noble" here means real, neither erroneous nor deceptive.

The Four Noble Truths are

1. The Noble Truth of Suffering,
2. The Noble Truth of the Origin of Suffering,
3. The Noble Truth of the Cessation of Suffering, and
4. The Noble Truth of the Path which leads to the Cessation of Suffering.

The characteristic of the First Noble Truth, the Noble Truth of Suffering, is "affliction." Suffering makes you miserable. It afflicts you, so the characteristic of suffering is affliction. Its function is to burn you, to make you miserable. It manifests as an occurrence, as a coming into being.

The Second Noble Truth is about the Origin of Suffering which is "craving." It has the characteristic of "originating," and its function is to prevent interruption. That means, it continues to cause indefinite origination and does not allow any interruption. The craving then manifests as an impediment.

The Third Noble Truth, which is about *nibbāna*, has the characteristic of "peace" and "peacefulness." Peacefulness means freedom from mental defilements — greed, hatred, delusion. Its function is neither to die nor to fade away. It manifests as being signless. Therefore, you cannot describe *nibbāna* either in terms of form or shape. *Nibbāna* has no attributes. Once, King Milinda asked the Venerable Nagasena whether it was possible to describe the shape or configuration or age or size of *nibbāna* and the sage answered that it was not![21]

The characteristic of the Fourth Noble Truth, the Path Leading to the Cessation of Suffering, is offering "a means or a way to escape." Its function is to abandon defilements. In fact, this truth consists of eight factors present at the moment of path consciousness, so that, at the moment of path consciousness, the mental defilements are abandoned. It manifests to meditators as release from the round of rebirth.

The First Noble Truth is called *dukkha* in Pāli. The meaning of *dukkha* here is "vile" (*du*) and "empty" (*kha*). Anything which is disgusting and empty, anything which is impermanent, without happiness, and without substance is called *dukkha*.

The Second Noble Truth is called *samudaya*. *Aya* means "cause," *udaya* means "arising," and *sam* means it is "combined with other conditions." Craving, arising together with ignorance, clinging, *kamma*, and other factors, supported by these other causes, originates *dukkha*. Therefore, it is called *samudaya*, the "origin of *dukkha*."

The Third Noble Truth is called *dukkha nirodha*. The prefix *ni* means "not" or "absence" and *rodha* means "prison." There is no prison of *dukkha*, of the round of rebirths, in *nibbāna*, since it is free from all rebirths. *Nibbāna* is called *dukkha nirodha*, because it is a condition for the cessation of suffering.

The Fourth Noble Truth has a long name, *dukkha nirodha gāminī paṭipadā*, which means the "Path" or "Way" or "Practice," *paṭipadā*, which "leads to," *gāminī*, the "cessation of suffering," *dukkha nirodha*. Actually, no phenomenon leads to any other place, it disappears wherever it arises. But this Noble Truth takes *nibbāna* or cessation of suffering as its object of practice when it arises. Therefore it is the way which leads to the cessation of suffering.

With regard to these Four Noble Truths, the Buddha said in the *sutta*,

> *a bhikkhu knows, according to reality, "This is suffering"; he knows, according to reality, "This is the origin of suffering"; he knows, according to reality, 'This is the cessation of suffering"; and he knows, according to reality, "This is the path leading to the cessation of suffering."*

This passage describes how meditators know or realize the Four Noble Truths. You know, according to reality, that this is birth, etc., and it is suffering. "According to reality" means according to what is. You know, according to reality, that this craving is the origin of suffering and that *nibbāna* is the cessation of suffering, and that this Noble Eightfold Path is the path which leads to the cessation of suffering.

The Noble Truth Of Suffering

The Buddha further explained the First Noble Truth,

> *And what, bhikkhus, is the Noble Truth of Suffering? Birth is suffering, aging is suffering, death is suffering, sorrow, lamentation, pain, grief and excessive distress are suffering, association with the disliked is suffering, separation from the liked is suffering, not to get what one wishes, that also is suffering; in brief, the five aggregates of clinging are suffering.*

This explanation can be found also in the *Dhammacakkappavattana Sutta,* which is the first sermon of the Buddha.

Birth is suffering because it is the basis or ground for subsequent suffering which you experience during your entire life. Aging is also suffering. Aging means getting old, maturing, and decaying. Aging is also the basis or the ground for suffering. Nobody wants to get old but everybody ages all the time. At every hour, every minute, every second, beings and things are getting older and older. There is not a single moment when you do not get older. You cannot escape this process of aging. You may be able to do away with some aspects of aging. Wrinkles can be removed by plastic surgery but you cannot stop the process of aging. Even on the operating table, while undergoing plastic surgery to remove wrinkles, people are getting older and older, second by second. Although they may look younger after surgery, they are not really younger. They cannot turn back the process of aging. You do not want to get older, but you are getting older, second by second. This is a cause of unhappiness. Therefore, aging is also the basis or ground for suffering and so aging is called "suffering."

That death is suffering is not difficult to understand. Nobody wants to die. Sorrow, lamentation, pain, grief, and excessive distress are suffering. You experience them in your lives. Sometimes, it is sorrow, at other times, it is lamentation. Lamentation means "crying aloud." There will be pain, physical pain, and grief which is mental pain and despair. Mental pain is *domanassa* or "unpleasant feeling" and despair is *dosa*, "ill will."

Association with those you dislike is suffering. When you have to see what you don't want to see, that is suffering. When you have to hear what you don't want to hear, that is suffering, and so on. When you have to live with people whom you dislike, that is suffering. Separation from what you like, whether from people or things, whether through death or only temporary separation, is suffering. Not to get what you wish, that also is suffering.

"Not to get what one wishes" means to not get what cannot be obtained. You almost constantly wish for what you do not have. Frustration, suffering in the mind is constant. Not getting older is something that is not obtainable and not getting what is unobtainable is suffering. We often find that getting what we want is also suffering.

In summary, the five aggregates of clinging are suffering. The five aggregates of clinging are everything in the world, animate as well as inanimate, all beings and things, which can become objects of clinging, craving, and wrong views. Therefore, all five aggregates of clinging are suffering.

Why birth is suffering and why aging is suffering is not hard to understand, but the last sentence about the five aggregates of clinging being the cause of suffering is somewhat difficult to understand, because we have moved from the popular meaning of the word *dukkha* to its philosophical meaning. The popular meaning of *dukkha* is "pain" or "suffering." This is not difficult to understand, but when you can claim that you have understood the philosophical meaning of the word *dukkha*, then you can say that you understand the First Noble Truth well.

To understand *dukkha* well, we have to know the three kinds of *dukkha*. The first is *dukkha dukkha*, suffering in the popular sense of the word. It is translated as "intrinsic suffering." It is painful physical feelings and painful mental feelings. You prick your finger with a needle and you will feel pain. This is *dukkha dukkha*, real pain, intrinsic suffering. When you are sad or feel sorry or are depressed, you have painful or unpleasant mental feelings. They are also *dukkha dukkha*.

The second kind of *dukkha* is *viparināma dukkha*, "suffering based on change." This suffering refers to pleasant physical or mental feelings. Even pleasant feelings are called *dukkha*, because when they change, when they go away, they cause sorrow and suffering. So, according to this explanation, even pleasant feelings, whether they are felt physically or mentally, are *dukkha*.

The third kind of *dukkha* is *sankhāra dukkha*, "suffering due to formations," suffering because there are formations. "Formations" mean things which are produced or caused by other things. Everything in the world is caused, so *sankhāra dukkha* constitutes everything in the world. Here it includes equanimous feeling and the remaining formations of the three planes. At no moment in your life are you free from this kind of *dukkha*.

Why are the five aggregates of clinging called *dukkha*? One criterion for *dukkha* is that whatever is impermanent will also be *dukkha*. According to this definition, pleasant, unpleasant or equanimous feelings and everything else are impermanent. Since everything is impermanent, everything is *dukkha*.

What is the definition of impermanence? Anything that has a beginning and an end is impermanent. When something has a beginning, it must have an end. When there is an arising, there must surely be disappearing or fading away. When something is rising or fading away, coming into being and disappearing, it is impermanent. It is said to be oppressed by this coming into being and disappearing at every moment. When something is oppressed, it is *dukkha*. Anything that has a beginning and an end is impermanent, and anything that is impermanent is *dukkha*, suffering.

The word *dukkha* is usually translated with "suffering," but this translation is too limited. It is a popular definition of the word. The word *dukkha* includes everything that has a beginning and an end, everything that is impermanent. Even when you may be enjoying something, good food or a movie or some sense pleasures, you are actually suffering, because the enjoyment does not last. It has a beginning and an end. It arises and disappears immediately after arising, so it is impermanent. Because it is impermanent, it is *dukkha*.

Some authors prefer not to translate this word and instead use the Pāli word, because there is no word in English which can adequately cover the meaning of the Pāli word *dukkha*.

By proclaiming the First Noble Truth, the Buddha showed the world reality, the facts of life, which is suffering. Many people don't like Buddhism because they think, it dwells on *dukkha* or suffering. They think Buddhism teaches pessimism. Actually, it is not pessimistic to say that everything is *dukkha* because everything really is *dukkha*. We cannot accuse a physician of being pessimistic when, after a thorough examination, he tells a patient that he has a disease. This is not pessimism. It is realistic and necessary so that a program for curing the disease may be designed.

If the Buddha had pointed to *dukkha* only, he might be accused of teaching pessimism, but he found the cause of this suffering and gave us hope by declaring that there is cessation of suffering, like the physician telling the patient that the disease can be cured. Not only did the Buddha find out that there is cessation of suffering, but he also pointed out that there is a way to achieve that cessation of suffering, that there is a way, a method, a practice by which to eradicate suffering. So, the Buddha's message with regard to the Noble Truth of Suffering is not pessimistic; if anything at all, it is realistic. The Buddha showed that there is peace and wisdom in the cessation of suffering.

The statement, "in brief, the Five Aggregates of Clinging are suffering," has to be understood in this light. The five aggregates of clinging are conditioned and so they are formations. As such, they have a beginning and an end, and are impermanent. Since they are impermanent, they are suffering.

The Buddha has given definitions of the terms used in explaining the Noble Truth of Suffering.

> *What, now, is birth? The birth of beings belonging to this or that order of beings, their being born, their origination, their conception, their springing into existence, the manifestation of the aggregates, the acquisition of sense-bases, this, bhikkhus, is called birth.*

"The birth of beings belonging to this or that order of beings" means the birth of beings in the human or the celestial worlds, and so on. "The manifestation of the aggregates" means the arising of the aggregates at the moment of rebirth. "The acquisition of sense-bases" means the arising of some sense-bases at that moment.

> *And what, bhikkhus, is aging?   The aging of beings belonging to this or that order of beings, their old age, decrepitude, breaking of teeth, greyness of hair, wrinkling of skin, the failing of their vital force, the wearing out of their sense faculties, this, bhikkhus, is called aging.*

In the *Aṭṭhasālinī*, it is stated that aging cannot be seen. What you see is the result of aging, the breaking of teeth, the greyness of your hair, etc. From the results, like breaking of teeth, you infer the cause which is aging. So aging is here described by recognizing its results.[22]

> *And what, bhikkhus, is death?   The departing and vanishing of beings out of this or that order of beings, their destruction, disappearance, dying, death, the completion of their life span, the dissolution of the aggregates, the discarding of the body, the destruction of the faculty to control the vital forces, this, bhikkhus, is called death.*

When the Buddha described and explained death, he used many examples. He used many synonyms, so a listener who did not understand the first explanation might be able to understand a second or third one. This is how the Buddha explained words, especially words in the *Abhidhamma* where many synonyms are given for one and the same thing.

> *And what, bhikkhus, is sorrow?   The sorrow of one afflicted by this or that loss, touched by this or that painful thing, the sorrowing, the sorrowful state of mind, the inner sorrow, the inner deep sorrow, this, bhikkhus, is called sorrow.*

Sorrow is an unpleasant feeling which is present in the two types of consciousness accompanied by *dosa*, ill will.

> *And what, bhikkhus, is lamentation?   The wail of one afflicted by this or that loss, touched by this or that painful*

feeling, lament, wailing and lamenting, the state of wailing and lamentation, this, bhikkhus, is called lamentation.

First, you feel sorrow and then you may voice this sorrow. You cry aloud and this crying aloud is called "lamentation." Lamentation is the disorderly sound or voice caused by the mind.

And what, bhikkhus, is pain? The bodily pain and bodily unpleasantness, the painful and unpleasant feeling resulting from mental contact, this, bhikkhus, is called pain.

Pain is an unpleasant feeling with regard to the body. When you hit yourself with something, you feel this pain. It is the feeling which accompanies the resultant type of body consciousness, concomitant with pain.

And what, bhikkhus, is grief? The mental pain and mental unpleasantness, the painful and unpleasant feeling resulting from mental contact, this, bhikkhus, is called grief.

It is an unpleasant feeling, concomitant with the types of consciousness which are accompanied by *dosa*, "ill will". When you investigate grief, you will find out how similar this feeling is to types of consciousness which arise with ill will.

And what, bhikkhus, is excessive distress? The distress of one afflicted by this or that loss, touched by this or that painful thing, distress, excessive distress, the state of being in distress, and the state of being in excessive distress, this, bhikkhus, is called excessive distress.

This *dosa* or "ill will" is concomitant with two types of consciousness which are accompanied by unpleasant feelings.

The difference between sorrow, lamentation and distress is mentioned in the *Visuddhimagga* as follows:

Sorrow is like the cooking of oil, etc., in a pot over a slow fire. Lamentation is like its boiling over from the pot when cooking over a quick fire. Distress is like what remains in the pot after it has boiled over and is unable to do so anymore, cooking in the pot till it dries up.[23]

And what, bhikkhus, is suffering that is association with the disliked? Herein, whatever undesirable, disagreeable, unpleasant objects there are, visible, audible, odorous, sapid and tangible; or whoever they are who are wishers of loss, wishers of harm, wishers of discomfort, and wishers of unrelease from bonds; that which is being together with them, coming together with them, fraternizing with them, and being mixed with them, this, bhikkhus, is called suffering that is association with the disliked.

And what, bhikkhus, is suffering that is separation from the liked? Herein, whatever desirable, agreeable, pleasant objects there are, visible, audible, odorous, sapid and tangible; or whoever they are who are wishers of welfare, wishers of benefit, wishers of comfort and wishers of release from bonds, mothers, fathers, brothers, sisters, friends, colleagues, relatives or blood relations; those who are not together with them, those who do not come together with them, who do not fraternize with them and are not mixed with them, this, bhikkhus, is called suffering that is separation from the liked.

And what, bhikkhus, is not to getting what one wishes? In being subject to birth, a wish may arise, "Oh, that we were not subject to birth! Oh, that no birth would come to us!" But this, indeed, cannot be attained by mere wishing. This is not getting what one wishes.

In beings subject to aging....

In beings subject to sickness....

In beings subject to death....

In beings subject to sorrow, lamentation, pain, grief and excessive distress, such a wish may arise, "Oh, that we were not subject to sorrow, lamentation, pain, grief and excessive distress! Oh, that no sorrow, lamentation, pain,

grief and excessive distress would come to us!" But, this,
indeed, cannot be attained by mere wishing. This, too, is
not to get what one wishes, and this also is suffering.

"Not to get what one wishes" means not to get what is
unobtainable. Every time you wish you would not be subject
to birth, and so on, you are wishing for something that cannot
be attained and therefore causes suffering.

And what, bhikkhus, is, "In brief, the five aggregates of
clinging are suffering?" They are the aggregate of cling-
ing to material form, the aggregate of clinging to feeling,
the aggregate of clinging to perception, the aggregate of
clinging to mental formations, the aggregate of clinging
to consciousness. These, bhikkhus, are called, "in brief,
the five aggregates of clinging which are suffering."

The Noble Truth of Suffering is explained in detail in this
sutta. The last explanation is the most important one because
it embraces everything in the world. It helps you to understand the First Noble Truth on the philosophical level.

When commenting on the sentence, "Not to get what one
wishes," this is also suffering, the commentator said that the
desire for what is unattainable, what you cannot get, is suffering. In the *sutta* itself, it is explained that desire for form, etc.,
is the object of the Second Noble Truth which is desire or
craving. Therefore, desire can be the object of another desire.
The Venerable Mahāsi Sayadaw teaches us that desire or
craving which has been accumulated in past lives and which
is the origin of aggregates in subsequent lives is the Second
Noble Truth. It is the desire for things which are unattainable,
the desire which belongs to the aggregates in subsequent lives.

The Noble Truth Of The Origin Of Suffering

The Second Noble Truth was explained by the Buddha as
follows:

And what, bhikkhus, is the Noble Truth of the Origin of
Suffering? It is that craving which gives rise to new
rebirths and, bound up with pleasure and lust, finds ever
new delight, now here, now there, to wit, the sensual

> *craving, the craving for eternal existence, and the craving*
> *for non-existence.*

This explanation also appears in the First Sermon. Buddhism is unique in the way it points out that craving is the origin of suffering and the origin of life. It does not accept creation or a creator as the origin of suffering. In fact, it does not even accept the existence of a creator. This statement hit people with a great force when it was first proclaimed.

Craving is a driving force. If you had no craving at all, you would not be reborn at all. When you desire to go, let's say, to Washington D.C., you will go and arrive there because you had the desire. When you have no desire to go there, you won't go and won't arrive there. In the same way, when you have craving for existence, then this craving will cause rebirth. That is why it has been said that craving gives rise to new rebirths. Even performing meritorious deeds, if motivated by craving for better rebirths, keeps you in the cycle of rebirth.

Craving is "bound up with pleasure and lust." "Bound up with," *sahagata*, here means "comes to be identical with." So, in reality, craving is nothing else but pleasure and lust.

It "finds ever fresh delight, now here, now there." This means it takes fresh delight, wherever beings are reborn. When a being is born into any existence, the first active thought that arises in that being is the thought of craving for existence, the thought of attachment to life. Beings begin their lives with attachment. When they are reborn as human beings, they are attached to their human lives, and when they are reborn as celestial beings, they are attached to their celestial lives.

There are three kinds of craving, namely, sensual craving, craving for existence, and craving for non-existence.

Sensual craving means craving for sensual things, desire for sensual pleasure. Wanting to see something agreeable, is sensual desire. Wanting to hear something good, and so on, is sensual desire. Desire for sense objects is sensual craving.

Craving for existence is, according to the commentaries, of four kinds. The first is craving for sense-sphere realms. That means, for those born in the sense-sphere, attachment to the existence they are born in, and the desire to be reborn in good human and lower celestial (*deva*) realms. The second is craving that arises together with the eternalist view, the view that takes beings and the world for eternal, existing for ever. There is a belief that there is, in beings, a permanent entity that goes from one life to another, purifying itself until it comes into union with the great or universal Self. Craving that accompanies such belief is, therefore, called craving for existence. Existence in this case means eternal existence. The third is craving for or attachment to the existences of two kinds of Brahmas, the fine material Brahmas and the immaterial Brahmas. The fourth is the attachment to *jhānas*. When meditators reach the *jhāna* states, they can become attached to these *jhānas*. These are the four kinds of craving for existence.

Craving for non-existence arises together with the annihilationist view. There are some people who believe that there is this life only. Nothing arises after the end of this life. There is no rebirth and so beings are annihilated at death. Such a belief is called "annihilationist view." The craving that goes with this view is called "craving for non-existence."

Whatever kind of craving it may be, it causes new rebirth. It is simply pleasure and lust, and it finds delight in this or that life. This craving is the origin or cause of suffering. There are other causes of suffering such as ignorance, but this is singled out as the origin of suffering because it is the specific cause of suffering. It causes suffering with the support of other causes.

The Buddha gives us the basis of this craving in detail:

> *And where, bhikkhus, does this craving, when arising arise, when settling, settle? Whatever in the world is a delightful thing, a pleasurable thing, therein this craving, when arising, arises and when settling, settles.*

Here, "arising" means the first arising, "settling" means repeated arising. Or, according to the sub-commentary, "arising" means also arising or coming up in the mind, and "settling" means to lie dormant or latent in the mind.

There are three stages of defilements: the latent stage, the arising stage, and the transgression or acting out stage. At this moment, we have no anger. We are not angry with anybody. Anger is now absent in us, but we have the potential to get angry. This is the latent stage. When there is some sort of provocation, we may become angry. When there is a cause, we get angry, anger arises in the mind, it rises to the surface. Formerly, it was not existent in the mind, but now, when we get angry, there is anger in us. This is the arising stage. The next stage is the transgression or acting out stage. We will act according to this anger. We may quarrel with somebody or hit somebody or we may even kill somebody. That is the grossest stage of anger. Here, by "settling," the first or latent stage is meant and by "arising," the second or coming up stage is meant. In things that are delightful, that are pleasurable, this craving arises and repeats itself; or it is latent in these things and arises or comes up, depending on these things.

> *And what in the world is a delightful thing, a pleasurable thing?*
>
> *Eye in the world is a delightful thing, a pleasurable thing, therein this craving, when arising, arises and, when settling, settles.*
>
> *Ear in the world....*
>
> *Nose in the world....*
>
> *Tongue in the world....*
>
> *Body in the world....*
>
> *Mind in the world is a delightful thing, a pleasurable thing; therein this craving, when arising, arises and when settling, settles.*[24]

Eye, ear, nose, tongue, body, and mind can be delightful things and you may be attached to them, so craving arises and settles in your mind with regard to them.

Visible forms, sounds, smells, tastes, tangible things, and *dhammas* can be delightful things. When you are attached to them, craving arises and settles in your mind with regard to them.

"Eyes consciousness" means consciousness dependent on the eye, or, in other words, seeing consciousness. The others are to be understood similarly.

"Eye contact" means mental contact which arises when visible object, eye, and seeing consciousness come together. It is one of the mental factors.

Depending on and along with contact, feeling arises.

Together with the eye-consciousness, etc., perception also arises. Perception, *saññā*, is making a sign or a mark as a condition for perceiving that "this is the same," like carpenters do on timber. When you see an object note, "This is a man, this is a woman," or "This is beautiful," perception arises in you.

"Volition" is that which wills. It is also a mental factor. It accomplishes its own and others' functions.

Craving for visual forms is the result of another craving. Craving for visual forms, etc., is the First Noble Truth, and the craving that arises from that craving is the Second Noble Truth. When you begin to understand that you have cravings for visual forms, you have understood the First Noble Truth. When you begin to understand that these cravings give rise to other cravings, you have understood the Second Noble Truth.

"Thought" here is what is known in the *Abhidhamma* as *vitakka*, initial application. It is a mental factor. "Discursive thought," in the *Abhidhamma*, is *vicāra*, "sustained application." It is also a mental factor. The difference between *vitakka* and *vicāra* is explained in the *Visuddhimagga* as follows:

> *Vitakka* is the first impact of the mind in the sense that it is both gross and inceptive, like the striking of a bell; *vicāra* is the act of keeping the mind anchored, in the sense that it is subtle with the individual essence of continued pressure, like the ringing of the bell.[25]

All those factors noted above are delightful. They are objects of craving. Craving arises and settles depending on them.

The Noble Truth Of The Cessation Of Suffering

The Third Noble Truth, the Noble Truth of the Cessation of Suffering, is popularly known as *nibbāna*. The Buddha described this Noble Truth as follows:

> *It is the total extinction, by removing of, or forsaking of, or discarding of, or the freedom from, and the non-attachment to that same craving.*

The Noble Truth of the Cessation of Suffering means the total extinction by removing the craving described in the

Second Noble Truth. "Total extinction by removing" is the translation of the Pali *asesa-virāga-nirodha*. The Pali can be translated differently, for example, "the total extinction and the total removing of" that same craving. According to this translation, the Third Noble Truth, the Noble Truth of the Cessation of Suffering, *nibbāna* is the extinction or removal of craving. It is like an instrument by which craving is removed or forsaken. When meditators realize the truth, when they experience attainment, there arises in them a kind of consciousness called "path consciousness." This consciousness takes *nibbāna* or the extinction of suffering as its object and has the function of eradicating craving or mental defilements.

In what way does path consciousness eradicate or remove the defilements? Does it eradicate past defilements? If so, it is fruitless, it eradicates nothing, because, at the moment of path consciousness, defilements are non-existent. Does it eradicate future defilements? If so, it is fruitless too, because, at the moment of path consciousness, these defilements have not yet come into existence. Then, does it eradicate present defilements? If so, it would amount to saying that path consciousness is accompanied by mental defilements. According to the *Abhidhamma*, wholesome and unwholesome states cannot arise together at the same moment, so path consciousness and the defilements cannot arise simultaneously. It would also amount to saying that defilements arise dissociated from or without consciousness, and there is no such thing as a present defilement, dissociated from consciousness. Therefore, it cannot be said that path consciousness eradicates the present defilements either and so it would seem to follow that path consciousness eradicates nothing.

Then, what does path consciousness eradicate? In the words of the commentator, it is the defilements "that have soil to grow on" which are eradicated by path consciousness. Here "soil" means the five aggregates in the three planes of existence, which are the object of *vipassanā*. "Having the soil" means defilements are capable of arising with respect to these aggregates. The defilements eradicated by path consciousness do neither belong to the past nor the future nor the present. What the path consciousness eradicates is the latent state of defilements or the potential of the defilements to arise. You have defilements but they are not always present in your mind. Since there is a possibility that they will arise in your mind when there are the conditions, you are said to have these defilements although they are not present at the moment. You are liable to have these defilements, and it is this liability of the defilements to arise that is eradicated.

There is a simile of a mango tree which applies to the eradication of defilements. If you do not want the tree to bear fruit, you accomplish this not by destroying the past, the present or the future fruit but by treating the tree with chemicals so that its ability to bear fruit in the future is destroyed. In the same way, it is not the past or the present or the future defilements that are eradicated, but their potential to arise in the future. At the moment of path consciousness, the potential for the defilements are destroyed and the path consciousness takes the Cessation of Suffering or *nibbāna* as its object.[26]

The Third Noble Truth or *nibbāna* is very difficult to describe because it does not belong to this world. Because we are used to this world, we look at things from a worldly point of view. It is difficult for us to understand *nibbāna*, because it is so different from what we know or have experienced.

Once, it is told, a tortoise left the water and walked on land, and then it went back into the sea. There it met a fish. The tortoise told the fish that it had been walking on land, and the fish said, "Oh, you must have been swimming." The tortoise said, "No, I was walking on land." The fish could not understand that there was such a thing as land, because it had never experienced it. It thought land must be another liquid in which it could swim.

In the same way, *nibbāna* is different from what you are used to and what you have experienced in this world. It is very difficult to understand and also very difficult to describe. Since *nibbāna* is opposite to the conditions in this world, it is often described in negative terms, such as the extinction of suffering, non-becoming, having no sign, not being born, not getting old, and not dying. It is described in negative terms, because it cannot be adequately described in positive terms. Suppose you are asked to describe what health is. How would you describe it? You will probably say that it is the absence of illness, a state where there are no ailments or diseases.

However, though *nibbāna* is described mostly in negative terms, this does not mean that *nibbāna* is negative. It is neither negative nor positive because it is non-existent. Only something that exists can be either negative or positive. It is neither a state nor a frame of mind nor a position. You simply cannot describe it. *Nibbāna* just means the destruction of defilements and the cessation of suffering.

Many people ask whether there is happiness in *nibbāna*. This question is also inappropriate. It presupposes that *nibbāna* is some place or existence or state of mind. Since *nibbāna* is neither a place nor a state of mind, you cannot say, there is suffering or there is happiness in *nibbāna*. It is the absence of suffering and the absence of mental defilements.

Moreover, *nibbāna* is not the result of the path leading to it. Only the realization of or reaching it is the result of the path, that is, the result of *vipassanā* meditation. If it would be the result of something, it would have a beginning and an end. If it had a beginning and an end, it could not be permanent and it could not be real happiness. *Nibbāna* is not the result of the path, just as a city is not the result of the road. But just as reaching the city is the result of taking the road, realization of or reaching *nibbāna* is the result of practicing *vipassanā* meditation. *Nibbāna* cannot be said to be the result of anything.

Nor can it be said that *nibbāna* has any shape or color or size or age. We recall King Milinda's question and the Venerable Nāgasena's answer in the previous chapter. Here is what the Venerable said, "Without a counterpart, oh king, it is not possible by simile or argument or cause or method to point out the shape or configuration or age or size of *nibbāna*."[27]

You cannot say that *nibbāna* is bright or round or square or big or small or has any attribute whatsoever. *Nibbāna* simply cannot be described in such terms. In the eleventh *sutta* of the *Dīgha Nikāya* and the forty-ninth *sutta* of the *Majjhima Nikāya*, *nibbāna* is described as *sabbatopabha*, which one of the commentators explains with "luminous in all respects." However, it should not be understood in a literal sense. It is described as "luminous" because it is not polluted by any of the defilements. Mahāsi Sayadaw explained it as follows:

> Matter can be polluted by dirt; mental properties like consciousness and mental factors can be associated with greed, hatred, and so on, and so they can become polluted; even wholesome mental states can be polluted when they are preceded and followed by greed, hatred, and so on. *Nibbāna*, however, cannot come into contact with any pollution, so that it is

exceptionally pure. This is what was meant when the commentators explained that "it [*nibbāna*] is luminous in all respects." Some say, depending on this commentarial explanation that *nibbāna* is a very bright light, but light is matter (and there is no matter in *nibbāna* and *nibbāna* itself is not matter) and so their saying is against the teachings of the Buddha. Only the interpretation that non-becoming or cessation is luminous in all respects because it is totally free from the pollution of conditioned things, is the suitable one.[28]

The Buddha described *nibbāna* in the first *sutta* mentioned above as follows:

> *Nibbāna* which is known [by the wisdom of the Noble Path] cannot be seen [by naked eyes], it has no limits [of arising, dissolution and otherness after having been], it is luminous in all respects. Here, no water element, no earth element, no fire element, and no air element gain a foothold. Here, no length, no shortness, no smallness, no greatness, no beauty, no ugliness gain a foothold. Here, mind and matter disappear altogether. With the cessation of consciousness [*kamma* consciousness and death consciousness of the Buddhas and *arahats*], all this [mind and matter] ceases.

You should not get the wrong impression that *nibbāna* is described only in negative terms. It is also described in positive terms, as "the truth, the other shore, the hard-to-see, the lasting, the auspicious, the safe, the marvelous, the intact, the purity, the island, the shelter, the highest bliss, and others."[29]

You should understand that, although *nibbāna* cannot be described adequately, although it does not exist in the sense that it has the three phases of existence, namely, the arising, the static, and the dissolution, it really *is*. It consists in the cessation of craving, the cessation of the defilements, and the cessation of suffering.

When describing the Third Noble Truth, the Buddha said, "It is the total extinction of that same craving." Thus, he described the extinction of suffering as the extinction of craving. Suffering ceases with the cessation of craving.

The commentators said that the Buddha behaved like a lion. Lions, they said, direct their strength toward the man who is shooting an arrow at them and not towards the arrow. In the same way, the Buddha deals with the cause and not with the fruit. When he taught the cessation of suffering, he dealt with the cause. When the cause, which is craving, ceases, the fruit, which is suffering, ceases also. So, it is craving which you attempt to eradicate in order to eradicate suffering.[30]

Although *nibbāna*, according to the characteristic of peace or peacefulness, is only one, it can be considered to be of two kinds. The first is *nibbāna* with the resultant aggregates remaining and the second is *nibbāna* without the remaining resultant aggregates. In Pāli, the first is called *sa-upādisesa nibbāna* and the second *anupādisesa nibbāna*. In an *arahat*, all mental defilements are eradicated. Although an *arahat* has no mental defilements anymore, there are still body and mind which are the results of past *kamma*. So, *nibbāna*, realized by *arahats* while they are still alive, is called *sa-upādisesa nibbāna*, the *nibbāna* with the resultant aggregates remaining. When an *arahat* dies, the remaining resultant aggregates, which are suffering, cease to exist. That cessation of suffering at the death of an *arahat* is called *anupādisesa nibbāna*, the *nibbāna* without the remaining resultant aggregates.

The first is also called *kilesa parinibbāna*, "total blowing out of defilements," and the second is called *khandha parinibbāna*, "total blowing out of aggregates." The first is experienced by *arahats* during their lifetime and the second becomes evident when they die.

The Buddha explained when craving is abandoned and when craving ceases. He uses similar words here as in his exposition of the Second Noble Truth.

> *And where, bhikkhus, is this craving, when being abandoned, abandoned and where does this craving, when ceasing, cease? Whatever in the world is a delightful thing, a pleasurable thing, therein this craving, when abandoned, is abandoned and when ceasing, ceases.*

Craving arises in regard to whatever is delightful in the world; and when it is abandoned and ceases, it is abandoned and ceases with regard to the same delightful things. It is said that craving for the delightful things is abandoned and ceases. The delightful things mentioned here are the same as those mentioned in the passages on the Second Noble Truth — eye, ear, nose, and so on.

The Noble Eightfold Path

The next Noble Truth is the Noble Truth of the Path Leading to the Cessation of Suffering. This is the well-known Noble Eightfold Path or the Middle Way of the Buddha.

> *And what, bhikkhus, is the Noble Truth of the Path leading to the Cessation of Suffering? It is simply this Noble Eightfold Path, namely, Right Understanding, Right Thought, Right Speech, Right Action, Right Livelihood, Right Effort, Right Mindfulness, Right Concentration.*

The eight factors mentioned above are collectively called the Noble Eightfold Path, the path which leads to the cessation of suffering. The Fourth Noble Truth is the Noble Eightfold Path.

> *And what, bhikkhus, is Right Understanding? Understanding of suffering, understanding of the origin of suffering, understanding of the cessation of suffering, and understanding of the path leading to the cessation of suffering. This, bhikkhus, is called Right Understanding.*

Here, Right Understanding means direct knowledge of the Four Noble Truths, gained through practice. There are other kinds of Right Understanding. They are understanding that beings have *kamma* and its results, and the direct knowledge of the three characteristics of all conditioned things.

> *And what, bhikkhus, is Right Thought? Thought associated with renunciation, thought associated with absence of ill will, thought associated with absence of cruelty. This, bhikkhus, is called Right Thought.*

"Thought associated with renunciation" means thoughts of going forth, becoming a *bhikkhu* or a recluse, practicing meditation for the attainment of *jhānas*, paths and fruition.

"Thought associated with absence of ill will" means thoughts of loving kindness. When you practice loving kindness meditation, this kind of Right Thought will be predominant in your mind. "Thought associated with absence of cruelty" means compassion. When you practice compassion, wishing, "May beings be able to get out of distress," and so on, Right Thought will be predominant in your mind.

Right Thought is explained in the *Visuddhimagga* as "directing the mind toward *nibbāna*." According to the *Abhidhamma*, Right Thought or *sammā sankappa* is the mental factor *vitakka*, i.e., initial application of the mind. The characteristic of *vitakka* is directing the mind to the object. With its help, the mind is directed toward the object, so that the correct understanding arises. Therfore, although it is translated as Right Thought, it is not thinking, but directing the mind in meditation toward the object.

The next factor is Right Speech. Right Speech means

> *abstaining from false speech, abstaining from slanderous speech, abstaining from harsh speech, abstaining from frivolous speech.*

"False speech" means telling lies. "Slanderous speech" means saying one thing to one person and another to another person so that they become divided. "Harsh speech" means harsh or abusive language and "frivolous speech" means talk that is not profitable or that is nonsense. Abstaining from these four unwholesome ways of speaking is called Right Speech. When you abstain from these four wrong ways of speech, this factor is present in your mind.

Right Action is

> *abstaining from killing beings, abstaining from taking what is not given, abstaining from sexual misconduct.*

Right Action means, therefore, abstaining from the three wrong physical actions.

The next factor is Right Livelihood. It is described in the *sutta* as follows,

> *Herein, bhikkhus, a noble disciple, having abandoned wrong livelihood, makes a living by means of Right Livelihood. This, bhikkhus, is called Right Livelihood.*

There are five kinds of trade which are described by the Buddha as being wrong. They are dealing in weapons, human beings, meat, liquor, and poison.[31] Avoiding these kinds of trade and making a living by blameless trades is called Right Livelihood. A person who claims to be a disciple of the Buddha should avoid the above-mentioned trades.

These three factors — Right Speech, Right Action, and Right Livelihood — are called *virati* or "abstentions" in the *Abhidhamma*. Right Livelihood means abstention from the four wrong doings when speaking and the three physical wrong doings with respect to livelihood.

There are three kinds of abstentions, namely, "abstention on occasion," "abstention by observance," and "abstention by total eradication." Sometimes, people don't observe any particular precept, but when they actually meet the situation in which they might do something wrong, they abstain from doing wrong, reflecting on their birth, age, experience, and so on, thinking, "It is not fit for me to do such a thing." Such abstention is called "abstention on occasion." Sometimes, they take precepts and later meet a situation in which they might do wrong and they abstain from doing wrong because they have taken the precepts, their abstention is said to be "abstention by observance." But when abstention is accomplished through total eradication of defilements at the moment of entering the Noble Path (*Ariya Magga*), it is called "abstention by total eradication."

The following stories, from the *Aṭṭhasālinī*, illustrate the first two kinds of abstention.

> There was in Ceylon a lay disciple called Cakkana. When he was young, his mother suffered from a disease and the doctor recommended fresh hare meat. Cakkana's brother then said, "Go, dear, roam the fields!" and he sent him out. Cakkana went and, at that time, a hare came to eat the tender crops. On seeing Cakkana, it quickly ran away and was caught in the creepers, crying, "kiri, kiri!" Cakkana went after the sound, caught the hare, and thought, "I shall make a medicine for mother." But he also thought, "It is not proper that, for the sake of my mother's life, I should take the life of another." He then freed the

hare, saying, "Go, enjoy grass and water with other hares in the jungle." When asked by his brother, "Well, dear, did you catch a hare?" he told him what had happened and the brother scolded him, but Cakkana went to his mother and, affirming the truth, said, "Since I was born, I do not remember having taken the life of any creature." The mother recovered right away.

The second story tells of a lay disciple who lived on the Mountain Uttaravaddhamana.

After taking the precepts in the presence of the Elder Pingalabuddharakhhita, who dwelt in the Ambariya Monastery, the disciple was ploughing his field and his ox got lost. While looking for it, he ascended the Uttaravaddhamana Mountain, where a big serpent seized him. He thought, "I will cut off its head with my sharp axe," but again he thought, "It is not proper that I, who have taken the precepts from my teacher, should break them." After having these thoughts for the third time, he thought, "I will sacrifice my life, but not the precepts," and he took the sharp axe from his shoulder and threw it away in the forest. Immediately, the boa constrictor released him and went away.[32]

The next factor is Right Effort. It means making effort for the non-arising of unwholesome states that have not arisen, for the abandoning of unwholesome states that have arisen, for the arising of wholesome states that have not yet arisen, and for the development of wholesome states that have arisen. So, there are two kinds of effort with regard to wholesome states.

How do you make an effort to abandon unwholesome states that have arisen? Actually, they have arisen and have already disappeared. So, what is the meaning of "abandoning unwholesome states that have arisen?" It means unwholesome states you had in the past. When you remember these states, you will acquire new unwholesome states because, while you remember them, you remember them with remorse. So, remembering past unwholesome states, makes you not only miserable, but it increases your unwholesome states. Therefore, the sensible way is to resolve not to have them in the future and to forget that you had them in the past. This is meant when the Buddha said,

> Now, headman, the disciple has confidence in that teacher and he thus ponders: "The Blessed One in diverse ways, censures, strongly censures, the taking of life, and He further said, 'Abstain ye from taking life.' But there are beings, this many or that many, deprived of life by me. That is not well done. That is not good. However, if I were to be remorseful as a result of that [taking of live], that evil deed would not become undone." So, pondering, he abandons taking of life and abstains from it in the future. Thus does he get beyond this evil deed.[33]

The best way, though, to abandon past unwholesome states or *kamma* is to practice *vipassanā* meditation and become an *arahat*. The Buddha said, in connection with the Venerable Angulimala, who had been a robber-murderer but later became an *arahat*, "Whoever, by good deed, covers the evil done, such one illumines this world like the moon freed from clouds."[34]

The next factor is Right Mindfulness. It is described as consisting of the Four Foundations of Mindfulness — mindfulness of the body, mindfulness of feelings, mindfulness of consciousness, and mindfulness of the *dhammas*.

The next factor is Right Concentration. In describing Right Concentration, the Buddha pointed to the four *jhānas* as examples for Right Concentration. The four *jhānas* actually belong to *samatha* meditation, but they can be the basis for *vipassanā* meditation, too. For those, who selected *samatha* as vehicle for enlightenment or, in other words, who first attain *jhānas* and then turn to *vipassanā* meditation, the *jhānas* can be made the object of *vipassanā* meditation and thus become the basis for *vipassanā*. But here you should understand that "momentary concentration" is also meant, because without it, there can be no *vipassanā* and no enlightenment. This concentration has been gained when meditators can keep their mind on the meditation object for some time, for ten or fifteen

minutes, for half an hour, or longer. There may be very few
distractions of the mind at that time and even when there is a
distraction, you will be able to dismiss it immediately. In this
sutta and in many other *suttas,* Right Concentration is
described as consisting of the four stages of *jhāna.*

> *Herein, bhikkhus, a bhikkhu, quite secluded from sense
> pleasures, quite secluded from unwholesome states, at-
> tains and dwells in the first jhāna, accompanied by sus-
> tained application, with rapture and happiness born of
> seclusion.*

Those who want to know more about the *jhānas* can find the
information in the fourth chapter of the *Visuddhimagga, The
Path of Purification.*

What is important to know, in general, about the *jhānas* is
that sense pleasures and *jhānas* are incompatible. Sense
pleasures are hindrances to *jhānas.* When you want to get
jhānas, you have to get away from sense pleasures and practice
samatha meditation. Sense pleasures are said to be opposites
of concentration. They are hindrances to *vipassanā* meditation,
too. You cannot mix *vipassanā* meditation with sense
pleasures. When you are practicing *vipassanā* meditation,
your practice has to be pure. It should not be mixed with
anything that involves sense pleasures.

As you have seen, there are altogether eight factors in the
Fourth Noble Truth, the Noble Truth of the Path that Leads to
the Cessation of Suffering. When you practice *vipassanā*
meditation, you are said to be following this path.

Five of these eight factors are active factors: the first, the
second, the sixth, the seventh, and the eighth. They are so
called because they function actively when meditators are
practicing. Without Right Thought, which is initial application, meditators cannot direct their mind to the object.
Without Right Effort, which is initial application, meditators
cannot direct their mind to the object. Without Right Mindfulness, the mind cannot hit the object or go into the object.
Without Right Concentration, the mind cannot stay on the
object. Without Right Understanding, the mind cannot
penetrate the true nature of things; it cannot see things as they
really are. Right Thought directs the mind to the object and
Right Effort supports Right Thought and other concomitants.

Right Mindfulness helps the mind to hit the object or to go deep into it and Right Concentration keeps the mind on the object for a longer period of time. Then, Right Understanding helps the mind to see things as they really are. When the meditation is going well, these five factors are actively and evenly functioning. That is why they are called "active factors," *kāraka maggaṅgas.*

What are the remaining three factors? They are virtually accomplished when you practice meditation. Before practicing meditation, you take precepts. This means you refrain from certain actions. These three abstentions may not be present in you at the time of meditation, because they can be present only when you meet the situation and abstain from transgression. They are accomplished already. Therefore, you can say that all eight factors are functioning when you practice meditation.

These eight factors constitute the Buddhist path of morality, concentration, and wisdom. The first two — Right Understanding and Right Thought — belong to the wisdom group. The next three — Right Speech, Right Action, and Right Livelihood — belong to the morality group, while the last three — Right Effort, Right Mindfulness, and Right Concentration — belong to the concentration group. When Right Thought does not direct or take the mind to the object, Right Understanding won't be able to see the object as it really is. Therefore, Right Thought is included in the wisdom group. So, you have this Buddhist path of morality, concentration, and wisdom in the Noble Eightfold Path. Followers of the Buddha should follow this path.

There are four functions connected with the Four Noble Truths. At the moment of penetrating the Truths, path knowledge is said to exercise four functions simultaneously. With regard to the First Noble Truth, the Noble Truth of Suffering, it is full understanding. The function of the Second Noble Truth is to abandon suffering. The function of the Third Noble Truth is to realize *nibbāna.* The function of the Fourth Noble Truth is to develop and to practice the Noble Eightfold Path. Path knowledge exercises these four functions at a single moment. Just as a lamp performs four functions simultaneously — burning the wick, dispelling darkness, making light appear, and using oil — so path knowledge penetrates suffering with full understanding, the origin of suffering with abandoning, the path with developing, and the cessation of suffering with realizing.

Meditators who comprehend their own truths, the truths of others, and both their own and other's truth, are said to contemplate on the truths internally, externally, and both internally and externally.

Mahāsi Sayadaw explained that when meditators, after being convinced of the goodness of the third and the fourth truth, and expecting to realize them, comprehend mindfully the first and the second truths evident in themselves, they are said to be contemplating on the truths internally. After seeing the internal things clearly in themselves, they decide and know that the external things are of the same nature. Deciding and comprehending in this way is contemplation on the external truths. Moreover, when meditators contemplate how others are comprehending sights, sounds, and so on, this is also contemplating on the truths externally. Although it is suggested you contemplate on the Four Truths, you contemplate only on the First and the Second Truth. The Third and the Fourth Truth cannot be contemplated because they are not the object of *vipassanā* and are not seen or attained with regard to worldlings (*puthujjanas*). The commentary and the sub-commentary explained that the functions of contemplating on these truths is accomplished just by hearing that these two are good and having the desire to know and attain them.

Origination and dissolution here should be understood as the arising and stopping of or retreating from suffering as has been taught in these Four Truths.

Meditators who comprehend the Four Noble Truths in this way, will not be attached to anything by way of craving and wrong view and will not cling to anything in this world of aggregates.

Thus meditators dwell contemplating the *Dhamma* in the *dhammas*.

5 Assurance of Attainment

Having studied the *sutta*, we turn to the Assurance of Attainment which was given by the Buddha himself. But, before we study this assurance, let us recapitulate what we have studied so far.

In this *sutta*, the Buddha taught the Four Foundations of Mindfulness in twenty-one different ways. The Four Foundations of Mindfulness are the Contemplation of the Body, the Contemplation of Feelings, the Contemplation of Consciousness, and the Contemplation of the *Dhammas*.

The Contemplation of the Body is described in fourteen ways: mindfulness of breathing, the postures of the body, clear comprehension of activities, reflection on the repulsiveness of the body, on the material elements, and the practice of the nine cemetery contemplations.

The Contemplation of Feelings is described only in one way which is the contemplation on consciousness because feelings are mental states which express the quality of sensations experienced with respect to an object.

The Contemplation of the *Dhammas*, however, is described in five ways: the contemplation of the five hindrances, the five aggregates of clinging, the six internal and six external sensebases, the seven factors of enlightenment, and the Four Noble Truths.

Among the twenty-one ways of *satipaṭṭhāna* meditation, mindfulness of breathing, reflection on the repulsiveness of the body, and the nine cemetery contemplations can lead to the attainment of *jhānas*. The remaining meditation topics can only produce "proximate concentration." The commentator said that, in the opinion of a teacher named Mahāsiva, the Reciter of the *Dīgha Nikāya*, the nine cemetery contemplations are taught to discern faults in the body. According to him, only the two — mindfulness of breathing, and reflection on the repulsiveness of the body — produce *jhānas* during *kammaṭṭhāna* meditation. The remaining topics produce "proximate concentration." This statement of the commentator leads us to think that "proximate concentration" can be equated with "momentary meditation" which the practitioners of *vipassanā* meditation experience, but it is not the same. "Proximate concentration" must precede *jhāna* concentration and the ten or nineteen meditation topics do not lead to *jhāna* concentration but to *vipassanā* goals.

After describing all these twenty-one ways of meditation on the Four Foundations of Mindfulness, the Buddha gave this assurance,

> *Verily, bhikkhus, whoever is practicing these Four Foundations of Mindfulness for seven years, can expect one of two results: highest knowledge here and now, or, if there be yet some remainder of clinging, the state of non-returner.*

This is the assurance: When you practice these Four Foundations of Mindfulness for seven years, you can expect one of two results — arahathood or the third stage of sainthood.) "Highest knowledge" here means the knowledge of the Path of arahathood. Meditators who are successful, do eradicate all defilements and become *arahats*. When they cannot eradicate all defilements and some defilements still remain, they will become an *anāgāmi*, a "non-returner." A "non-returner" is a person who has reached the third stage of sainthood and who consequently won't return, by rebirth, to this sense--sphere, the world of human beings, or to the celestial worlds. Although only the two highest stages of sainthood are mentioned here, you must not take it to mean that meditators cannot reach the first two stages. Without attaining the first two stages, you cannot attain the third and the fourth stages. In fact, meditators who practice this meditation for seven years can reach all four stages of sainthood and become Noble Persons, who have realized *nibbāna* and who have gained enlightenment.

> *Let alone seven years, bhikkhus, should any person practice these Four Foundations of Mindfulness in this man-*

ner for six years...five years...four years...three years...two years...for one year, then he may expect one of two results: highest knowledge here and now, or, when there be yet a remainder of clinging, the state of non-returner.

Let alone one year, bhikkhus, should any person practice these Four Foundations of Mindfulness in this manner for seven months...six months...five months...four months...three months...two months...one month...for half a month, then he may expect one of two results: highest knowledge here and now, or, when there is yet a remainder of clinging, the state of non-returner.

Let alone half a month, bhikkhus, should any person practice these Four Foundations of Mindfulness for seven days, he may expect one of two results: highest knowledge here and now, or when there is yet a remainder of clinging, the state of non-returner.

This statement is made for people of average intelligence. For people whose intelligence is not so keen, it will take longer and for people who have keen intelligence and quick understanding, it will take less time. Such meditators may not even need seven days to become enlightened. In the eighty-fifth *sutta* of the *Majjhima Nikāya*, in response to the question put to him by Prince Bodhi, the Buddha said, a *bhikkhu* who has the five qualities of striving, i.e., faith, health, honesty, energy, and wisdom, and who has the Buddha as teacher, will attain arahathood in any length of time, beginning with seven years down to less than a day. The Buddha said, in the end, a *bhikkhu* can attain arahathood in the morning after having been instructed in the evening, or can attain arahathood in the evening after having been instructed in the morning.[35]

There are many people who attained enlightenment in a very short time. Sometimes, they just listened to the teachings of the Buddha and, immediately after the discourse, they reached enlightenment. One person among those who gained enlightenment in a very short time was the former ascetic Subhadda who became the last disciple to be taught personally by the Buddha. He belonged to a different faith and did not seem to have much respect for the Buddha, but when he heard that the Buddha was about to pass away, he thought, "I have some doubts about the claims made by other religious teachers. The recluse Gotama may be able to remove these doubts, and my teachers have said that such a person like the recluse Gotama rarely appears in the world. He is reported to pass away in the last watch of the night." He went where the Buddha was at that time and asked the Venerable Ānanda to let him see the Buddha. The Buddha was only a few hours away from his death, so the Venerable Ānanda refused to give Subhadda permission to see the Buddha. The Buddha overheard their conversation and told Ānanda to let him in. When he received permission, Subhadda approached the Buddha and asked him whether the esteemed religious teachers had really attained realization as they claimed or not, or whether some of them had and others not. The Buddha put his question aside and taught him the truth that only where the teaching of the Noble Eightfold Path is found, can there be persons who attain realization. The Buddha thus answered Subhadda's question indirectly. Subhadda was pleased with the Buddha's answer and requested to be admitted to the Order. The Buddha asked the Venerable Ānanda to ordain Subhadda. Immediately after the ordination, the Buddha taught him meditation and gave him a meditation topic. Subhadda, then, went to a secluded place and practiced meditation. The commentary said that he practiced meditation walking back and forth. He might have practiced walking meditation as you practice now. In a very short time, within a few hours, Subhadda developed *vipassanā* and reached the highest stage of sainthood. He became the last disciple ever to be personally taught by the Buddha.

People who have practiced meditation in their past life and so have accumulated experience, can attain in a short time, but people who don't have such experiences need much longer to reach enlightenment.

At the beginning of this *sutta*, it was said that it has been delivered in the land of the Kurus to the Kuru people. The Kuru country can be found near New Delhi. That part of the country was called Indraprasttha in Sanskrit. Why did the Buddha preach this *sutta* to the Kuru people? Was it a mere coincidence? The commentary says, "no." It is said that the Kuru country was blessed with a perfect climate. It neither got too cold nor too hot. And, the Kuru people enjoyed other comforts such as good food and drink. Since they enjoyed these comfortable conditions, they were always happy in body and in mind. Helped by their healthy bodies and minds, their power of wisdom matured and they were capable of receiving profound teachings, i.e., *satipaṭṭhāna*. That is why the Buddha preached this *sutta* to them. But this does not mean that the Buddha preached this *sutta* only to the people of Kuru. During the forty-five years of his teaching, the Buddha preached the *satipaṭṭhāna* method at many different places on different occasions.

In the collection of the *Kindred Sayings*, there is a *satipaṭṭhāna* chapter. It consists of 104 *suttas*. They are short *suttas* which were delivered at different places. But it was only to the people of Kuru that the Buddha taught this *sutta* in greater detail.

The commentary mentions that the people of Kuru were so well-endowed with a good climate and good food, that their minds became mature. All classes of people practiced *satipaṭṭhāna* meditation. So, if people who were asked what kind of *satipaṭṭhāna* meditation they were practicing said, "none," they were reproached and the people of Kuru would teach them one of the kinds of *satipaṭṭhāna* meditation. But when they answered that they were practicing such and such Foundation of Mindfulness, they were praised, "Well done! Your life is blessed, your life as a human being is worth living. It is for such people like you that the Buddha appeared in the world." The commentary goes even so far as to say that even animals practiced *satipaṭṭhāna* meditation in the Kuru country.

The commentator mentions a story of a parrot. There was a dancer who lived like a gypsy. He went from one place to another. He had a parrot and he trained that parrot to sing and to dance. Wherever the dancer travelled, he stayed at monasteries and nunneries, because, at these places, he could get free food and a free place to sleep. Once, he happened to spend some time in a certain nunnery. When he left that place, he forgot to take his parrot with him. So, the parrot was taken care of by the female novices in the nunnery. He was given the name Buddharakkhita, "One Protected by the Buddha." One day, when the parrot was sitting in front of the chief nun who was the abbess, she asked the parrot, "Do you practice any meditation?" When the parrot answered, "No," she said, "People who live with ascetics, monks or nuns, should not be heedless. Since you are an animal, you cannot do much, therefore, just repeat, 'bones, bones, bones.'" So, the nun taught the parrot the repulsiveness of the body meditation. The parrot kept repeating "bones, bones, bones." One day, when the parrot was basking in the sun on top of a gate, a big bird swooped down, seized the parrot with its claws and flew away. The parrot made a noise which sounded like "kiri-kiri." When the novices heard the noise, they said, "Buddharakkhita has been abducted by a bird." They took sticks and stones and scared the big bird so that it released the parrot. When the novices brought the parrot to the abbess, she asked, "Buddharakkhita, what were you thinking when you were taken away by that bird?" And the parrot answered, "I didn't think of anything else but that a skeleton is taking a skeleton away. I don't know where it will be scattered. That is the only thing I thought of when I was taken away by the bird." The abbess was pleased and told the parrot, "It will serve you as a cause for the cessation of existence in the future." This is the story of the parrot who practiced *satipaṭṭhāna* meditation.

It is said that the Kuru country was blessed with a perfect climate and its people enjoyed good food and drink and other amenities of life. What about the American people and all the people in the West who enjoy a perfect climate, at least indoors? Even at places with extreme climate, very cold or very hot, you can control the indoor climate with a thermostat. When it is too hot, you turn on the air-conditioner, and when it is too cold, you turn on the heater. So, like the Kuru people, the American people enjoy a very good climate. Food in the West is also very rich and good, and when you care about what you eat, you can have health food. And there are other facilities. Westerners have even a better chance than the Kuru people. Perhaps, *vipassanā* meditation is more suitable for people in the West than for people in other countries.

It is a custom of the Buddhist authors to pay homage to the Buddha, and also to the *Dhamma*, and the *Sangha*, and, sometimes, to one's teacher or teachers before writing a book. This is done for two reasons. One is to have no dangers or interferences during the course of writing the book. The other reason is to bring the book to a successful end. We have paid homage to the Buddha, the *Dhamma*, and the *Sangha* at the beginning of this book. Our paying homage to the Triple Gem has now born fruit. We have come to the end of the *sutta* and to the end of the discussion.

"Homage to the Blessed One, the Worthy One, the Fully Enlightened One."

Thank you all for giving me the opportunity to share with you whatever knowledge I have of the *Dhamma* and its practice. I came to this country to give whatever I can to its people. So, I thank all those who read this book.

The *sutta* concludes as it begun:.

> *Because of this, it was said, "This is the only way, bhik-khus, for the purification of beings, for the overcoming of sorrow and lamentation, for the disappearance of pain and grief, for reaching the Noble Path, for the realization of nibbāna, namely, the Four Foundations of Mindfulness."*
> *This, the Blessed One said. Glad in their hearts, the bhikkhus welcomed the words of the Blessed One.*

Part Two
The Great Discourse on the Foundations of Mindfulness

The Great Discourse on the Foundations of Mindfulness

NAMO TASSA BHAGAVATO ARAHATO
SAMMĀSAMBUDDHASSA

HOMAGE TO THE BLESSED ONE, THE WORTHY ONE THE FULLY-ENLIGHTENED BUDDHA

Thus have I heard.

At one time, the Blessed One was living in Kurus, where there was a market town of the Kurus, named Kammasadamma. There the Blessed One addressed the bhikkhus thus: "Bhikkhus," and the bhikkhus replied to him, "Venerable Sir." And the Blessed One spoke as follows:

This is the only way, bhikkhus, for the purification of beings, for the overcoming of sorrow and lamentation, for the disappearance of pain and grief, for reaching the Noble Path, for the realization of Nibbāna, namely, the Four Foundations of Mindfulness.

What are the four?

Herein [in this teaching], bhikkhus, a bhikkhu dwells contemplating the body in the body, ardently, clearly comprehending and mindful, removing covetousness and grief in the world; he dwells contemplating the feeling in the feelings, ardently, clearly comprehending and mindful, removing covetousness and grief in the world; he dwells contemplating the consciousness in the consciousness, ardently, clearly comprehending and mindful, removing covetousness and grief in the world; he dwells contemplating the Dhamma in the dhammas, ardently, clearly comprehending and mindful, removing covetousness and grief in the world.

1. THE CONTEMPLATION OF THE BODY IN THE BODY

Mindfulness of Breathing

And how, bhikkhus does a bhikkhu dwell contemplating the body in the body? Here, bhikkhu, a bhikkhu having gone to the forest, to the foot of a tree, or to a secluded place, sits down cross-legged, keeps his upper body erect, and directs mindfulness towards the object of meditation. Ever mindful, he breathes in, ever mindful he breathes out.

Breathing in a long breath, he knows, "I breathe in long;" breathing out a long breath, he knows, "I breathe out long."

Breathing in a short breath, he knows, "I breathe in short;" breathing out a short breath, he knows, "I breathe out short."

"Making clear the entire in-breath body, I shall breathe in," thus he makes effort [literally, he trains himself]; "making clear the entire out-breath body, I shall breath out," thus he makes effort.

"Calming the gross in-breath [literally, body-conditioned object], I shall breathe in," thus he makes effort; "calming the gross out-breath, I shall breathe out," thus he makes effort.

As a skillful turner [of a lathe] or his apprentice, making a long turn, knows, "I make a long turn," or making a short turn, knows, "I make a short turn," just so the bhikkhu, breathing in a long breath, knows, "I breathe in long;" breathing out a long breath," he knows, "I breathe out long." Breathing in a short breath, he knows, "I breathe in short;" breathing out a short breath, he knows, "I breathe out short." "Making clear the entire in-breath body, I shall breathe in," thus he makes effort; "making clear the entire out-breath body, I shall breathe out," thus he makes effort. "Calming the gross in-breath, I shall breathe in," thus he makes effort; "calming the gross out-breath, I shall breathe out," thus he makes effort.

Thus he dwells contemplating the body in the body internally, or he dwells contemplating the body in the body externally, or he dwells contemplating the body in the body both internally and externally.

He dwells contemplating the origination factors in the breath-body, or he dwells contemplating the dissolution factors in the breath-body, or he dwells contemplating both the origination and dissolution factors in the breath-body.

Or his mindfulness is established as "there is breath-body only." And that mindfulness is established to the extent necessary to further knowledge and mindfulness.

Not depending on (or attached to) anything by way of craving and wrong view, he dwells.

Nor does he cling to anything in the world of the five aggregates of clinging.

Thus too, bhikkhus, a bhikkhu dwells contemplating the body in the body.

The Postures of the Body

And again, bhikkhus, a bhikkhu knows, "I am going," when he is going; he knows, "I am standing," when he is standing; he knows, "I am sitting," when he is sitting; he knows, "I am lying down," when he is lying down, or just as his body is disposed so he knows it.

Thus he dwells contemplating the body in the body internally, or he dwells contemplating the body in the body externally, or he dwells contemplating the body in the body both internally and externally.

He dwells contemplating the origination factors in the body, or he dwells contemplating the dissolution factors in the body, or he dwells contemplating both the origination and dissolution factors in the body.

Or his mindfulness is established as "there is the body only." And that mindfulness is established to the extent necessary to further knowledge and mindfulness.

Not depending on (or attached to) anything by way of craving and wrong view, he dwells.

Nor does he cling to anything in the world of the five aggregates of clinging.

Thus too, bhikkhus, a bhikkhu dwells contemplating the body in the body.

Mindfulness with Clear Comprehension

And again, bhikkhus, a bhikkhu in going forward and in going back, [he] applies clear comprehension; in looking straight ahead and in looking away from the front, [he] applies clear comprehension; in wearing the three robes, and in carrying the bowl, [he] applies clear comprehension; in eating, drinking, chewing and savoring, [he] applies clear comprehension;

in obeying the calls of nature, [he] applies clear comprehension; in walking, standing, sitting, falling asleep, waking, speaking, and in keeping silent, [he] applies clear comprehension.

Thus he dwells contemplating the body in the body internally, or he dwells contemplating the body in the body externally, or he dwells contemplating the body in the body both internally and externally.

He dwells contemplating the origination factors in the body, or he dwells contemplating the dissolution factors in the body, or he dwells contemplating both the origination and dissolution factors in the body.

Or his mindfulness is established as "there is the body only." And that mindfulness is established to the extent necessary to further knowledge and mindfulness.

Not depending on (or attached to) anything by way of craving and wrong view, he dwells.

Nor does he cling to anything in the world of the five aggregates of clinging.

Thus too, bhikkhus, a bhikkhu dwells contemplating the body in the body.

Reflection on the Repulsiveness of the Body

And again, bhikkhus, a bhikkhu reflects upon this very body, upward from the soles of his feet, downward from the tips of his hair, enclosed by the skin and full of diverse impurities, thus, "There are in this body

head hair, body hair, nails, teeth, skin	5
flesh, sinews, bones, marrow, kidneys	5
heart, liver, intestines, spleen, lungs	5
bowels, stomach, undigested food, feces, brain	5
bile, phlegm, pus, blood, sweat, fat	6
tears, lymph, saliva, nasal mucus, oil of the joints, urine.	6

As if there were a double-mouthed provision bag filled with various kinds of grain such as hill paddy, paddy, green gram, cowpea, sesame, husked rice, a man with sound eyes, having opened it, should examine it thus, "This is hill paddy, this is paddy, this is green gram, this is cowpea, this is sesame, this is husked rice." Just so, bhikkhus, a bhikkhu reflects upon his very body, upward from the soles of his feet, downward from the tips of his hair, enclosed by the skin and full of diverse impurities, thus, "There are in this body head hair, body hair [see above list]...urine."

Thus he dwells contemplating the body in the body internally, or he dwells contemplating the body in the body externally, or he dwells contemplating the body in the body both internally and externally.

He dwells contemplating the origination factors in the body, or he dwells contemplating the dissolution factors in the body, or he dwells contemplating both the origination and dissolution factors in the body.

Or his mindfulness is established as "there is the body only." And that mindfulness is established to the extent necessary to further knowledge and mindfulness.

Not depending on (or attached to) anything by way of craving and wrong view, he dwells.

Nor does he cling to anything in the world of the five aggregates of clinging.

Thus too, bhikkhus, a bhikkhu dwells contemplating the body in the body.

Reflection on the Material Elements

And again, bhikkhus, a bhikkhu reflects upon this very body just as it is placed or disposed, with regard to its primary elements, "There are in this body the earth element, the water element, the fire element, and the air element."

As a skillful butcher and his apprentice, having slaughtered a cow and divided it into portions, were sitting at the junction of four highways, just so, bhikkhus, a bhikkhu reflects upon this very body just as it is placed or disposed, with regard to its primary elements, "There are in this body the earth element, the water element, the fire element, and the air element."

Thus he dwells contemplating the body in the body internally, or he dwells contemplating the body in the body externally, or he dwells contemplating the body in the body both internally and externally.

He dwells contemplating the origination factors in the body, or he dwells contemplating the dissolution factors in the body, or he dwells contemplating both the origination and dissolution factors in the body.

Or his mindfulness is established as "there is the body only." And that mindfulness is established to the extent necessary to further knowledge and mindfulness.

Not depending on (or attached to) anything by way of craving and wrong view, he dwells.

Nor does he cling to anything in the world of the five aggregates of clinging.

Thus too, bhikkhus, a bhikkhu dwells contemplating the body in the body.

The Nine Cemetery Contemplations

i. And again, bhikkhus, when a bhikkhu sees a body one day dead, or two days dead, or three days dead, swollen, blue, and festering, discarded in the charnel ground, he then applies [this perception] to his own body, "Truly, this body too is of the same nature. It will become like that and will not go beyond that nature."

Thus he dwells contemplating the body in the body internally, or he dwells contemplating the body in the body externally, or he dwells contemplating the body in the body both internally and externally.

He dwells contemplating the origination factors in the body, or he dwells contemplating the dissolution factors in the body, or he dwells contemplating both the origination and dissolution factors in the body.

Or his mindfulness is established as "there is the body only." And that mindfulness is established to the extent necessary to further knowledge and mindfulness.

Not depending on (or attached to) anything by way of craving and wrong view, he dwells.

Nor does he cling to anything in the world of the five aggregates of clinging.

Thus too, bhikkhus, a bhikkhu dwells contemplating the body in the body.

ii. And again, bhikkhus, when a bhikkhu sees a body discarded in the charnel ground, being devoured by crows, by hawks, by vultures, by herons, by dogs, by leopards, by tigers, by jackals, being devoured by various kinds of worms, he then applies [this perception] to his own body, "Truly, this body too is of the same nature. It will become like that and will not go beyond that nature."

Thus, he dwells contemplating the body in the body internally, or he dwells contemplating the body in the body externally, or he dwells contemplating the body in the body both internally and externally.

He dwells contemplating the origination factors in the body, or he dwells contemplating the dissolution factors in the body, or he dwells contemplating both the origination and dissolution factors in the body.

Or his mindfulness is established as "there is the body only." And that mindfulness is established to the extent necessary to further knowledge and mindfulness.

Not depending on (or attached to) anything by way of craving and wrong view, he dwells.

Nor does he cling to anything in the world of the five aggregates of clinging.

Thus too, bhikkhus, a bhikkhu dwells contemplating the body in the body.

iii. And again, bhikkhus, when a bhikkhu sees a body discarded in the charnel ground, reduced to a skeleton, held together by the tendons, with some flesh adhering to it, he then applies [this perception] to his own body, "Truly, this body too is of the same nature. It will become like that and will not go beyond that nature."

Thus he dwells contemplating the body in the body internally, or he dwells contemplating the body in the body externally, or he dwells contemplating the body in the body both internally and externally.

He dwells contemplating the origination factors in the body, or he dwells contemplating the dissolution factors in the body, or he dwells contemplating both the origination and dissolution factors in the body.

Or his mindfulness is established as "there is the body only." and that mindfulness is established to the extent necessary to further knowledge and mindfulness.

Not depending on (or attached to) anything by way of craving and wrong view, he dwells.

Nor does he cling to anything in the world of the five aggregates of clinging.

Thus too, bhikkhus, a bhikkhu dwells contemplating the body in the body.

iv. And again, bhikkhus, when a bhikkhu sees a body discarded in the charnel ground, reduced to a skeleton, held together by the tendons, blood-smeared, fleshless, he then applies [this perception] to his own body, "Truly this body too is of the same nature. It will become like that and will not go beyond that nature."

Thus he dwells contemplating the body in the body internally, or he dwells contemplating the body in the body externally, or he dwells contemplating the body in the body both
internally and externally.

He dwells contemplating the origination factors in the body,
or he dwells contemplating the dissolution factors in the body,
or he dwells contemplating both the origination and dissolution factors in the body.

Or his mindfulness is established as "there is the body only."
And that mindfulness is established to the extent necessary to
further knowledge and mindfulness.

Not depending on (or attached to) anything by way of
craving and wrong view, he dwells.

Nor does he cling to anything in the world of the five
aggregates of clinging.

Thus too, bhikkhus, a bhikkhu dwells contemplating the
body in the body.

v. And again, bhikkhus, when a bhikkhu sees a body discarded in the charnel ground, reduced to a skeleton, held
together by the tendons, without flesh and blood, he then
applies [this perception] to his own body, "Truly, this body
too is of the same nature. It will become like that and will not
go beyond that nature."

Thus he dwells contemplating the body in the body internally, or he dwells contemplating the body in the body externally, or he dwells contemplating the body in the body both
internally and externally.

He dwells contemplating the origination factors in the body,
or he dwells contemplating the dissolution factors in the body,
or he dwells contemplating both the origination and dissolution factors in the body.

Or his mindfulness is established as "there is the body only."
And that mindfulness is established to the extent necessary to
further knowledge and mindfulness.

Not depending on (or attached to) anything by way of
craving and wrong view, he dwells.

Nor does he cling to anything in the world of the five
aggregates of clinging.

Thus too, bhikkhus, a bhikkhu dwells contemplating the
body in the body.

vi. Again, bhikkhus, when a bhikkhu sees a body discarded
in the charnel ground, reduced to loose bones scattered in all

directions — here bones of the hand, there bones of the foot, shin bones, thigh bones, pelvis, spine and skull — he then applies [this perception] to his own body, "Truly, this body too is of the same nature. It will become like that and will not go beyond that nature."

Thus he dwells contemplating the body in the body internally, or he dwells contemplating the body in the body externally, or he dwells contemplating the body in the body both internally and externally.

He dwells contemplating the origination factors in the body, or he dwells contemplating the dissolution factors in the body, or he dwells contemplating both the origination and dissolution factors in the body.

Or his mindfulness is established as "there is the body only." And that mindfulness is established to the extent necessary to further knowledge and mindfulness.

Not depending on (or attached to) anything by way of craving and wrong view, he dwells.

Nor does he cling to anything in the world of the five aggregates of clinging.

Thus too, bhikkhus, a bhikkhu dwells contemplating the body in the body.

vii. And again, bhikkhus, when a bhikkhu sees a body discarded in the charnel ground, reduced to bleached bones of shell-like color, he then applies [this perception] to his own body, "Truly, this body too is of the same nature. It will become like that and will not go beyond that nature."

Thus he dwells contemplating the body in the body internally, or he dwells contemplating the body in the body externally, or he dwells contemplating the body in the body both internally and externally.

He dwells contemplating the origination factors in the body, or he dwells contemplating the dissolution factors in the body, or he dwells contemplating both the origination and dissolution factors in the body.

Or his mindfulness is established as "there is the body only." And that mindfulness is established to the extent necessary to further knowledge and mindfulness.

Not depending on (or attached to) anything by way of craving and wrong view, he dwells.

Nor does he cling to anything in the world of the five aggregates of clinging.

Thus too, bhikkhus, a bhikkhu dwells contemplating the body in the body.

viii.   And again, bhikkhus, when a bhikkhu sees a body discarded in the charnel ground, reduced to bones more than a year old, lying in a heap, he then applies [this perception] to his own body, "Truly, this body too is of the same nature. It will become like that and will not go beyond that nature."

Thus he dwells contemplating the body in the body internally, or he dwells contemplating the body in the body externally, or he dwells contemplating the body in the body both internally and externally.

He dwells contemplating the origination factors in the body, or he dwells contemplating the dissolution factors in the body, or he dwells contemplating both the origination and dissolution factors in the body.

Or his mindfulness is established as "there is the body only." And that mindfulness is established to the extent necessary to further knowledge and mindfulness.

Not depending on (or attached to) anything by way of craving and wrong views, he dwells.

Nor does he cling to anything in the world of the five aggregates of clinging.

Thus too, bhikkhus, a bhikkhu dwells contemplating the body in the body.

ix.   And again, bhikkhus, when a bhikkhu sees a body discarded in the charnel ground, reduced to rotten bones, crumbling to dust, he then applies [this perception] to his own body, "Truly, this body too is of the same nature. It will become like that and will not go beyond that nature."

Thus he dwells contemplating the body in the body internally, or he dwells contemplating the body in the body externally, or he dwells contemplating the body in the body both internally and externally.

He dwells contemplating the origination factors in the body, or he dwells contemplating the dissolution factors in the body, or he dwells contemplating both the origination and dissolution factors in the body.

Or his mindfulness is established as "there is the body only." And that mindfulness is established to the extent necessary to further knowledge and mindfulness.

Not depending on (or attached to) anything by way of craving and wrong view, he dwells.

Nor does he cling to anything in the world of the five aggregates of clinging.

Thus too, bhikkhus, a bhikkhu dwells contemplating the body in the body.

2. THE CONTEMPLATION OF FEELINGS

And how, bhikkhus, does a bhikkhu dwell contemplating the feeling in the feelings?

Here, bhikkhus, when experiencing a pleasant feeling, the bhikkhu knows, "I experience a pleasant feeling"; when experiencing a painful feeling, he knows, "I experience a painful feeling"; when experiencing a neutral feeling, he knows, "I experience a neutral feeling"; when experiencing a pleasant worldly feeling, he knows, "I experience a pleasant worldly feeling"; when experiencing a pleasant non-worldly feeling, he knows, "I experience a pleasant non-worldly feeling"; when experiencing a painful worldly feeling, he knows, "I experience a painful worldly feeling"; when experiencing a painful non-worldly feeling, he knows, "I experience a painful non-worldly feeling"; when experiencing a neutral worldly feeling, he knows, "I experience a neutral worldly feeling"; when experiencing a neutral non-worldly feeling, he knows, "I experience a neutral non-worldly feeling."

Thus he dwells contemplating the feeling in the feelings internally, or he dwells contemplating the feeling in the feelings externally, or he dwells contemplating the feeling in the feelings both internally and externally.

He dwells contemplating the origination factors in the feelings, or he dwells contemplating the dissolution factors in the feelings, or he dwells contemplating both the origination and dissolution factors in the feelings.

Or his mindfulness is established as "there is feeling only." And that mindfulness is established to the extent necessary to further knowledge and mindfulness.

Not depending on (or attached to) anything by way of craving and wrong view, he dwells.

Nor does he cling to anything in the world of the five aggregates of clinging.

Thus too, bhikkhus, a bhikkhu dwells contemplating the feeling in the feelings.

3. THE CONTEMPLATION OF CONSCIOUSNESS

And how, bhikkhus, does a bhikkhu dwell contemplating the consciousness in the consciousness?

Here, bhikkhus, a bhikkhu knows the consciousness with lust as consciousness with lust, the consciousness without lust as consciousness without lust, the consciousness with hate as consciousness with hate, the consciousness without hate as consciousness without hate, the consciousness with delusion as consciousness with delusion, the consciousness without delusion as consciousness without delusion, the constricted consciousness as constricted consciousness, the scattered consciousness as scattered consciousness, the consciousness that has become great as consciousness that has become great, the consciousness that has not become great as consciousness that has not become great, the surpassable consciousness as surpassable consciousness, the unsurpassable consciousness as unsurpassable consciousness, the concentrated consciousness as concentrated consciousness, the unconcentrated consciousness as unconcentrated consciousness, the freed consciousness as freed consciousness, the unfreed consciousness as unfreed consciousness.

Thus he dwells contemplating the consciousness in the consciousness internally, or he dwells contemplating the consciousness in the consciousness externally, or he dwells contemplating the consciousness in the consciousness both internally and externally.

He dwells contemplating the origination factors in the consciousness, or he dwells contemplating the dissolution factors in the consciousness, or he dwells contemplating both the origination and dissolution factors in the consciousness.

Or his mindfulness is established as "there is consciousness only." And that mindfulness is established to the extent necessary to further knowledge and mindfulness.

Not depending on (or attached to) anything by way of craving and wrong view, he dwells.

Nor does he cling to anything in the world of the five aggregates of clinging.

Thus too, bhikkhus, a bhikkhu dwells contemplating the consciousness in the consciousness.

4. THE CONTEMPLATION OF THE DHAMMAS

And how, bhikkhus, does a bhikkhu dwell contemplating the Dhamma in the dhammas?

The Five Hindrances

Here, bhikkhus, a bhikkhu dwells contemplating the Dhamma in the dhammas in the five hindrances. And how, bhikkhus, does a bhikkhu dwell contemplating the Dhamma in the dhammas in the five hindrances?

Here, bhikkhus, when sense-desire is present in him, the bhikkhu knows, "There is sense-desire in me," or when sense-desire is absent in him, he knows, "There is no sense-desire in me." He also knows the reason why the arising of non-arisen sense-desire comes to be; he also knows the reason why the abandoning of arisen sense-desire comes to be; and he also knows the reason why non-arising in the future of the abandoned sense-desire comes to be.

When ill will is present in him, he knows, "There is ill will in me," or when ill will is absent in him, he knows, "There is no ill will in me." He also knows the reason why the arising of non-arisen ill will comes to be; he also knows why the abandoning of arisen ill will comes to be; and he also knows the reason why non-arising in the future of the abandoned ill will comes to be.

When sloth and torpor are present in him, he knows, "There are sloth and torpor in me," or when sloth and torpor are absent in him, he knows, "There are no sloth and torpor in me." He also knows the reason why the arising of non-arisen sloth and torpor comes to be; he also knows the reason why the abandoning of arisen sloth and torpor comes to be; and he also knows the reason why non-arising in the future of the abandoned sloth and torpor comes to be.

When restlessness and remorse are present in him, he knows, "There are restlessness and remorse in me," or when restlessness and remorse are absent in him, he knows, "There are no restlessness and remorse in me." He also knows the reason why the arising of non-arisen restlessness and remorse comes to be; he also knows the reason why the abandoning of arisen restlessness and remorse comes to be; he also knows the reason why non-arising in the future of the abandoned restlessness and remorse comes to be.

When doubt is present in him, he knows, "There is doubt in me," or when doubt is absent in him, he knows, "There is no doubt in me." He also knows the reason why the arising of non-arisen doubt comes to be; he also knows the reason why the abandoning of arisen doubt comes to be; and he also knows the reason why non-arising in the future of the abandoned doubt comes to be.

Thus he dwells contemplating the Dhamma in the dhammas internally, or he dwells contemplating the Dhamma in the dhammas externally, or he dwells contemplating the Dhamma in the dhammas both internally and externally.

He dwells contemplating the origination factors in the dhammas, or he dwells contemplating the dissolution factors in the dhammas, or he dwells contemplating both the origination and dissolution factors in the dhammas.

Or his mindfulness is established as "there are dhammas only." And that mindfulness is established to the extent necessary to further knowledge and mindfulness.

Not depending on (or attached to) anything by way of craving and wrong view, he dwells.

Nor does he cling to anything in the world of the five aggregates of clinging.

Thus too, bhikkhus, a bhikkhu dwells contemplating the Dhamma in the dhammas in the five hindrances.

The Five Aggregates of Clinging

And again, bhikkhus, a bhikkhu dwells contemplating the Dhamma in the dhammas in the five aggregates of clinging. And how, bhikkhus, does a bhikkhu dwell contemplating the Dhamma in the dhammas in the five aggregates of clinging?

Here, bhikkhus, a bhikkhu knows, "This is material form, this is the arising or cause of material form, this is the passing away or cause of passing away of material form. This is feeling, this is arising or cause of feeling, this is the passing away or cause of passing away of feeling. This is perception, this is the arising or cause of perception, this is passing away or cause of passing away of perception. These are mental formations, this is the arising or cause of mental formations, this is the passing away or cause of passing away of mental formations. This is consciousness, this is the arising or cause of consciousness, this is the passing away or cause of passing away of consciousness."

Thus he dwells contemplating the Dhamma in the dhammas internally, or he dwells contemplating the Dhamma in the dhammas externally, or he dwells contemplating the Dhamma in the dhammas both internally and externally.

He dwells contemplating the origination factors in the dhammas, or he dwells contemplating the dissolution factors in the dhammas, or he dwells contemplating both the origination and dissolution factors in the dhammas.

Or his mindfulness is established as "there are dhammas only." And that mindfulness is established to the extent necessary to further knowledge and mindfulness.

Not depending on (or attached to) anything by way of craving and wrong view, he dwells.

Nor does he cling to anything in the world of the five aggregates of clinging.

Thus too, bhikkhus, a bhikkhu dwells contemplating the Dhamma in the dhammas, in the five aggregates of clinging.

The Six Internal and the Six External Sense-Bases

And again, bhikkhus, a bhikkhu dwells contemplating the Dhamma in the dhammas in the six internal and the six external sense-bases. And how, bhikkhus, does a bhikkhu dwell contemplating the Dhamma in the dhammas in the six internal and the six external sense-bases?

Herein, bhikkhus a bhikkhu knows the eye, knows the visible forms and also knows the fetter that arises dependent on both. He also knows the reason why the arising of non-arisen fetter comes to be; he also knows the reason why the abandoning of the arisen fetter comes to be; and he also knows the reason why non-arising in the future of the abandoned fetter comes to be.

He knows the ear, knows the sounds, and also knows the fetter that arises dependent on both. He also knows [for continuation see above paragraph on the eye].

He knows the nose, knows the smells, and also knows the fetter that arises dependent on both. He also knows [for continuation see above paragraph on the eye].

He knows the tongue, knows the flavors, and also knows the fetter that arises dependent on both. He also knows [for continuation see above paragraph on the eye].

He knows the body, knows the tactile objects, and also knows the fetter that arises dependent on both. He also knows [for continuation see above paragraph on the eye].

He knows the mind, knows the dhammas, and also knows the fetter that arises dependent on both. He also knows [for continuation see above paragraph on the eye].

Thus he dwells contemplating the Dhamma in the dhammas internally, or he dwells contemplating the Dhamma in the dhammas externally, or he dwells contemplating the Dhamma in the dhammas internally and externally.

He dwells contemplating the origination factors in the dhammas, or he dwells contemplating the dissolution factors in the dhammas, or he dwells contemplating both the origination and dissolution factors in the dhammas.

Or his mindfulness is established as "there are dhammas only." And that mindfulness is established to the extent necessary to further knowledge and mindfulness.

Not depending on (or attached to) anything by way of craving and wrong view, he dwells.

Nor does he cling to anything in the world of the five aggregates of clinging.

Thus too, bhikkhus, a bhikkhu dwells contemplating the Dhamma in the dhammas in the six internal and in the six external sense-bases.

The Seven Factors of Enlightenment

And again, bhikkhus, a bhikkhu dwells contemplating the Dhamma in the dhammas in the seven factors of enlightenment. And how, bhikkhus, does a bhikkhu dwell contemplating the Dhamma in the dhammas in the seven factors of enlightenment.

Here, bhikkhus, when the enlightenment-factor of mindfulness is present in him, the bhikkhu knows, "There is the enlightenment-factor of mindfulness in me," or when the enlightenment-factor of mindfulness is absent in him, he knows, "There is no enlightenment-factor of mindfulness in me." He also knows the reason why the arising of the non-arisen enlightenment-factor of mindfulness comes to be; he also knows the reason why the perfection through cultivation of the enlightenment-factor of mindfulness comes to be.

When the enlightenment-factor of the investigation of dhammas is present in him, he knows, "There is the enlightenment-factor of investigation of dhammas in me," or when the enlightenment-factor of the investigation of dhammas is absent in him, he knows, "There is no enlightenment-factor of the investigation of dhammas in me." He also knows the reason why the arising of the non-arisen enlightenment-factor of the investigation of dhammas comes to be; he also knows the reason why the perfection through cultivation of the enlightenment-factor of the investigation of dhammas comes to be.

When the enlightenment-factor of energy is present in him, he knows, "There is the enlightenment factor of energy in me," or when the enlightenment-factor of energy is absent in him, he knows, "There is no enlightenment-factor of energy in me." He also knows the reason why the arising of the non-arisen enlightenment factor of energy comes to be; he also knows the reason why the perfection through cultivation of the enlightenment-factor of energy comes to be.

When the enlightenment-factor of rapture is present in him, he knows "There is the enlightenment-factor of rapture in me," or when the enlightenment-factor of rapture is absent in him, he knows, "There is no enlightenment-factor of rapture in me." He also knows the reason why the arising of the non-arisen enlightenment-factor of rapture comes to be; he also knows the reason why the perfection through cultivation of the arisen enlightenment-factor of rapture comes to be.

When the enlightenment-factor of tranquility is present in him, he knows, "There is the enlightenment-factor of tranquility in me," or when the enlightenment-factor of tranquility is absent in him, he knows, "There is no enlightenment-factor of tranquility in me." He also knows the reason why the arising of the non-arisen enlightenment-factor of tranquility comes to be: he also knows the reason why the perfection through cultivation of the arisen enlightenment-factor of tranquility comes to be.

When the enlightenment-factor of concentration is present in him, he knows, "There is the enlightenment-factor of concentration in me," or when the enlightenment-factor of concentration is absent in him, he knows, "There is no enlightenment-factor of concentration in me." He also knows the reason why the arising of the non-arisen enlightenment-factor of concentration comes to be; he also knows the reason why the perfection through cultivation of the arisen enlightenment-factor of concentration comes to be.

When the enlightenment-factor of equanimity is present in him, he knows, "There is the enlightenment-factor of equanimity in me," or when the enlightenment-factor of equanimity is absent in him, he knows, "There is no enlightenment-factor of equanimity in me." He also knows the reason why the arising of the non-arisen enlightenment-factor of equanimity comes to be; he also knows the reason why the perfection through cultivation of the arisen enlightenment-factor of equanimity comes to be.

Thus he dwells contemplating the Dhamma in the dhammas internally, or he dwells contemplating the Dhamma in the dhammas externally, or he dwells contemplating the Dhamma in the dhammas both internally and externally.

He dwells contemplating the origination factors in the dhammas, or he dwells contemplating the dissolution factors in the dhammas, or he dwells contemplating both the origination and dissolution factors in the dhammas.

Or his mindfulness is established as "there are dhammas only." And that mindfulness is established to the extent necessary to further knowledge and mindfulness.

Not depending on (or attached to) anything by way of craving and wrong view, he dwells.

Nor does he cling to anything in the world of the five aggregates of clinging.

Thus too, bhikkhus, a bhikkhu dwells contemplating the Dhamma in the dhammas in the seven factors of enlightenment.

The Four Noble Truths

And again, bhikkhus, a bhikkhu dwells contemplating the Dhamma in the dhammas in the Four Noble Truths.

And how, bhikkhus, does a bhikkhu dwell contemplating the Dhamma in the dhammas in the Four Noble Truths?

Here, bhikkhus, a bhikkhu knows, according to reality, "This is suffering"; he knows, according to reality, "This is the origin of suffering"; he knows, according to reality, "This is the cessation of suffering"; he knows, according to reality, "This is the path leading to the cessation of suffering."

And what, bhikkhus, is the Noble Truth of Suffering? Birth is suffering, aging is suffering, death is suffering, sorrow, lamentation, pain, grief, and excessive despair are suffering;

association with the disliked is suffering; separation from the liked is suffering; not to get what one wishes, that also is suffering. In brief, the five aggregates of clinging are suffering.

What, now, is birth? The birth of beings belonging to this or that order of beings, their being born, their origination, their conception, their springing into existence, the manifestations of the aggregates, the acquisition of the sense-bases. This, bhikkhus, is called birth.

And what, bhikkhus, is aging? The aging of beings belonging to this or that order of beings, their old age, decrepitude, breaking of teeth, greyness of hair, wrinkling of skin, the failing of their vital force, the wearing out of their sense faculties. This, bhikkhus, is called aging.

And what, bhikkhus, is death? The departing and vanishing of beings out of this or that order of beings, their destruction, disappearance, dying, death, the completion of their life period, dissolution of the aggregates, the discarding of the body, the destruction of the controlling faculty of vital principle. This, bhikkhus, is called death.

And what, bhikkhus, is sorrow? The sorrow of one afflicted by this or that loss, touched by this or that painful thing, the sorrowing, the sorrowful state of mind, the inner sorrow, the inner deep sorrow. This, bhikkhus, is called sorrow.

And what, bhikkhus, is lamentation? The wailing of one afflicted by this or that loss, touched by this or that painful thing, lament, wailing and lamenting, the state of wailing and lamentation. This, bhikkhus, is called lamentation.

And what, bhikkhus, is pain? The bodily pain and bodily unpleasantness, the painful and unpleasant feeling produced by bodily contact. This, bhikkhus, is called pain.

And what, bhikkhus, is grief? The mental pain and mental unpleasantness, the painful and unpleasant feeling produced by mental contact. This, bhikkhus, is called grief.

And what, bhikkhus, is excessive distress? The distress of one afflicted by this or that loss, touched by this or that painful thing, excessive distress and the state of excessive distress, this, bhikkhus, is called excessive distress.

And what, bhikkhus, is suffering which is association with the disliked? Whatever undesirable, disagreeable, unpleasant objects there are visible, audible, odorous, tasteable, and tangible; or whoever those wishers of loss, wishers of harm,

wishers of discomfort and wishers of non-release from bonds
are, it is that being together with them, coming together with
them, fraternizing with them, and being mixed with them.
This, bhikkhus, is called suffering which is association with
the disliked.

And what, bhikkhus, is suffering that is separation from the
liked? Whatever desirable, agreeable, pleasant objects there
are visible, audible, odorous, tasteable, and tangible; or
whoever those wishers of welfare, wishers of benefit, wishers
of comfort, and wishers of release from bonds are - mothers,
fathers, brothers, sisters, friends, colleagues, relatives, or
blood relations, it is that not being together with them, not
coming together with them, not fraternizing with them, and
not being mixed with them. This, bhikkhus, is called suffering
that is separation from the liked.

And what, bhikkhus, is "not to get what one wishes, that also
is suffering?" In being subject to birth such a wish arises, "Oh,
that we were not subject to birth! Oh, that no birth would come
to us!" But this, indeed, cannot be attained by mere wishing.
This is "not to get what one wishes, that also is suffering."

In being subject to aging such a wish arises, "Oh, that we
were not subject to aging! Oh, that no aging would come to
us!" But this, indeed cannot be attained by mere wishing. this
is "not to get what one wishes, that also is suffering."

In being subject to sickness such a wish arises, "Oh, that we
were not subject to sickness! Oh, that no sickness would come
to us!" But this, indeed, cannot be attained by mere wishing.
This is "not to get what one wishes, that also is suffering."

In being subject to death such a wish arises, "Oh, that we
were not subject to death! Oh, that no death would come to
us!" But this, indeed, cannot be attained by mere wishing.
This is "not to get what one wishes, that also is suffering."

In being subject to sorrow, lamentation, pain, grief, and
excessive distress such a wish arises, "Oh that we were not
subject to sorrow, lamentation, pain, grief, and excessive distress! Oh, that no sorrow, lamentation, pain, grief, and excessive distress would come to us!" But this, indeed, cannot be
attained by mere wishing. This is "not to get what one wishes,
that also is suffering."

And what, bhikkhus, is "in brief, the five aggregates of
clinging are suffering?" They are the aggregate of clinging to
material form, the aggregate of clinging to feeling, the ag-

gregate of clinging to perception, the aggregate of clinging to mental formations, and the aggregate of clinging to consciousness. This, bhikkhus, is called, "in brief, the five aggregates of clinging are suffering."

This, bhikkhus, is called the Noble Truth of Suffering.

And what, bhikkhus, is the Noble Truth of the Origin of Suffering? It is that craving which gives rise to further rebirth and, bound up with pleasure and lust, finds ever fresh delight, now here, now there — to wit, the sensual craving, the craving for existence, and the craving for non-existence.

And where, bhikkhus, does this craving, when arising, arise, and, when settling, settle? Whatever in the world is a delightful thing, a pleasurable thing, therein this craving, when arising, arises and, when settling, settles.

What in the world is a delightful thing, a pleasurable thing? Eye in the world is a delightful thing, a pleasurable thing; therein this craving, when arising, arises and, when settling, settles.

Ear in the world is a delightful thing, a pleasurable thing; therein this craving, when arising, arises and, when settling, settles.

Nose in the world is a delightful thing, a pleasurable thing; therein this craving when arising, arises, and, when settling, settles.

Tongue in the world is a delightful thing, a pleasurable thing; therein this craving when arising, arises and, when settling, settles.

Body in the world is a delightful thing, a pleasurable thing; therein this craving when arising, arises and, when settling, settles.

Mind in the world is a delightful thing, a pleasurable thing; therein this craving, when arising, arises and, when settling, settles.

Visible forms in the world are delightful things, pleasurable things; therein this craving, when arising, arises and, when settling, settles.

Sounds in the world are delightful things, pleasurable things; therein this craving, when arising, arises and, when settling, settles.

Smells in the world are delightful things, pleasurable things; therein this craving, when arising, arises and, when settling, settles.

Tastes in the world are delightful things, pleasurable things; therein this craving, when arising, arises and, when settling, settles.

Tangible objects in the world are delightful things, pleasurable things; therein this craving, when arising, arises and, when settling, settles.

Dhammas in the world are delightful things, pleasurable things; therein this craving, when arising, arises and, when settling, settles.

Eye-consciousness in the world is a delightful thing, a pleasurable thing; therein this craving, when arising, arises and, when settling, settles.

Ear-consciousness in the world is a delightful thing, a pleasurable thing; therein this craving, when arising, arises and, when settling, settles.

Nose-consciousness in the world is a delightful thing, a pleasurable thing; therein this craving, when arising, arises and, when settling, settles.

Tongue-consciousness in the world is a delightful thing, a pleasurable thing; therein this craving, when arising, arises and, when settling, settles.

Body-consciousness in the world is a delightful thing, a pleasurable thing; therein this craving, when arising, arises and, when settling, settles.

Mind-consciousness in the world is a delightful thing, a pleasurable thing; therein this craving, when arising, arises and, when settling, settles.

Eye-contact in the world is a delightful thing, a pleasurable thing; therein this craving, when arising, arises and, when settling, settles.

Ear-contact in the world is a delightful thing, a pleasurable thing; therein this craving, when arising, arises and, when settling, settles.

Nose-contact in the world is a delightful thing, a pleasurable thing; therein this craving, when arising, arises and, when settling, settles.

Tongue-contact in the world is a delightful thing, a pleasurable thing; therein this craving, when arising, arises and, when settling, settles.

Body-contact in the world is a delightful thing, a pleasurable thing; therein this craving, when arising, arises and, when settling, settles.

Mind-contact in the world is a delightful thing, a pleasurable thing; therein this craving, when arising, arises and, when settling, settles.

The feeling born of eye-contact in the world is a delightful thing, a pleasurable thing; therein this craving, when arising, arises and, when settling, settles.

The feeling born of ear-contact in the world is a delightful thing, a pleasurable thing; therein this craving, when arising, arises and, when settling, settles.

The feeling born of nose-contact in the world is a delightful thing, a pleasurable thing; therein this craving, when arising, arises and, when settling, settles.

The feeling born of tongue-contact in the world is a delightful thing, a pleasurable thing; therein this craving, when arising, arises and, when settling, settles.

The feeling born of body-contact in the world is a delightful thing, a pleasurable thing; therein this craving, when arising, arises and, when settling, settles.

The feeling born of mind-contact in the world is a delightful thing, a pleasurable thing; therein this craving, when arising, arises and, when settling, settles.

The perception of visual forms in the world is a delightful thing, a pleasurable thing; therein this craving, when arising, arises and, when settling, settles.

The perception of sounds in the world is a delightful thing, a pleasurable thing; therein this craving, when arising, arises and, when settling, settles.

The perception of smells in the world is a delightful thing, a pleasurable thing; therein this craving, when arising, arises and, when settling, settles.

The perception of tastes in the world is a delightful thing, a pleasurable thing; therein this craving, when arising, arises and, when settling, settles.

The perception of touches in the world is a delightful thing, a pleasurable thing; therein this craving, when arising, arises and, when settling, settles.

The perception of dhammas in the world is a delightful thing, a pleasurable thing; therein this craving, when arising, arises and, when settling, settles.

The volition concerning visual forms in the world is a delightful thing, a pleasurable thing; therein this craving, when arising, arises and, when settling, settles.

The volition concerning sounds in the world is a delightful thing, a pleasurable thing; therein this craving, when arising, arises and, when settling, settles.

The volition concerning smells in the world is a delightful thing, a pleasurable thing; therein this craving, when arising, arises and, when settling, settles.

The volition concerning tastes in the world is a delightful thing, a pleasurable thing; therein this craving, when arising, arises and, when settling, settles.

The volition concerning touches in the world is a delightful thing, a pleasurable thing; therein this craving, when arising, arises and, when settling, settles.

The volition concerning the dhammas in the world is a delightful thing, a pleasurable thing; therein this craving, when arising, arises and, when settling, settles.

The craving for visual forms in the world is a delightful things, a pleasurable thing; therein this craving, when arising, arises and, when settling, settles.

The craving for sounds in the world is a delightful things, a pleasurable thing; therein this craving, when arising, arises and, when settling, settles.

The craving for smells in the world is a delightful thing, a pleasurable thing; therein this craving, when arising, arises and, when settling, settles.

The craving for tastes in the world is a delightful thing, a pleasurable thing; therein this craving, when arising, arises and, when settling, settles.

The craving for touches in the world is a delightful thing, a pleasurable thing; therein this craving, when arising, arises and, when settling, settles.

The craving for the dhammas in the world is a delightful thing, a pleasurable thing; therein this craving when arising, arises and, when settling, settles.

The thought for visual forms in the world is a delightful thing, a pleasurable thing; therein this craving, when arising, arises and, when settling, settles.

The thought for sounds in the world is a delightful thing, a pleasurable thing; therein this craving, when arising, arises and, when settling, settles.

The thought for smells in the world is a delightful thing, a pleasurable thing; therein this craving, when arising, arises and, when settling, settles.

The thought for tastes in the world is a delightful thing, a pleasurable thing; therein this craving, when arising, arises and, when settling, settles.

The thought for touches in the world is a delightful thing, a pleasurable thing; therein this craving, when arising, arises and, when settling, settles.

The thought for dhammas in the world is a delightful thing, a pleasurable thing therein this craving, when arising, arises and, when settling, settles.

The discursive thought for visual forms in the world is a delightful thing, a pleasurable thing; therein this craving, when arising, arises and, when settling, settles.

The discursive thought for sounds in the world is a delightful thing, a pleasurable thing; therein this craving, when arising, arises and, when settling, settles.

The discursive thought for smells in the world is a delightful thing, a pleasurable thing; therein this craving, when arising, arises and, when settling, settles.

The discursive thought for tastes in the world is a delightful thing, a pleasurable thing; therein this craving, when arising, arises and, when settling, settles.

The discursive thought for touches in the world is a delightful thing, a pleasurable thing; therein this craving, when arising, arises and, when settling, settles.

The discursive thought for dhammas in the world is a delightful thing, a pleasurable thing; therein this craving, when arising, arises and, when settling, settles.

This, bhikkhus, is the Noble Truth of the Origin of Suffering.

And what, bhikkhus, is the Noble Truth of the Cessation of Suffering? It is the total extinction by removing of, forsaking of, discarding of, freedom from, and non-attachment to that same craving.

And where, bhikkhus, is this craving, when being abandoned, abandoned, and when does this craving, when ceasing, cease? Whatever in the world is a delightful thing, a pleasurable thing, therein this craving, when being abandoned, is abandoned and, when ceasing, ceases.

What in the world is a delightful thing, a pleasurable thing? Eye in the world is a delightful thing, a pleasurable thing; therein this craving, when being abandoned, is abandoned and, when ceasing, ceases.

Ear in the world is a delightful thing, a pleasurable thing; therein this craving, when being abandoned, is abandoned and, when ceasing, ceases.

Nose in the world is a delightful thing, a pleasurable thing; therein this craving, when being abandoned, is abandoned and, when ceasing, ceases.

Tongue in the world is a delightful thing, a pleasurable thing; therein this craving, when being abandoned, is abandoned and, when ceasing, ceases.

Body in the world is a delightful thing, a pleasurable thing; therein this craving, when being abandoned, is abandoned and, when ceasing, ceases.

Mind in the world is a delightful thing, a pleasurable thing; therein this craving, when being abandoned, is abandoned and, when ceasing, ceases.

Visual forms in the world are delightful things, pleasurable things; therein this craving, when being abandoned, is abandoned and, when ceasing, ceases.

Sounds in the world are delightful things, pleasurable things; therein this craving, when being abandoned, is abandoned and, when ceasing, ceases.

Smells in the world are delightful things, pleasurable things; therein this craving, when being abandoned, is abandoned and, when ceasing, ceases.

Tastes in the world are delightful things, pleasurable things; therein this craving, when being abandoned, is abandoned and, when ceasing, ceases.

Tangible objects in the world are delightful things, pleasurable things; therein this craving, when being abandoned, is abandoned and, when ceasing, ceases.

Dhammas in the world are delightful things, pleasurable things; therein this craving, when being abandoned, is abandoned and, when ceasing, ceases.

Eye-consciousness in the world is a delightful thing, a pleasurable thing; therein this craving, when being abandoned, is abandoned and, when ceasing, ceases.

Ear-consciousness in the world is a delightful thing, a pleasurable thing; therein this craving, when being abandoned, is abandoned and, when ceasing, ceases.

Nose-consciousness in the world is a delightful thing, a pleasurable thing; therein this craving, when being abandoned, is abandoned and, when ceasing, ceases.

Tongue-consciousness in the world is a delightful thing, a pleasurable thing; therein this craving, when being abandoned, is abandoned and, when ceasing, ceases.

Body-consciousness in the world is a delightful thing, a pleasurable thing; therein this craving, when being abandoned, is abandoned and, when ceasing, ceases.

Mind-consciousness in the world is a delightful thing, a pleasurable thing; therein this craving, when being abandoned, is abandoned and, when ceasing, ceases.

Eye-contact in the world is a delightful thing, a pleasurable thing; therein this craving, when being abandoned, is abandoned and, when ceasing, ceases.

Ear contact in the world is a delightful thing, a pleasurable thing; therein this craving, when being abandoned, is abandoned and, when ceasing, ceases.

Nose-contact in the world is a delightful thing, a pleasurable thing; therein this craving, when being abandoned, is abandoned and, when ceasing, ceases.

Tongue-contact in the world is a delightful thing, a pleasurable thing; therein this craving, when being abandoned, is abandoned and, when ceasing, ceases.

Body-contact in the world is a delightful thing, a pleasurable thing; therein this craving, when being abandoned, is abandoned and, when ceasing, ceases.

Mind-contact in the world is a delightful thing, a pleasurable thing; therein this craving, when being abandoned, is abandoned and, when ceasing, ceases.

The feeling born of eye-contact in the world is a delightful, a pleasurable thing; therein this craving, when being abandoned, is abandoned and, when ceasing, ceases.

The feeling born of ear-contact in the world is a delightful, a pleasurable thing; therein this craving, when being abandoned, is abandoned and, when ceasing, ceases.

The feeling born of nose-contact in the world is a delightful, a pleasurable thing; therein this craving, when being abandoned, is abandoned and, when ceasing, ceases.

The feeling born of tongue-contact in the world is a delightful thing, a pleasurable thing; therein this craving, when being abandoned, is abandoned and, when ceasing, ceases.

The feeling born of mind-contact in the world is a delightful thing, a pleasurable thing; therein this craving, when being abandoned, is abandoned and, when ceasing, ceases.

The perception of visual forms in the world is a delightful thing, a pleasurable thing; therein this craving, when being abandoned, is abandoned and, when ceasing, ceases.

The perception of sounds in the world is a delightful thing, a pleasurable thing; therein this craving, when being abandoned, is abandoned and, when ceasing, ceases.

The perception of smells in the world is a delightful thing, a pleasurable thing; therein this craving, when being abandoned, is abandoned and, when ceasing, ceases.

The perception of tastes in the world is a delightful thing, a pleasurable thing; therein this craving, when being abandoned, is abandoned and, when ceasing, ceases.

The perception of touches in the world is a delightful thing, a pleasurable thing; therein this craving, when being abandoned, is abandoned and, when ceasing, ceases.

The perception of dhammas in the world is a delightful thing, a pleasurable thing; therein this craving, when being abandoned, is abandoned and, when ceasing, ceases.

The volition concerning visual forms in the world is a delightful thing, a pleasurable thing; therein this craving, when being abandoned, is abandoned and, when ceasing, ceases.

The volition concerning sounds in the world is a delightful thing, a pleasurable thing; therein this craving, when being abandoned, is abandoned and, when ceasing, ceases.

The volition concerning smells in the world is a delightful thing, a pleasurable thing; therein this craving, when being abandoned, is abandoned and, when ceasing, ceases.

The volition concerning tastes in the world is a delightful thing, a pleasurable thing; therein this craving, when being abandoned, is abandoned and, when ceasing, ceases.

The volition concerning touches in the world is a delightful thing, a pleasurable thing; therein this craving, when being abandoned, is abandoned and, when ceasing, ceases.

The volition concerning the dhammas in the world is a delightful thing, a pleasurable thing; therein this craving, when being abandoned, is abandoned and, when ceasing, ceases.

The craving for visual forms in the world is a delightful thing, a pleasurable thing; therein this craving, when being abandoned, is abandoned and, when ceasing, ceases.

The craving for sounds in the world is a delightful thing, a pleasurable thing; therein this craving, when being abandoned, is abandoned and, when ceasing, ceases

The craving for smells in the world is a delightful thing, a pleasurable thing; therein this craving, when being abandoned, is abandoned and, when ceasing, ceases.

The craving for tastes in the world is a delightful thing, a pleasurable thing; therein this craving, when being abandoned, is abandoned and, when ceasing, ceases.

The craving for touches in the world is a delightful thing, a pleasurable thing; therein this craving, when being abandoned, is abandoned and, when ceasing, ceases.

The craving for dhammas in the world is a delightful thing, a pleasurable thing; therein this craving, when being abandoned, is abandoned and, when ceasing, ceases.

The thought for visual forms in the world is a delightful thing, a pleasurable thing; therein this craving, when being abandoned, is abandoned and, when ceasing, ceases.

The thought for sounds in the world is a delightful thing, a pleasurable thing; therein this craving, when being abandoned, is abandoned and, when ceasing, ceases.

The thought for smells in the world is a delightful thing, a pleasurable thing; therein this craving, when being abandoned, is abandoned and, when ceasing, ceases.

The thought for tastes in the world is a delightful thing, a pleasurable thing; therein this craving, when being abandoned, is abandoned and, when ceasing, ceases.

The thought for touches in the world is a delightful thing, a pleasurable thing; therein this craving, when being abandoned, is abandoned and, when ceasing, ceases.

The thought for dhammas in the world is a delightful thing, a pleasurable thing; therein this craving, when being abandoned, is abandoned and, when ceasing, ceases.

The discursive thought for visual forms in the world is a delightful thing, a pleasurable thing; therein this craving, when being abandoned, is abandoned and, when ceasing, ceases.

The discursive thought for sounds in the world is a delightful thing, a pleasurable thing; therein this craving, when being abandoned, is abandoned and, when ceasing, ceases.

The discursive thought for smells in the world is a delightful thing, a pleasurable thing; therein this craving, when being abandoned, is abandoned and, when ceasing, ceases.

This, bhikkhus, is the Noble Truth of the Cessation of Suffering.

And what, bhikkhus, is the Noble Truth of the Path leading to the Cessation of Suffering? It is simply the Noble Eightfold Path, namely, Right Understanding, Right Thought, Right Speech, Right Action, Right Livelihood, Right Effort, Right Mindfulness, Right Concentration.

And what, bhikkhus, is Right Understanding? Understanding of suffering, understanding of the origin of suffering, understanding of the cessation of suffering, understanding of the path leading to the cessation of suffering. This, bhikkhus, is called Right Understanding.

And what, bhikkhus, is Right Thought? Thought associated with renunciation, thought associated with absence of ill will, thought associated with absence of cruelty. This, bhikkhus, is called Right Thought.

And what, bhikkhus, is Right Speech? Abstaining from false speech, abstaining from slanderous speech, abstaining from harsh speech, abstaining from frivolous speech. This, bhikkhus, is called Right Speech.

And what, bhikkhus, is Right Action? Abstaining from killing beings, abstaining from taking what is not given, abstaining from sexual misconduct. This, bhikkhus, is called Right Action.

And what, bhikkhus, is Right Livelihood? Here, bhikkhus, a noble disciple having abandoned wrong livelihood, makes a living by means of Right Livelihood. This, bhikkhus, is called Right Livelihood.

And what, bhikkhus, is Right Effort? Here, bhikkhus, a bhikkhu engenders wishes, makes effort, arouses energy, exerts the mind, and strives for the non-arising of evil, unwholesome states that have not arisen; engenders wishes, makes effort, arouses energy, exerts the mind, and strives for the abandoning of evil, unwholesome states that have arisen; engenders wishes, makes effort, arouses energy, exerts the mind, and strives for the arising of wholesome states that have not arisen; engenders wishes, makes effort, arouses energy, exerts the mind, and strives for the stabilizing, for the collation, for the increase, for the maturity, for the development, for the perfection through cultivation of wholesome states that have arisen. This, bhikkhus, is called Right Effort.

And what, bhikkhus, is Right Mindfulness? Here, bhikkhus, a bhikkhu dwells contemplating the body in the body, ardently, clearly comprehending, and mindfully, removing covetousness and grief in the world. He dwells contemplating the feeling in the feelings, ardently, clearly comprehending, and mindfully, removing covetousness and grief in the world. He dwells contemplating the consciousness in the consciousness, ardently, clearly comprehending, and mindfully, removing covetousness and grief in the world. He dwells contemplating the Dhamma in the dhammas, ardently, clearly comprehending, and mindfully, removing covetousness and grief in the world. This, bhikkhus, is called Right Mindfulness.

And what, bhikkhus, is Right Concentration? Here, bhikkhus, a bhikkhu, quite secluded from sense pleasures, secluded from unwholesome states, attains and dwells in the first jhāna accompanied by initial application, accompanied by sustained application, with rapture and happiness born of seclusion; with the non-appearance of initial application and sustained application, he attains and dwells in the second jhāna, which is internal, accompanied by confidence, which causes singleness of mind to grow, which is without initial application and sustained application, which is born of concentration and which is with rapture and happiness; with the overcoming of rapture as well as of initial application and sustained application, he dwells in equanimity, is mindful and clearly comprehending, experiences happiness with his body and mind. He attains and dwells in the third jhāna, on account of which the noble ones announce, "With equanimity and mindfulness, he dwells in happiness." With the abandoning of pleasure and pain, and with the previous disappearance of joy and grief, he attains and dwells in the fourth jhāna, which has neither pain nor pleasure and has purity of mindfulness caused by equanimity. This, monks, is called Right Concentration.

This, bhikkhus, is the Noble Truth of the Path leading to the Cessation of Suffering.

Thus he dwells contemplating the Dhamma in the dhammas internally, or he dwells contemplating the Dhamma in the dhammas externally, or he dwells contemplating the Dhamma in the dhammas both internally and externally.

He dwells contemplating the origination factors in the dhammas, or he dwells contemplating the dissolution factors in the dhammas, or he dwells contemplating both the origination and dissolution factors in the dhammas.

Or his mindfulness is established as "there are dhammas only." And that mindfulness is established to the extent necessary to further knowledge and mindfulness.

Not depending on (or attached to) anything by way of craving and wrong view, he dwells.

Nor does he cling to anything in the world of the five aggregates of clinging.

Thus too, bhikkhus, a bhikkhu dwells contemplating the Dhamma in the dhammas in the Four Noble Truths.

Assurance of Attainment

Verily, bhikkhus, whoever is practicing these Four Foundation of Mindfulness for seven years, he can expect one of two results — highest knowledge here and now, or, if there still be a remainder of clinging, the state of non-returner.

Let alone seven years, bhikkhus, should any person practice these Four Foundations of Mindfulness for six years....five years....four years....three years....two years....for one year, then he may expect one of two results — highest knowledge here and now, or, if there still be a remainder of clinging, the state of non-returner.

Let alone one year, bhikkhus, should any person practice these Four Foundations of Mindfulness for seven months....six months....five months....four months....three months....two months....a month....half-a-month, then he may expect one of two results — highest knowledge here and now, or, if there still be a remainder of clinging, the state of non-returner.

Let alone half-a-month, bhikkhus, should any person practice these Four Foundations of Mindfulness in this manner for seven days, he may expect one of two results — highest knowledge here and now, or, if there still be a remainder of clinging, the state of non-returner.

Because of this, it has been said: "This is the only way, bhikkhus, for the purification of beings, for the overcoming of sorrow and lamentation, for the disappearance of pain and grief, for reaching the Noble Path, for the realization of nibbana, namely, the Four Foundations of Mindfulness."

This the Blessed One said. Glad in their hearts, the bhikkhus welcomed the words of the Blessed One.

Part Three
Meditation Instructions

Meditation Instructions

To practice meditation, you have to look first for a suitable place. A suitable place is a place which offers you the necessary seclusion for your meditation. You may find secluded places in nature, however, when you are meditating inside a house, you have to look for the place which is most suitable for meditation and you will then use this place for meditation each time. You may want to put up a statue or a picture of the Buddha, some flowers, a candle or some incense to assist your meditation, but these items are not so important as the necessity for a secluded place where you will always practice your meditation in the future.

To begin your meditation, you sit down cross-legged, keeping the upper portion of your body erect. If the cross-legged position is too difficult for you, you may sit in the half-lotus position, putting one leg on top of the other, i.e., not intertwining your legs. If this is still to difficult, you may sit in the "easy" or "Burmese" position, putting one leg in front of the other. Because some comfort is necessary to continue the practice of meditation, you may even sit on a cushion, a chair or a bench. Though the cross-legged position is the ideal position for meditation, you have to decide for yourself in which position you can maintain your meditation best. Important in all positions is that you keep the upper portion of your body erect.

We will look at three kinds of meditation. The first is Forgiveness, the second Loving Kindness and the last *vipassanā* meditation.

We practice forgiveness to remove any guilt feelings. Sometimes you did something wrong to somebody and then you have this feeling of guilt. Especially, when you are meditating, you want to keep your mind pure but these thoughts come to you again and again and spoil your meditation. Like cleaning the slate, you first ask forgiveness from others. This is one aspect. The other aspect is to forgive others. There may be somebody who has done something wrong to you and you have some anger or grudge against that person. You have to get rid of this anger or grudge, too. In order to practice loving kindness, you must be able to forgive people. If you cannot forgive people, you cannot practice meditation. So, loving kindness and forgiveness go together. If you cannot forgive somebody, you cannot send loving kindness to that person. So you get rid of the ill feeling toward anybody who may have done something wrong to you. And thirdly, you forgive yourself. Sometimes, you find it more difficult to forgive yourself than to forgive others. If you cannot forgive yourself, the same feeling of anger and hatred about yourself will disturb your meditation. Therefore, before entering meditation, you have to practice forgiveness; after that you practice loving kindness meditation.

Loving kindness is a kind of love, a genuine desire for the well-being of all beings. It is love, not connected with attachment, not connected with lust. It is pure love and pure desire for all beings, including ourselves. So when you practice loving kindness and wish for your own happiness, "May I be well, happy, and peaceful!" this should not be interpreted as selfishness because, in order to send out loving kindness to others, we have to generate these thoughts first in ourselves. Also, when you send thoughts to yourself, you can take yourself as example. That means, when you say, "May I be well, happy and peaceful," you think, "I want to be well. I want to be happy. I want to be peaceful. May the other person also be well, happy, and peaceful." To be able to practice loving kindness toward other beings, you first have to practice loving kindness toward yourself. Then you send your thoughts to other beings. You can send these thoughts in different ways. You can send thoughts to all beings by location. You send loving kindness to all beings in this house, all beings include all animals, insects, etc. Then you send loving kindness to all beings in this area, in this city, in this county, in this state, in this country, in this world, in this universe, and last, to all beings in general. When you say the sentences to yourself, please, mean them and try to see and visualize the beings you mention as well, happy, and peaceful. Your thoughts of loving kindness will be going to them and make them really well, happy, and peaceful. It will take about fifteen minutes. When practicing forgiveness, please, fold your hands.

> If by deed, speech or thought,
> foolishly I have done wrong,
> may all forgive me honored ones,
> who are in wisdom and compassion strong.
> I freely forgive anyone
> who may have hurt or insured me.
> I freely forgive myself.

Now you can practice loving kindness meditation. When practicing loving kindness meditation, please, repeat each sentence silently to yourself, about ten times.

> May I be well, happy, and peaceful!
> May all beings in this house be well, happy, and peaceful!
> May all beings in this area be well, happy, and peaceful!
> May all beings in this city be well, happy, and peaceful!
> May all beings in this county be well, happy, and peaceful!
> May all beings in this state be well, happy, and peaceful!
> May all beings in this country be well, happy, and peaceful!
> May all beings in this world be well, happy, and peaceful!
> May all beings in this universe be well, happy, and peaceful!
> May all beings be well, happy, and peaceful!

Loving kindness can also be practiced by way of persons:

> May I be well, happy, and peaceful!
> May my teachers be well, happy and peaceful!
> May my parents be well, happy, and peaceful!
> May my relatives be well, happy, and peaceful!
> May my friends be well, happy, and peaceful!

May the indifferent persons be well, happy, and
peaceful!
May the unfriendly persons be well, happy, and
peaceful!
May all meditators be well, happy, and peaceful!
May all beings be well, happy, and peaceful!

May suffering ones be suffering free
and the fear-struck fearless be!
May the grieving shed all grief,
and all beings find relief!

After you have sent loving kindness to the whole world and
all beings, you practice *vipassanā* meditation.

In-breath and out-breath each last about four or five
seconds. Be really mindful of the in-breath. You may feel a
sensation of the air at the tip of your nose or in your nose. Be
mindful of it. When you exhale, be really mindful of the
out-breath for the whole duration of four or five seconds and
concentrate on the nature of breath, the moving nature or the
supporting nature of breath rather than the shape or form of
the breath. Try to see the in-breath and out-breath as two
separate things not just one and the same breath going in and
coming out. Do not follow the breath into your body or
outside the body. Your mind is like a gatekeeper standing at
the gate, taking note of people going in and coming out. Do
not force or strain yourself. Just calmly be mindful and watch
the breath. You may make a mental note when you breathe in
and when you breathe out, as "in" and "out," or "in, out." If
you think you should recognize what is interfering with your
concentration, you need not to do that. Just be mindful of the
breath. Your mindfulness is important and not the knowing
of "what is going on." However, for some people, it is important to know what helps them to keep their mind on the object
and what not. If it helps you, you may use labels or investigate
"what is going on," but when it interferes with your concentration, you don't have to say "what is going on," just be mindful.

When your mind can be on the breath only, that is very good.
However, the mind has the tendency to wander. If your mind
wanders or goes out and you are aware of it, be mindful of the
going out. Or you may say to yourself, "going out, going out,
going out," two or three times and then go back to the breath.

If you see something or someone in your thoughts, be mindful of seeing or say to yourself, "seeing, seeing, seeing," until that object disappears from your mind, then go back to the breath. If you hear somebody talking in your thoughts, be mindful of hearing or say to yourself, "hearing, hearing, hearing," and then go back to the breath. If you talk to someone in your thoughts or if you talk to yourself, be mindful of talking or say to yourself, "talking, talking, talking," and then go back to the breath. If you speculate about something, if you analyze something, be mindful of analyzing. If you make judgments, be mindful of making judgments. If you remember something in the past, be mindful of the remembrance or say to yourself, "remembering, remembering, remembering" or "thinking, thinking, thinking," and then go back to the breath. If you think of the future and make plans, be mindful of it or say to yourself, "planning, planning, planning," and then go back to the breath. If you become lazy, be mindful of your laziness or say, "lazy, lazy, lazy." The laziness will go away after some moments, then go back to the breath. If you feel bored, be mindful of boredom or say to yourself, "bored, bored, bored," until boredom goes away, then go back to the breath. If you have resistance, be mindful of it or say to yourself, "resisting, resisting, resisting." When resistance disappears, go back to the breath. If you have thoughts of attachment or greed or lust, be mindful of these thoughts or say to yourself, "attachment, attachment, attachment," or "greed, greed, greed," or "lust, lust, lust," until they disappear and then go back to the breath. If you are upset or angry for any reason, just be mindful of that anger, in other words, make that anger the object of meditation. Concentrate on your anger or you may say to yourself, "anger, anger, anger" or "angry, angry, angry" or "upset, upset, upset." After some moments, the anger will disappear and when it has disappeared, go back to the breath.

If you want to swallow your saliva, first be mindful of the intention or desire to swallow, saying to yourself, "intention, intention, intention," or "desire, desire, desire." And when you have gathered the saliva in your mouth, be mindful of gathering or say to yourself, "gathering, gathering, gathering." When you swallow, be mindful of swallowing or say to yourself, "swallowing, swallowing, swallowing," then go back to the breath.

If you have an itching sensation, do not scratch it right away. Concentrate on the place of that itching and be mindful of it, saying to yourself, "itching, itching, itching." In most cases, itching will go away after some time. When it goes away, return to the breath. Sometimes, the itching will not go away. It may become more intense, then be with it, taking note of it and be aware of it, as long as you can. If you think you cannot bear it any longer you may scratch. But before scratching, be mindful of the intention or desire to scratch. When you move your hand to the place where you experience the itch, be mindful of moving. Move your hand slowly, following the movement with mindfulness. When your fingers touch the place, say "touching, touching, touching." When you scratch, say "scratching, scratching, scratching." When you take the hand back, say "taking, taking, taking" or "moving, moving, moving." When your hand touches your lap, the knee or the other hand again, be mindful of touching or say to yourself, "touching, touching, touching." Then go back to the breath.

If you have painful feelings in the body, numbness, stiffness, heat, focus your mind on the place of these feelings and be mindful of them. If you have pain somewhere in the body, focus on the place of that pain, be mindful of that pain and say to yourself, "pain, pain, pain." You will have to be very patient with painful feelings. Pain will not easily go away. You have to be patient and be mindful of it. It may go away or it may become more acute. Stay with it as long as you can. Actually pain is a very good object for meditation. It is a strong object. Your mind is pulled towards the place where there is pain. So be mindful of it and try to see that it is first of all a sensation. Do not identify pain with yourself. Don't say either, "It is not *my* pain" or "*I* feel pain." There is just the pain, just the sensation. If the pain becomes so intense, you think you cannot bear it any longer, you may ignore pain altogether and go back to the breath. Or you may move and change posture to ease pain. But when you move or change posture, first note the intention to change, be mindful of the intention to change and then make movements slowly, one at a time, following each movement with mindfulness. And when you have made changes, go back to the breath.

So the breath is the whole object of your meditation. Whenever there are no other objects to be mindful of, you just continue with being mindful of the breath. If there are more prominent objects, then you take note of them, become aware of them, mindful of them, and then go back to the breath. Do not use force, do not strain yourself, just calmly watch the objects, take note of them, be mindful of them. Do not try to push distractions or emotions or feelings in the body away, just watch them and let them go by themselves.

For some people, it is difficult to concentrate on the breath at the tip of the nose. Such people can keep their mind on the abdomen and be mindful of the rising and falling movements of the abdomen. When you inhale, the abdomen extends or rises and when you exhales, it contracts or falls. These movements of rising and falling can be the home object of meditation instead of the breath. Keep your mind on the abdomen and be really mindful of the rising from the beginning to the end, and also the falling movement from the beginning to the end. Your mind is like a jockey riding a horse, your mind and your breath are both moving. You may even put your hand on the abdomen to feel the rising and falling movements. After some time, you may be able to follow the rising and falling movements without your hand on the abdomen. If you are comfortable with just watching the breath, you need not go to the abdomen.

Do not have any expectations at this time of practice, do not expect to experience something strange or to see visions or whatever. Expectation is a mild form of greed or attachment which is a hinderance to concentration and has to be eliminated. If you have expectations, just be mindful of them or say to yourself, "expecting, expecting, expecting." Then go back to the breath or the movements of the abdomen.

Having meditated for ten or more minutes, you can practice walking meditation.

When you practice *vipassanā* meditation, it is important to keep mindfulness with you always. So, when you change from sitting to standing, keep mindfulness with you. Before standing up, therefore, be mindful of the intention to stand up or to get up. You may say to yourself "intention, intention, intention," or "desire, desire, desire." Then get up slowly, keeping your mind on your whole body, on the upward movements of your body or saying to yourself, "getting up, getting up, getting up." And when you are standing, be mindful of the standing position or say to yourself, "standing, standing, standing."

When you walk, it is better to chose a walking path and stay on it. Walk on it back and forth. When you walk, you walk slowly, keeping your mind on the foot or the movements of the foot, being aware of at least four stages of each step.

In order to make a step, first you raise your foot. Keep your mind on the foot and be mindful of the raising or lifting, "lifting, lifting, lifting." Then you push your foot forward, you move your foot forward. Be mindful of that moving, saying to yourself, "moving, moving, moving." When you put your foot down on the floor, be mindful of the putting down or just say, "putting, putting, putting." Then you shift weight to make the other step. Keep your mind on the whole body and say, "shifting, shifting, shifting." Then make the next step, being mindful of lifting, pushing, putting down, and shifting, moving slowly. Keep your eyes open and look at the floor about four or five feet in front of you. Do not close your eyes. You may fall if you close your eyes. Keep them a little open and look at the floor, look down.

When you reach the end of the walking space, you stop and be mindful of stopping or say to yourself, "stopping, stopping, stopping." When you want to turn around, be mindful of the desire or intention to turn around or say to yourself, "intention, intention, intention," or "desire, desire, desire," then you turn slowly. Be mindful of the turning movement or say to yourself, "turning, turning, turning." Then walk again, taking note of the different stages in each step, lifting, pushing, putting down, shifting, and so on, until you reach the other end of the walking space. Stop there and be mindful of stopping. Wanting to turn around, be mindful of turning around and then walk again. Also, when you walk, you may keep your hands in front or in the back or on the sides. So, you walk back and forth until the end of the walking period.

Walking is designed to exercise the body. When you are practicing for half an hour or one hour, walking may not be necessary but when you are on a retreat and practice the whole day, you need to move your body. At the end of the walking period, the sitting period begins again. So you go back to the sitting place, walking slowly, making notes, being aware of the different stages and steps. Before lowering yourself, be mindful of the desire to sit down. Then lower yourself slowly, keeping your mind on the whole body. When the body touches the floor, say "touching, touching, touching."

Arrange your legs and hands, say "arranging, arranging, arranging." And then, go back to the breath and be mindful of the in-breath and out-breath. This way, you alternate sitting and walking and maintain your mindfulness, trying not to lose it at any moment during the retreat. During retreats, eating is also done with meditation. Everything has to be done with mindfulness. Even the activities in the bathroom should not escape your mindfulness.

After meditation, we share merit. It is a good practice to share merit with all beings whenever we have done some meritorious deeds.

> May all beings share this merit
> which we have thus acquired
> for the acquisition of
> all kinds of happiness.
>
> May beings inhabiting space and earth,
> deities and others of mighty power,
> share this merit of ours!
> May they long protect the Teachings!

Notes

INTRODUCTION

1 Passages that are indented and italicized are quotations from the translation of the *Mahā Satipaṭṭhāna Sutta*.
2 *The Expositor*, p. 19.

CHAPTER ONE: CONTEMPLATION OF THE BODY IN THE BODY

3 *Majjhima Nikāya*, 1979, i., p. 181.
4 *The Path of Purification (Visuddhimagga)*, 1976, Ch. VIII, p. 290.
5 Ibid., p. 286.
6 Ibid., pp. 294-295.
7 *The Way of Mindfulness*, 1975, p. 81.
8 *Aṅguttara*, i.43.
9 *Aṅguttara*, i.45.
10 *The Path of Purification*, 1976, pp. 403-406.
11 Ibid.

CHAPTER FOUR: CONTEMPLATION OF THE DHAMMAS

12 *Aṅguttara*, iv, p. 85ff.
13 *Dhammasangani*, p. 197.
14 *Visuddhimagga, 1976, Ch.. XIV, p. 523.*
15 *Visuddhimagga*, 1976, Ch. IV, pp. 95-97.
16 *The Progress of Insight*, p. 13.
17 For details on the recollections, see *Visuddhimagga, 1976*, Ch. IV; also *The Way of Mindfulness*, 1975, p. 186.
18 *The Way of Mindfulness*, 1975, p. 186.
19 Ibid.

20   *Visuddhimagga*, 1976, Ch.IV, pp. 166-168.
21   *The Questions of King Milinda*, ii, pp. 151ff.
22   *The Expositor*, p. 428.
23   *The Path of Purification*, 1976, Ch. XVI, p. 574.
24   Please, find the remaining passages on the causes of suffering in the translation of the *sutta* in Part II.
25   *The Path of Purification*, 1976, Ch. IV, p. 148.
26   *The Path of Purification*, 1976, Ch. XII, para 78-91.
27   *The Questions of King Milinda*, ii, 151.
28   *On the Nature of Nibbāna*, Burmese language edition, pp. 252-253.
29   *Dhammapada*, verse 204.
30   *The Path of Purification*, 1976, Ch. XVI, p. 577.
31   *The Book of the Gradual Sayings*, iii, p. 153.
32   *The Expositor*, pp. 136-137.
33   *Saṃyutta Nikāya*, iv, p.321; see, also *Kindred Sayings*, iv, pp. 225-226.
34   *Dhammapada*, verse 173.

CHAPTER FIVE: ASSURANCE OF ATTAINMENT

35   *The Middle Length Sayings*, ii, pp. 281-283.

Glossary

Abhidhamma: The highest teachings of the Buddha; the Third Basket of the *Tipiṭaka;* Buddhist philosophy and psychology; metaphysical teachings which deal with the ultimate nature of things.

Abhiññā: Supernatural faculty, intuitive knowledge.

Akusala: Morally bad, sinful, unwholesome.

Anāgāmi: Non-Returner; disciple who has reached the third of the four stages of emancipation. One who has destroyed sensual delight and ill will completely and will not return to the world of the sense-spheres, i.e., not be reborn, again.

Ānāpāna-sati: Mindfulness of in- and out-breathing.

Anatta: Non-self, together with *dukkha* and *anicca,* one of the three characteristics of phenomenal existence.

Anicca: Impermanence, together with *anatta* and *dukkha,* one of the three characteristics of phenomenal existence.

Anumodanā: A monk's blessings after receiving *dāna* (a meal or a gift).

Arahat or *Arahant:* One who is worthy, who has attained the highest level of spiritual development, who is free, who will not be reborn again.

Ariyasaccani: Noble Truth; see also *cattari ariyasaccani,* the Four Noble Truths.

Āsava: Literally, "flux." Taints of mind, corruptions, biases. There are four: *kamasava,* taint of sense-desire; *bhāvasava,* desire for continued existence; *diṭṭhasava,* taint of wrong views, and *avijjasava,* taint of ignorance.

Aṭṭhaṅgika magga: The Eightfold Path: *sammā diṭṭhi,* right understanding; *sammā samkappa,* right thought; *sammā vācā,* right speech; *sammā kammanta,* right action; *sammā ājīva,* right livelihood; *sammā vāyāma,* right effort; *sammā sati,* right mindfulness; and *sammā samādhi,* right concentration.

223

Avijjā: Ignorance.

Āyatana: Sense field. The external or objective fields are the five sense objects and the mind objects. The internal or subjective fields are the five sense organs and the mind.

Bhava: Becoming.

Bhikkhu: Mendicant; Buddhist monk (who keeps the 227 precepts).

Bhikkhunī: Buddhist nun.

Bodhi: Perfect knowledge; enlightenment; the wisdom at the moment when Path Consciousness arises.

Bodhisatta: One who is destined for enlightenment; the Buddha in his previous existences.

Brahma vihāras: The Four Divine States: *mettā,* loving kindness; *karunā,* compassion; *muditā,* altruistic joy, and *upekkhā,* equanimity.

Buddha: The Enlightened One, epithet of Prince Siddhattha Gotama, son of King Suddhodana and Queen Maya. He renounced his kingdom at the age of twenty-nine. After studying with several teachers and practicing strict penances for six years, he chose the Middle Way and became enlightened by his own efforts. In his first sermon, *Dhammacakka-pavatthana Sutta,* he talked about the Noble Eightfold Path (*ariya aṭṭhaṅgika magga*) and the Four Noble Truths (*cattāri ariyasaccāni*).

Cāga: Generosity.

Cattāri ariyasaccāni: The Four Noble Truths:

> The Noble Truth of Suffering (*dukkha*) — Birth is suffering, old age is suffering, disease is suffering, death is suffering, to be separated from the pleasant is suffering, not to be separated from the unpleasant is suffering, not to receive what one craves for is suffering, i.e., the five aggregates of attachment are suffering.

> The Noble Truth of the Cause/Arising (*samudaya*) of Suffering — Craving for sensual pleasures, *kāmatanhā;* for existence, *bhāvatanhā;* and for annihilation, *vibhavatanhā,* leads to rebirth.

> The Noble Truth of Cessation (*nirodha*) of Suffering — Total cessation is forsaking of craving, breaking loose, and being delivered.

The Noble Truth of the Path (*magga*) leading to the Cessation of suffering. This is the Noble Eightfold Path (see *aṭṭhaṅgikamagga*).

Concentration: See *samādhi*.

Consciousness: The distinguishing feature of mental activity; capacity for experiencing awareness and for knowing the external world, etc.

Dāna: Giving; the first of the Ten Good Deeds, see *pāramī*.

Dasa kasina: Ten meditation objects: the four elements, the four colors (blue, yellow, red, white), space, and light. These meditation objects cause a calming of the passions.

Defilements: See *kilesas*.

Deva: Literally, "shining one"; god, invisible to mortal eyes but having a subtle physical body, living on celestial planes, i.e., six celestial planes in the Realm of Desire, *kāmaloka*, and sixteen celestial planes in the Realm of Form, *rūpaloka*.

Dhamma: The Buddha's Teachings; the Law; truth.

Dhamma vicaya: Investigation of *dhammas*.

Dhammas: Things, phenomena; nature.

Dhutaṅgas: Ascetic practices to remove the defilements.

Dosa: Aversion, hatred.

Dukkha: Unsatisfactoriness, suffering, misery; the first of the Four Noble Truths: *dukkha dukkha*, intrinsic suffering; *dukkha nirodha*, removal of suffering; *dukkha nirodha gāminī paṭipādā*, the Path which goes to the cessation of suffering; *saṅkhāra dukkha*, suffering due to formations; *vipariṇama dukkha*, suffering due to change.

Five Faculties: See *pancendriya*.

Four Noble Truths: See *cattari ariyasaccāni*.

Hindrances: See *nīvaraṇas*.

Indriyas: Faculties.

Jhāna: Meditative absorption of the mind, e.g., in a moral object as to cause dispelling or burning up of the defilements.

Kalyāṇa mitta: A virtuous friend, a spiritual friend.

Kamma: Volition accompanying actions, words, and thoughts. Whatever *kamma* has been accumulated in the past and is being accumulated in the present, will have results in this or future lives, depending on the quality of the *kamma*.

Kammaṭṭhāna: Meditation.

Karaka maggangas: Active factors.
Karunā: Compassion.
Kasina: Meditation object, e.g., earth disk.
Kāya: Body, form.
Khandas: Aggregates. Man is considered to be composed of a group of five: *rūpa,* form, matter; *vedanā,* feeling; *saññā,* notion, perception, memory; *saṅkhāra,* volition, motivation, impulse, mental formations; and *viññāna,* consciousness.
Kilesas: Defilements; those factors which cause the mind to become defiled. Defilements are capable of arising even when their conditions have been eradicated.
Kilesa parinibbāna: Total eradication of defilements.
Kusala: Good, skillful, wholesome.
Lobha: Greed.
Lokiya: Mundane, worldly.
Lokuttara: Otherwordly, transcendental.
Magga: The Path.
Mahāyāna: Great Vehicle. After the Indian Emperor Asoka had tried to unify the Sangha in the middle of the third century B.C., some Buddhist schools developed traditions of their own. The Mahāsaṅghika had already split from the Sthavira after the Second Council in the fifth century B.C. Mahāyāna schools maintain, for example, that a *bodhisattva* forgoes his final *nibbāna* so that he can teach and save all sentient beings, while Theravāda schools encourage the practitioner "to work out his own salvation with diligence," referring to the last words of the Buddha (see *Mahāparinibbāna Sutta*). *Vaipulya suttas* were added and codified in the Sanskrit Canon. Mahāyāna Buddhism was introduced to Central Asia by merchants and monks under the Kushans in India during the first two centuries A.D. and spread to Tibet, China, Siberia, Korea, Japan, and Vietnam later on. From the eight to the thirteenth century A.D., it was also practiced in Cambodia, Java, Sumatra, and on the Malayan Peninsula.
Mettā: Loving kindness.
Moha: Delusion.
Mudita: Altruistic joy.
Nāma: Mind; literally, that which inclines toward objects and that which causes others to incline to them; a collective term for all mental processes.
Nibbāna: Literally, "blowing out"; extinction.

Nimitta: Literally, "sign"; mental image appearing in meditation, indicating a high degree of mental concentration.

Nirodha: Annihilation, cessation.

Nīvarana: Hindrances. The five states of desiring sense pleasures — hatred, restlessness and remorse, sloth, and torpor, and doubt — are considered to be the main hindrances to reaching enlightenment.

Non-Returner: See *Anāgāmi.*

Pacceka Buddha: Someone who found enlightenment on his own but cannot teach his insights to others.

Pāli: Row, series, text; middle Indo-Aryan language, close to Māgadhi Prakrit; presumably the language of the Buddha, sacred language of the Theravāda Canon, the collection of the Buddha's teachings which were orally transmitted after the Buddha's death, until they were written down on Sri Lanka in the first century B.C.

Pancendriya: Five Faculties. A meditation term for the five mental states: confidence, *saddhā;* mindfulness, *sati;* effort, *vīriya;* concentration, *samādhi;* and wisdom, *paññā.* When maintained to an equal degree, they cause the occurrence of *jhāna* by suppressing the hindrances.

Paññā: Wisdom, intuitive knowledge.

Paramatha sacca: Ultimate truth (in opposition to *sammuti sacca,* the conventional truth); indescribable truth which is perceived directly and not bound by conceptual thought.

Pārāmi: Perfection, wisdom gone beyond. The ten perfections are: *dāna,* generosity; *sīla,* morality; *nekkhama,* renunciation; *paññā,* wisdom; *vīriya,* exertion, efforts; *khanti,* forbearance; *sacca,* truthfulness; *adhiṭṭhāna,* perseverance, determination; *mettā,* loving kindness; and *upekkhā,* equanimity.

Passaddhi: Calmness, tranquility.

Paticca samuppada: Dependent orgination; basis of the Buddha's teachings; with *avijja,* ignorance as cause of *sankhāra,* moral or immoral activities. Depending on *sankhāra* are *viññāna,* rebirth consciousness, linking the past with the present and other resultant consciousness; *nāma* and *rūpa,* mind and body/form come into being and lead to the formation of the six senses, *salāyatana.* Then contact, *phassa,* occurs leading to feeling, *vedanā.* These five links are the effects of past actions. They are called the passive side of life. From feeling arises craving, *tanhā,* which results in grasping, *upādāna* that, in turn, causes conditioning, *bhāva* and rebirth, *jāti*, being the inevitable cause of old age and death, *jarā-maraṇa*. These causes have to be removed, ignorance being the last link to be removed before attaining full enlightenment.

Pātimokkha: The set of rules (227 for monks and 3ll for nuns), mentioned in the *Vinaya*, the First Basket of the *Tipitaka*. They are binding for all monks and nuns and should be recited on the observance, *uposatha*, day, i.e., every two weeks, according to the phases of the moon.

Phassa: Literally, "contact"; sense impression.

Piṇḍapāta: Monks' almsround, food received in the alms bowl.

Pīti: Joy, contentment; happiness, pleasurable interests.

Precepts: See *sīla*.

Puthujjanas: Worldlings.

Rūpa: Form, matter.

Saddhā: Confidence.

Sahagata: Bound up with, comes to be identical with.

Samādhi: Concentration; state of being absorbed in a single mental object. There are three kinds of concentrations: preparatory, *parikamma;* near to *jhāna* but yet in the sense planes, *upacara;* and that of attainment or *jhāna, appanā*.

Samatha bhāvanā: Tranquility meditation; meditation with forty topics whose ultimate aim is the procurement of a state of peace or tranquility by suppressing certain defilements, e.g., the hindrances.

Sambojjhaṅga: Factors of enlightenment. The Seven Factors of Enlightenment are *sati* (mindfulness), *dhamma vicaya* (investigation of *dhammas*), *vīriya* (effort or energy), *pīti* (joy, contentment), *passaddhi* (calmness or tranquility), *samādhi* (concentration), *upekkhā* (equanimity).

Sampajaññā: Clear Comprehension.

Samudaya: Arising.

Samudaya dhammas: Origination factors.

Samutti sacca: Conventional truth, e.g., saying "I" although ultimately there is no ego.

Sangha: Assembly; community of monks who uphold the Buddha's teachings and observe the 227 *Vinaya* rules; the third of the Three Jewels.

Saṅkhāra: Conditioned; conditioned states; volition, impulse; motivation; mental formations.

Saññā: Notion, ideas; perception; memory.

Sati: Mindfulness.

Satipaṭṭhāna: Establishment of mindfulness; practice of Insight meditation by contemplating on the Four Foundations of Mindfulness — the body, the feelings, the consciousness, and the phenomena, *dhammas.*

Sīla: Morality; rules of conducts; one of the training rules of the Eightfold Path, preceding *samādhi* and *paññā;* taken together with the Three Refuges, to affirm that one is a Buddhist. The first five *(pancasīla)* are:

> *Pānātipāta veramanī sikkhāpadaṁ samādiyāmi,*
> I take the precept to abstain from taking life.

> *Adinnādānā veramanī sikkhāpadaṁ samādiyāmi,*
> I take the precept to abstain from taking what is not given.

> *Kāmesu micchācārā veramanī sikkhāpadaṁ samādiyāmi,*
> I undertake the precept to abstain from wrong sexual conduct.

> *Musāvādā veramanī sikkhāpadaṁ samādiyāmi,*
> I undertake the precept to abstain from telling lies.

> *Surāmeraya majja pamāda ṭṭhāna veramanī sikkhāpadaṁ samādiyāmi,*
> I undertake the precept to abstain from intoxicating liquor which leads to heedlessness.

Sotāpanna: Stream enterer; disciple who has reached the first stage of sainthood. One who will never be reborn again into the lower worlds and will become enlightened as an *arahat* within seven rebirths.

Sukkha: Happiness.

Sutta: Thread; discourse. Second Basket of the *Tipiṭaka,* containing all sermons taught by the Buddha.

Tanhā: Thirst, craving, desire which leads to rebirth.

Theravāda: The Word of the Elders. The only surviving school of the first eighteen schools which developed after the Buddha's *nibbāna.* The Elders recited all Teachings at the First Council after the Buddha's *nibbāna* and thus consolidated the tradition which is still maintained in Burma, Cambodia, Laos, Sri Lanka, and Thailand.

Three Roots of Evil: *Moha,* delusion; *dosa,* aversion; and *lobha,* greed.

Tipitaka: Three Baskets. The Three Baskets of the Theravāda Canon are the *Vinaya,* disciplinary rules; *Sutta,* the sermons of the Buddha; *Abhidhamma,* the metaphysical teachings of the Buddha.

Tisaraṇa: Three Refuges:

> *Namo tassa Bhagavato arahato sammā sambuddhasa,*
> Hail to the Enlightened One, the Arahat, the truly fully Enlightened One.
>
> *Buddhaṁ saraṇaṁ gacchāmi,*
> I go to the Buddha for refuge.
>
> *Dhammaṁ saraṇaṁ gacchāmi,*
> I go to the Teachings for refuge.
>
> *Saṅghaṁ saraṇaṁ gacchāmi,*
> I go to the Order of Monks for refuge.

Triple Gems: The Buddha, the *Dhamma,* and the *Sangha.*
Uddhata: Restlessness; literally, "to shake about."
Upadāna: Taking fully hold.
Upasama: Peace.
Upekkhā: Equanimity.
Vaya dhammas: Dissolution factors.
Vedanā: Feeling, sensation.
Vicāra: Act of keeping the mind anchored.
Vinaya: Discipline, training, guidance; the first Basket of the *Tipitaka.*
Viññāṇa: Consciousness.
Vipassanā: Insight.
Virati: Abstentions.
Vīriya: Effort.
Vitakka: Initial application of the mind, deliberation, consideration.
Visuddhimagga: *The Path of Purification,* a treatise on Buddhist meditation, composed by Buddhaghosa in the fourth century A.D.

A Select Bibliography

The *Mahā Satipaṭṭhāna Sutta* appears in two places in the Pāli Canon. It is the twenty-second *sutta* of the *Dīgha Nikāya*, the "Collection of Long Discourses" and the tenth *sutta* of the *Majjhima Nikāya*, the "Collection of Middle Length Discourses." The *Dīgha Nikāya* version is, therefore, longer than the *Majjhima Nikaya* version. The difference is that in the *Majjhima Nikāya* version the detailed expositions on the Four Noble Truths are omitted. In this book, I have followed the *Dīgha Nikāya*.

There is an ancient commentary on the *sutta* by the celebrated commentator, the Venerable Buddhaghosa, and there is a sub-commentary on the commentary by the equally famous author, the Venerable Dhammapāla. Both are written in Pāli.

With respect to the translations of the *sutta*, I would like to refer to the book, *The Way of Mindfulness*, by the Venerable Soma Thera, published by the Buddhist Publication Society in Kandy, Sri Lanka, 1975. It contains the translation of most of the commentaries and many marginal notes from the sub-commentaries and is indispensable for the detailed study of the *sutta*.

Other translations can be found in the following books:

1. *Buddhism in Translations*, by Henry Clark Warren. New York: Atheneum, 1963. The translation of the *sutta* appears in the Table of Contents as "The Four Intent Contemplations" (pp. 353-375). It follows the *Dīgha Nikāya* version.

2. *Some Sayings of the Buddha*, by F.L. Woodward. Oxford: Oxford University Press, 1973. The translation appears under the title, "The Only Way" and follows the *Majjhima Nikāya* version, but the *Dīgha Nikāya* version is also mentioned.

3. *The Heart of Buddhist Meditation*, by Nyānaponika Thera. York Beach, Maine: Samuel Weiser, Inc., 1988. The translation forms Part Two of this book and follows the *Dīgha Nikāya* version.

4. *The Foundations of Mindfulness*, by Nyānasatta Thera. Kandy, Sri Lanka: Buddhist Publication Society, Wheel Publication No. 19, 1974.

5. *The Foundations of Mindfulness*, ed. Chogyam Trungpa, Rinpoche. Berkeley: Shambhala Publications, Inc., 1967. This book contains an abridged form of Nyānasatta Thera's translation, followed by an exposition of the *sutta*.

6. *What the Buddha Taught*, by Walpola Rahula. New York: Grove Press, 1974. The translation appears in an abridged form.

7. *Thus Have I Heard*, translated and edited by Maurice Walshe. London: Wisdom Publications, 1987. This is a translation of the *Dīgha Nikāya*.

For other *suttas* on the Four Foundations of Mindfulness, see the Pāli Canon, *The Book of Kindred Sayings*, Part V, Book III, pp. 119-169, and Part III of *The Heart of Buddhist Meditation*, by Nyānaponika Thera, mentioned above.

The following two books were used as primary sources for this book:

1. *The Path of Purification*, transl. Bhikkhu Nyānamoli. Boulder: Shambhala Publications, Inc., 1976. The edition published by the Buddhist Publication Society is currently available.

2. *The Questions of King Milinda*, transl. T.W. Rhys Davids. New York: Dover Publications, Inc., 1963.

Wisdom Publications

Wisdom Publications is a registered, non-profit charity dedicated to preserving and transmitting the resources of Buddhism throughout the world. Through its worldwide network Wisdom distributes not only its own titles but also over 1500 books on Buddhism and Tibet from more than eighty other publishers.

Wisdom specializes in publishing books and other materials on Buddhism, Tibet and related East-West themes. The books are published in various series encompassing Buddhist theory and practice, biography, history, art and literature for children.

RECENTLY PUBLISHED

The second half of 1989 saw the publication of four new titles. *Song of the Profound View* (a Wisdom Intermediate Book: White Series) is a personal account of a long retreat spent meditating on emptiness by the late Geshe Rabten, one of Tibet's outstanding contemporary masters and a leading teacher of Buddhism in the West. *Dependent-Arising and Emptiness* (a Wisdom Advanced Book: Blue Series) is a detailed study of emptiness based on the *Lam-rim Chen-mo*, the major work of Lama Je Tsong Khapa, one of Tibet's greatest yogis and scholars, by Elizabeth Napper.

From our East-West Series come *The Social Face of Buddhism: An Approach to Political and Social Activism*, by Ken Jones ("...vital reading for all those who feel that a spiritual perspective is missing from a socio-political approach to world issues" - Christopher Titmuss), and *Beckett and Zen: A Study of Dilemma in the Novels of Samuel Beckett*, by Paul Foster, where the author applies his understanding of Zen Buddhism to the "absurdity" of Beckett, which he sees as an expression of deepest spiritual anguish.

Forthcoming in 1990

Two major projects, in preparation for over five years, will come to fruition in 1990. *The Nyingma School of Tibetan Buddhism: Its History and Fundamentals* (A Wisdom Advanced Book) is a two-volume, two-thousand-page book that is the definitive presentation of the history and fundamentals of the Nyingma tradition by its late supreme head, the great scholar and enlightened master Dudjom Rinpoche. *Liberation in the Palm of Your Hand* (A Wisdom Intermediate Book) is Trijang Rinpoche's presentation of Pabongkha Rinpoche's great teaching on the *Lam-rim*, the graduated path to enlightenment. A descriptive brochure about each of these two works is available from Wisdom.

As a non-profit organization Wisdom selects publishing projects primarily on the basis of importance and merit of the work, and not on commercial saleability alone. Thus books are often of specialized interest and produced in relatively short print runs. Consequently, sponsors play a critical role in enabling Wisdom to fulfil its mission of preserving, translating and distributing these great works. Wisdom is very grateful to the many benefactors whose contributions have made this work possible.

Wisdom Books from the Theravada Tradition

The Wisdom edition of Maurice Walshe's new translation of the longer discourses of the Buddha, the *Dīghā Nikāya*, has been universally acclaimed by Theravada practitioners and scholars as fresh, accurate and penetrating. "Dr Walshe's translation is very good and his fluent, readable style makes these scriptures highly accessible." - Venerable Bhikkhu Bodhi

We have also published Dr Hammalawa Saddhatissa's *Buddhist Ethics*, the only reliable work in this fundamentally important area of Buddhist practice and scholarship, and Ayya Khema's *Being Nobody, Going Nowhere*, winner of the Buddhist Society's annual Christmas Humphreys Award for the best introductory Buddhist book.

Two new books are in the pipeline.

Venerable U Pandita Sayadaw's *In This Very Life: The Liberation Teachings of the Buddha* is a significant new work by a highly respected master from the Burmese tradition of Theravada Buddhism. In an inspiring manner, U Pandita Sayadaw demonstrates how meditation practice embodies the truths of Buddhism in each moment and leads to full realization in this very life.

Continuing our series of new translations from the Pali Canon is Bhikkhu Bodhi's masterful revised translation of the *Majjhima Nikāya*, the middle length discourses of the Buddha, based on an earlier, largely unpublished translation by the late renowned scholar Nyanamoli Mahathera. A new translation of the *Samyutta Nikāya* is also planned.

Wisdom Catalogue of Buddhist Books

Wisdom announces its new 128-page Catalogue—a comprehensive reference work of Buddhist books published worldwide. Compiled through extensive research and effort, it contains more than 1,500 titles from over eighty publishers.

These books cover a wide range of subjects from all traditions of Buddhism. There are books for practitioners; philosophical and scholarly works; books on the dialogue of East and West in science, spirituality, psychology and the arts; language books; children's books; and publications on health and alternative medicine. There is also a large selection of Buddhist art— cards, posters, prints, and the best-selling Tibetan Art Calendar—as well as audio and video tapes.

In addition to popular classics, we offer rare and specialized publications, which are often difficult to obtain, from publishers such as Motilal Barnasidass and the Library of Tibetan Works and Archives in India; the Buddhist Publication Society of Sri Lanka; the Buddhist Missionary Society of Malaysia; Rinsen and Kosei of Japan; and many more publishers, large and small, both in the East and in the West. And, Wisdom has recently been appointed exclusive North American distributor for the Pali Text Society, the leading publisher of texts and translations from the Pali Canon and its commentaries since 1881.

To receive a copy of this catalogue please send US$3.95/£1.95/ A$4.95 to your nearest Wisdom office:

Wisdom USA	Wisdom UK	Wisdom Australia
361 Newbury Street	402 Hoe Street	P.O. Box 1326
Boston, MA 02115	London E17 9AA	Chatswood, NSW
(617) 536-3358	(01) 520-5588	2067
		(02) 922-6388

Wisdom Trust Fund

For the purpose of fulfilling our publishing mission a Wisdom Trust Fund has been established. Through the generosity of Wisdom Trustees, the contributors to this Fund, we are able to complete current projects, reprint our best-selling titles which have sold out, and undertake new publishing projects. If you would like to enable Wisdom to continue this work by making a tax-deductible contribution to the Wisdom Trust Fund, contact Wisdom Publications, 361 Newbury Street, Boston, MA 02115 U.S.A. Telephone (617) 536-3358, Fax (617) 536-1897.